Doubt

Innovation. Faith.

If there is no downturn, there is no joyride.

Decentralization is the next tier for humankind. But most can't understand it when they are still centralized thinkers.

Why natural forces like gravity are needed for a rollercoaster to get up to the other side.
And why crypto will revolutionize the entire world.

Chapters co-written with:
Lars Tvede Investor – Author - Serial entrepreneur
Lars Seier Christensen – Investor - Blockchain entrepreneur.
Farzam Kamalabadi – Investor - "The Most Influential Foreign Figure in Modern China History"

-1-

Thanks to MidJourney.com for A.I. pictures for the cover page.

Written by:
Steffen Kirkegaard

Audiobook read by the author.

Copyright ISBN 9798223969457

This book you are about to read has taken me 50 years to start. Why is that? I have often doubted what the world was about. Why do people live as they do? Why do they strive for certain things in life, and occasionally, they get them, and occasionally, they don't?

This book is my journey into the unknown of innovation and how it works. I have read most of the books on how innovation works and how it comes to life. While reading them, I questioned the reasons why it comes to life and how it comes to life.

My life until now has been an exploration into the minds of people who innovate, but also into the minds of most people who does not dare to.

Contents

If there is no downturn, there is no joyride. 0

Preface ix

If there is no downturn, there is no joyride. 12

Chapter 1: Self-doubt...1
Have you ever wondered why your neighbour leads the life they do? 1

Social economy 1
You believe...3
Power structures..4
The madness of the crowd 6
People believe what they will believe 8
The tipping points...10
Madness and virus 11
Cognitive dissonance... 12
The smartphone syndrome 14
You cannot un-innovate innovations 15

Chapter 2: Mysticism...16
From a tribal to a space odyssey...16

Artificial intelligence, the next frontier 17
Tribal to social economy 19
Consensus and the waterfall method...................................19
Tribal thinking...20
Space odyssey...21
Business networks 23

Chapter 3: Employment 25
Do you want money? 25

Don't steal my plate.. 25

Network 26

Battles between truth and doubt.................................... 27

Autonomy.. 28

Free owner 30

Anonymity and privacy 32

Chapter 4: Fraud and bullshit detection 34

How to detect a bug 34

The trap 34

The scammer.. 34

The high roller and the player 35

Anonymity and privacy 37

Bug fixing.. 38

I found a bug 39

Peer pressure 41

Family 43

DNA 45

Religion 47

Money 49

Socialism 50

Chapter 5: Doubt and Beliefs 53

You're not wrong when you're right.................................. 53

Scammers.. 53

Physics 54

The press and the clickbait 57

You're wrong.. 60

You're right 61

The righteous people 65

Holism 68

Space and time 72

So EIN ding 74

Chapter: 6 Lars Tvede on Innovation, Skepticism and Doubt 76
Interview with Lars Tvede..76

The Supertrends institute 76
The bullshit filters 77
Fraud and psychology...80
Immigrant in Switzerland 82
Pattern recognition...84
Why are there so many crooks? 87
What is the difference between speculation and
investment? 89
What is your take on crypto?...92
Decentralization?...94

Chapter 7: Money Laundering and Fraud..................................97
Who are the sharks and who are the whales?...........................97

A small fish 97
A big fish 99

Chapter 8: Breaking the Barriers...101
Tier two; crossing the chasm, and tipping points.................101

Crossing 101
The hamster-wheel 103
The chasm and the hype..106
The barriers..108
The tipping points...109
The tipping ideas 111
Tier two   114
Commitment is voluntary... 116

Chapter 9: Innovation Matters...117
Innovation ideas – where do they come from? How and why?
Why can't innovation be revoked?...117

Being innovative 117

Crossing the chasm 118

Trial and error 121

Innovation drivers.. 125

Innovation structural drivers 129

What is not understood 132

Exponential growth.. 133

Crushing innovation 135

Chapter 10: Decentralized government 141
DAO. Decentralized Autonomous Organization 141

Why DAOs?... 141

What is a DAO? 142

Decentralization in the public sector 144

Smart contracts in the Healthcare management 145

DAO projects.. 148

Collective intelligence 149

Chapter 11: An Entrepreneurial Mindset....................... 154
Why do you do this? Do you want to be rich, or do you want to change the world? 154

The mind155

Manipulation and change.. 156

Ownership... 157

Faith 158

Government.. 158

Private corporations.. 159

Chapter 12: Lars Seier Christensen................................ 163
Interview with Lars Seier Christensen 163

Why is innovation important? 163

What is bleeding edge innovation? 167

Table of Contents

What has been your biggest doubt in your life? 171

Is there a formula for success in building companies? 174

What is the success story for Y Combinator?...........................176

How did you get the idea on the ID layer and the KYC for blockchains? 176

Why is crypto important? 179

Decentralization versus centralization - what kind of society are we building right now? 182

What is your take on Decentralized Autonomous Organizations? 185

How can we build autonomy in the organizations?..........188

What is your best advice to others when it comes to innovation and blockchains?..........190

Gas fees - how do you control them?..........195

Nirvana in crypto. 197

Chapter 13: Evolution 198
Anthropology through times and the plastic frontal loops. 198

Doubt is the reason we explore and do science 198

The plastic brains 200

Jumping levels 201

Different belief systems..........212

Cognitive dissonance..........214

Objects and objectivity 217

Chapter 14: Why innovation? 221
A society at a standstill is doomed to die. 221

Why innovation?..........221

Controversies..........222

Innovation and strategy..........227

Pick the winners? 231

Combined knowledge? 235

If you can dream it, can you build it? 239

Society plagues and wars 240

Innovation cannot be stopped 243

Chapter 15: Farzam Kamalabadi 247
Interview with Farzam Kamalabadi. "The Most Influential Foreign Figure in Modern Chinese History" 247

What did you help China with? 247

It takes a lot of courage 255

Politicians try to steer their populations 257

How does decentralization help people? 262

How does the digital economy help the world? 265

The whole world in a grain of sand? 269

How does web3 run the world from now on? 271

Why is it hard to get funding? 273

What do you want to add? 275

Thanks   276

Epilogue 279
Innovation is built on doubt... 279
Notes. 282

Preface

> If you believe in one thing, you might doubt another. You might believe in what a group of people is telling you, and thereby not doubt what the meaning of it all is. You might believe in physics and find it natural to know that gravity always works in a specific way. But you can doubt even this if a whole group tells you that it is not so. Many experiments show that we are highly sensitive to peer pressure.

This book is my testimony, and I no longer doubt my beliefs. I have been curious all my life, and I was curious about why things were the way they were. This book is therefore the thoughts of the author and a thought experiment about how things are. It is OK if you believe that the world has a different shape, but for the most part, we accept that it is an ellipse, and it circles the sun. It is in a solar system and gravity is a real phenomenon. Gravity has been explained, but how do we know how, and most of all why it is here, and why does it work the way it does?
We all strive for money. We go to school to learn then go to university to get an education to get a job, so that we can trade the hours of our lives, to get money. We all know that money is the driver in this world. But who issues the money today and who controls them. The centralized banks are the main way the world is governed today. What will decentralized crypto bring to this world, and how will it work?

"Tell me and I forget. Teach me and I remember. Involve me and I learn." Benjamin Franklin

> ...people will forget what you said, people will forget what you did, but people will never forget how you made them feel.
>
> MAYA ANGELOU

I'm not writing this book to prove anything. I'm writing it because I hope to find people who also think and are on the edge of what is possible. Innovation is the number one driver for human wealth, prosperity and survival. One innovation leads to another; innovations are the reason the worlds' population is moving out of poverty and famine. The two quotations above about feeling and learning are intended to highlight something that I have a strong belief in.

This book is also about the pitfalls that I fell into the rabbit holes that caused me to fail. In my opinion, those were the starting points of trails. If you do not try to make a bulb and a spark of light, you will never make a lightbulb. On that subject, Edison once said "I have not failed. I've just found 10,000 ways that won't work."

I have had doubts about the crypto economy. I never doubted the technology it used. But how did I know what it was and what it was not? I have met numerous people in the last eight years who showed doubt in what I told them about this new technology. But we are on the edge of a whole new world order. We are at a tipping point, as Malcolm Gladwell explained in his book of the same name.

A single sick person can start an entire epidemic. The same goes for the start of fashion trends.

This tipping point is what builds religious and social movements, roads or railroads, and societies. It can also build metaverses. A virus has a lot in common with the way viral campaigns work. And this is why the madness of crowds is still a force today, even though we thought we would have left the tulip bubble by now.

The Wolf of Wall Street has a lot to teach us about how supply and demand are factors, just like gravity. That can provide us with great powers. And one of the doubts that exist today when it comes to the crypto economy is the question of whether it will float or sink.

I will go deeper into this in the following chapters. And in my way, I will try to explain some of the pitfalls I fell into, why I did this and why I understand the doubt that exists around something this big.

Cognitive dissonance is something any inventor struggles with. There is a blue ocean, and no one believes it, so they live in fear and doubt.

The good thing is that we do not have to do that; we can start today to live in a prosperous world where more people have a lot, and less have too little.

And why are decentralized economies better than centralized ones? This book will focus on the peer-to-peer technology built into the blockchain; now they exist, these technologies can't be revoked. Innovation can't be un-invented.

Doubt

If there is no downturn,
there is no joyride.

Have you ever wondered why your neighbour leads the life they do?

Have you ever looked at others and thought, '*This is not the way*'? Or maybe you have thought, '*Wow they have a great attitude and style*'. Sometimes, you might observe others and learn from or imitate them. Occasionally, you may even just look for beauty, and every so often you steer for the opposite. We are social beings, after all.

Social economy

One of my first ventures was in the early days of the internet. In 1995, in the early days of email, I had set up an account for a study I had attended. A few years before that, I had written a report in my technical gymnasium about the French telecom system Minitel.

I was fascinated about this option of dial-up and its potential for increasing ease, convenience and comfort. At the touch of your fingertips, you could order a pizza or a taxi. Anything was possible. Unfortunately, it soon became apparent that it was built in the wrong way. Numerous people thought this form of technology would never catch on. They were not able to distinguish the differences between Minitel and modern phones. Couldn't you already order a pizza by simply calling the restaurant? This demonstrated that this format was made in the wrong way. It was centralized; it was too complicated for companies to be a part of. Because of the complexity, or the need for alterations to how people might interact with each other, most public innovation fails. Some innovations have worked and are successfully built within the public sector, but most of them fail because they are too complex. This is particularly unfortunate because innovators simply want to make everybody happy. Minitel was a success until it got surpassed by the internet, which we are currently so dependent on.
The internet was specifically designed to be decentralized, meaning it could be operated from various locations. In 1968, during the Cold War, the US army were aware of the

possibility that the enemy could take out their information system. Information and intelligence are crucial components of winning a war. Therefore, the communication system had to be decentralized, so the enemy did not have the ability to send a bomb to smash the whole system in one fell swoop. Unix mainframe systems were a thing of the past in their mind. So, smaller units had to be built; thus, the internet was born.

You believe

It is not what you are told that achieves the indoctrination, it is what you are not told that does it.
  -Steffen Kirkegaard

I attended the same school as everyone else in the small, centralized country of Denmark. But there was something rotten in the state. As though you are merely a herd, socialistic teachers who subscribe to the beliefs of Karl Marx's *Das Kapital* teach adolescents about the economy: but never with true clarity about how it works. They never divulge clear and concise information, leaving the students in a perpetual state of confusion. It is a mild form of brainwashing. It took me years to find out simple things, even after the internet was invented. This was because I simply did not know what to ask; my world views stayed with me, like so many others who have cognitive dissonance.

"The term cognitive dissonance is used to describe the mental discomfort that results from holding two conflicting beliefs, values, or attitudes. People tend to seek consistency in their attitudes and perceptions, so this conflict causes feelings of unease or discomfort."

I tried to look at the classmate next to me in the classroom, but they were just as paralysed as I was. In Denmark, there are things you can't ask, even if you are in an educational setting.

My fascination with technology began when I received my first game pad or "bip bip game" as we called them back then in 1978. It was a Galaxy Invader. I played it for half a year before handing it off a schoolmate after I had grown bored with it. Later, in the early eighties, we had game pads that we played with 24/7. It felt like there was no end to what technology could do for us kids; the options were endless.

But even with all this new technology surrounding us, we still could not ask a teacher about how the economy worked. Why do socialists think the way they do? Why do they always mention the greater good, and why should we pay around 50% of income for taxes? These questions are simply not answered, let alone... 'STOP!' I hear someone shout. Well now it is my book, so I will continue talking about this as I always do when I find out why people are lying.

Power structures

Subscribing to any belief allows for power structures to develop. If you believe in religion, the church will corrupt your thoughts and convince you that you need to invest at least 10% in the church to further convince your God to absolve you of your sins. When it comes to socialism, the same thing occurs. The welfare state steals an extreme amount of money from people and invests that money into a public sector that is inefficient and lacking recent innovations. Never, as in 99.9% of the time. Efficiency is measured in surplus over the year.

I had a fun discussion with a teacher I met through Facebook about privatizing the primary school. She said that the children should not be treated like stocks in a company. I told her that it was not the children that were the stocks, it was her, and her education skills. For instance, if she performs taught purely for the children, who are the beneficiaries, the buyers interested in her teaching abilities would lose interest. This is a perfect example of how poorly they understand the market.

There are many small blob-like countries but most of them fail. For example, in a small nation like Denmark, the rotten part is the political parties. Firstly, there are far too many. Currently, we have 9 for a population of 5.5 million people. Recently, two politicians just broke away from one of the larger parties and created their own. So now Denmark will have 12 parties vying for power during the next election. Another country that is a great example of how the political project has gone wrong is Greece. For their population of about 10 million citizens, there are 10 political parties. There is more or less a political party for every group in the working population. A fun fact is that the hairdressers have their own party that managed to get legislation through saying the hairdressers could receive their pension when they were 42 years old. For such a small population, it is highly divided. But why so many? Most parties function as lobbyists for a specific part of the population. Most teachers vote socialist, so your children won't know how the market, or supply and demand work. They are happy without this knowledge. After all, Denmark is on the list of the happiest nations in the world. Just to clarify, we are also one of the nations in the world that has most people using Prozac and other mild forms of "happiness" medicine. Approximately 500,000 Danes are using these to make their day go by better.

So, are we happy? The rotten part is that the population vote for a party that say they will reform their business sector. Therefore, the teachers vote for Folk Socialists, the gymnasium/high school teachers vote for another left-wing party, and the nurses another, and thereby they keep themselves on a stick, without knowing it. In Greece, it is extreme. Their parties can't give them what they ask for because, at the end of the day, they aren't willing to reduce their quality of living; if they did, the voters would refuse to vote for them. Egoism will never allow the state to share wealth evenly amongst its citizens. If you look at Greece, the country is in a bad state. Other centralized nations will surely follow. We see this all over the world – specific groups of people get more than others. This is why centralisation will always corrupt people. Power structures where one leader sits at the end of the table will always be biased. And that is why crypto, and the decentralized economy are so different and so much fairer.

There are things you can't ask when you are growing up. If everyone accepts this belief system, they assume they are safe. This is the madness of the crowd; they all accept that this is something we do not talk about.

That is also one of the reasons why I failed to invest heavily in Bitcoin in the early years. Doubt.

The madness of the crowd

Wearing a medical grade face mask over your mouth when COVID-19 broke out didn't help you. It only provided comfort and allowed people to exhibit their care for others. Oh dear, how many angry eyes did I see over the facemask the last two years from 2020 until 2022 when we stopped having this circus in town. But why did we do this? Why do people wear a mask when there is proof that it does not work? Early in 2020, there was a gigantic survey of around 6,000 people. One half was tested for COVID-19 having not worn the face shield, and another who had been wearing it also got tested. It showed that in the 3,000 of them who had worn it, 19 had got COVID-19, and 22 of the group who had not worn it had got COVID-19. But then something strange happened; the (socialistic) government convinced the population to invest in wearing masks by using predominantly fear-based tactics. This was creepy. It reminded me of the second world war, when most Germans believed work camps were fiction, because they believed the propaganda of the government. Due to the spreading of misinformation, they simply did not know about what was going on. Now we see people doing exactly that with the vaccines.

I have my vaccines, but studies show that people still get sick with COVID-19, even after the third jab. I had COVID-19 twice, the first time without vaccines, the second time after two vaccines. Both times I only experienced mild headaches and dizziness. We can't presume one anecdotal experience accurately reflects the average COVID patient's symptoms. However, by observing the statistics, we can see a significant difference in fatalities when compared to earlier pandemics. Some of these plagues killed up to 200 million people, as opposed to five million from Covid-19. The Black Death ransacked Europe from 1334 to 1353; it was 20 years of death. In parts of Germany, about 40% of the known inhabitants disappeared. The plague might have reduced the world population from c. 475 million to 350–375 million in the 14th century (Link). Analysing this provides insight into why Covid-19 was not as devastating as other pandemics. People believe the vaccine had a say, and it might have done. But it also might have had a small impact considering that the majority of those who contracted the virus only suffered mild symptoms. People did not die from Covid-19 to the same degree as with the plague; I think we can make this clear. This conveniently intersects with my next point. Politicians propagated their campaigns around how well they responded to the pandemic, those whose lives they helped as a result and why that was an accurate depiction of their character. Some of them told us that it was mild, and we had to protect ourselves, but it should be with less fear than others wanted us to have. Again, the world was split in half. Some went anti-vax; others could not get enough of vaccines. The madness was that these groups of people hated each other. Even I was asked if I was an anti-vaxxer – obviously not, because I received two jabs. But people went crazy on this topic. If I had said 'no' it would probably not have made a difference because, as I said, I caught it anyway.

People believe what they will believe

Even though I find it scary, most people don't think about it at all. It's only a mask. It's only a vaccine. When confronted with the madness they believe in, they go haywire. Some of them want to go outside and have a fistfight. Others say that they can't talk to you because you are too extreme for their taste. The narrative is so strong that they will tell you that you're mad, even if you can prove whatever it is you are claiming. Even if you inform them that the earth is an ellipse that rotates around the sun, they will inform you that you're a flat-earther. Consensus-driven collectivists can be as strong in their beliefs as the religious zealotsin Clare Grave's level four people. Matthias Desmet, Professor of Clinical Psychology at Ghent University, wrote the book *The Psychology of Totalitarianism* (LINK), in which he points out why we run with the madness of the crowd. Now, it is dull bureaucrats and technocrats who lead the mass psychosis. Before it was people like Stalin and Hitler, Matthias states in the linked interview. Emerging during the 20th century, technocratic totalitarianism is a new state system predicated on mass formation. As opposed to classic dictatorships, totalitarian states are based on a more complex and more impressive psychological mechanism. With a deep and innate belief in their system, the radicals become blinded to everything that challenges them. They are ready to sacrifice everything. They become intolerant of dissonant vices to the extent that they will typically stigmatize people who do not go along with them. In the end, they will try to destroy people who do not go along with them. And they will do this as if it is their ethical duty to do so. The most fundamental principle of humanity is that you try to articulate ideas that seem honest and sincere. This is what you have to do as a person, so the truth can become stronger, eventually to the point that the mass psychosis starts to fade out. If they take this approach, the minority can become the majority.
Matthias has mapped out what a mass psychosis is and

how it works. The truth is set aside for some belief systems. If you cannot find out whether or not your truth is universal, examine how it affects your group within the consensus driven collectivistic system. In the COVID-19 case, the *we* thinkers on level six are still tribal and think how they can benefit from wearing a mask. I know I have to protect others if I'm sick, but was it not first aimed at protecting themselves from becoming sick? We know that masks did not work at all. Even surgeons' face and mouth masks give no protection against a microbial virus of this size. The physics won't allow it. The filter has big holes on the side and the fibre in the "filter" is one big open door for these microbes. But if you can't see it, you won't believe it. People simply took the politicians' words for the truth. Why did 99% of the population wear these? Only a short while later, the government recanted and announced people did not need wear masks. They all more or less followed this guidance too. If this is not mass psychosis, I don't know what is.

The whole case is a bad respray when you sell a used car. You make up some things to control the population and it worked, and still works. Even with the internet, people still believe what the government says here in Denmark; 20% of the population will remain social democrats, and over 50% will vote for a left-wing party with an overly sympathetic approach. The conclusion must be that this is not thought out in physical possibilities, and that the best thing for the people has not been thought through. Nothing is thought through beyond how something can directly benefit the individual. Just like the mask, it felt like the right thing to do. I recall the displeasure in the eyes of passers-by as I strolled through Copenhagen maskless. To me it was quite comical, but it was incredibly clear that it was not funny to them.

The tipping points

When does a virus go viral? When does a clip, on YouTube go viral? Why is it that people believe in a tulip bubble, an IT bubble, or a crypto bubble? And when is something even a bubble?
Another bell curve is Gardener's hype cycle; this explains how things are marketed. When a product gets air under its wings and flies on its own, when is the market strong enough to keep it afloat? Why do some things burst, and others don't? We know that some people said no to smartphones back in the early 2000s and continued to so for years. There was a similar response to owning cell phones in the 90s. Laggards who dislike the advances in new technology only experiences the normal realization of the convenience of smartphones once they finally give into the frenzy. Doh!
Another lunatic fringe is people who have to have the technology the day it comes out of the factory. One man even bought Bitcoin in 2013 to later use it for buying beer, just because he could. After the financial Bitcoin boom went viral, many people, just like me, wondered why they had not invested heavily in this earlier. Personally, I had my doubts. Soon after Bitcoin reached $1, its value suddenly dropped to next to nothing for a long time. The people around me all told me that it was a fad - nothing you should believe in; nothing to invest in. Why did I listen to them? Was I not strong enough on my own? Maybe not. To rectify this mishap, I tried to raise money for a few other crypto projects before going all-in on Gamer's Gold, where I am now.

Madness and virus

Extraordinary Popular Delusions and the Madness of Crowds

First published in 1841, Charles Mackay authored this book, which depicts the way our curious delusions began in history. The observation is that crowds become frenzied and influence how the market operates as we saw in 1929 before the big crash on Wall Street. What happened? Why did people go crazy about the bond market, and why did financiers like the Wolf of Wall Street exploit those on low incomes for financial gain once again in the 90s? The same apprehensive mindset influenced people regarding Bitcoin. In 2013, very few people were willing to invest, but in 2017, after they witnessed its potential, they wanted to invest heavily Nevertheless, many people do not understand what a blockchain is and how cryptocurrencies work. We still have the surrounding hype, and we have not seen the end of it yet.

A virus spreads through the air; the particles are small enough to spread like pollen on a sunny spring day. If you have allergies, you know how that feels. But one thing is for sure; the COVID-19 particle is even smaller than pollen. That is why people still get sick even if they wear FFP2 standard masks on their face. However, who cares about the size of a particle? Funnily enough, back in the Dark Ages people did not wash themselves every day, as they did not believe in the virtues of hygiene until the 1600s. It is rather strange because, before the Dark Ages, people had saunas in many societies. Due to the low hygiene standards, illnesses such as the Black Death and flu varieties flourished in this environment.

Cognitive dissonance

When people's beliefs are challenged, they get upset. Cognitive dissonance is hard to control.

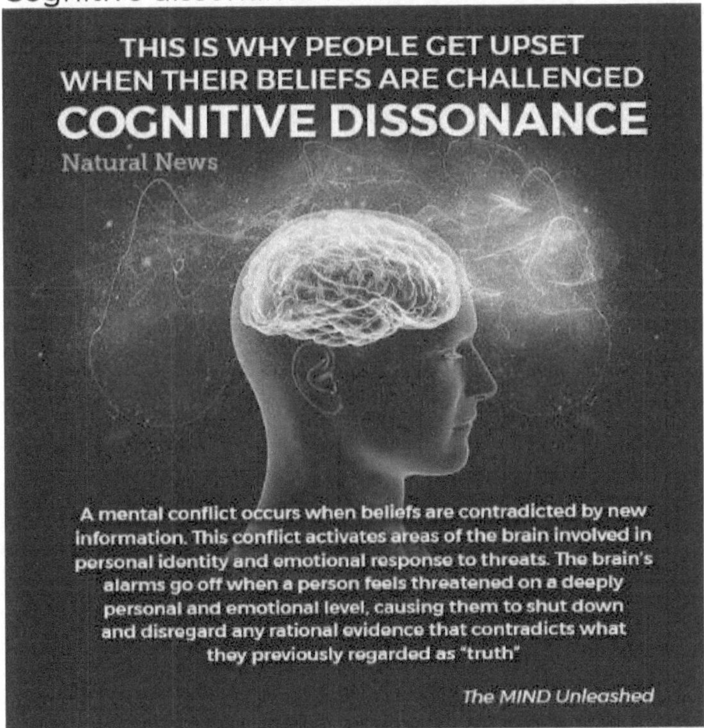

In the film *Meet the Fockers*, Jack Byrnes (Robert De Niro) speaks to Greg Focker (Ben Stiller) about the circle of trust. Jack successfully convinces Greg of the advantages of existing within the circle of trust, rather than outside of it. Why this is so funny is because he does not know when he is inside or outside the circle; it is a means of control. The manipulative tactic is exactly like the politicians who make the socialistic laws in Denmark, and any other party, for that matter. You never get a tax cut, but they might give you a check to spend, so they know what kind of money they are giving and who gets it. They are voters too, of course. Tax cuts would benefit everyone, which is something the government opposes. They only want control. But when politicians evoke the same tactics, they are met with backlash. People believe it is a clever idea, and they don't even see that the prime minister who does this to them are acting like Jack Byrnes. They do not even see that government is pulling their leg and making a fool out of them.

The sad truth is that the nurses working overtime during the COVID-19 crisis received extra money, but this only invited worse inflation in some countries after the crisis. But in Denmark, the nurses still vote for a party that does not even give them a decent pay cheque even though there is process in place which is supposed to guarantee this. It is truly remarkable and inexplicable. It would seem as though the brain shoots down and disregards any rational evidence that contradicts what they previously believed to be the "truth". But why does it happen? Why do they not break out of this control scenario? Why are the politicians playing cat and mouse with them? They have no self-beliefs or any objective thoughts. Even if they do have differing thoughts, they will probably not act on them for fear of potential backlash. But this is the precise narrative that needs to change. Their inaction is excused by their need to provide for their children and for themselves. Because of this, they are unwilling to take risks. So, they remain in their comfort zone, only to later complain about the injustice of it all.

Innovative cognitive dissonance is a real problem when it comes to investors needing to understand what lucrative potential is sitting before them. What is it that they are looking at? Why would they invest in this? We must know that investors are also people; some of them acquired money because they were lucky, had the right job, or found the correct investment early in life and became good at investing in the stock market. Some of them had a shady business where they made a lot of money and then got legitimate after. They moved on to the riskier business of start-ups. But to understand if an idea is good or great is hard. And it also comes down to the team. A bad team with a great idea is often not a worthwhile investment, but a bad idea with a talented team can be. The reason is that the talented team knows how to pivot an idea and make it into a great idea. It is simply hard to know, and it takes an ecosystem of believers who back each other. They also have to have some degree of group thinking. It is better to take the decision with others when it is a risky one.

The smartphone syndrome

I have met some people who did not want to buy a smartphone. They ask why it would be so much better than their phone, if theirs can already adequately send/receive texts and phone calls. I informed them that with a smartphone, I could look up things on a map with GPS. I told them I had direct access to my emails, and I told them every other perk that a smartphone allows due to its use of data and Wi-Fi. They told me they had an encyclopaedia at home they could look everything up in if they needed information; email was not that important... and so they argued against all of the benefits.
In my opinion, they simply wanted to remain laggards: maybe they think the good life lies in being last, or whatever logic they use. Nowadays, they laugh because the Bitcoin price has gone down, and I tell them not to buy it. Their honest, obnoxious laughter overwhelms me. My only response to them is to scold them for being unaware that they are only laughing because they do not currently own any Bitcoin, to which the answer is silence.
Trying to explain to a person with this mindset what blockchain will do to our society is cumbersome and usually pointless. Fortunately, they are not my target audience, so it is no skin off my nose. First, they laugh; then they attempt to silence you; then they attempt to save face by announcing the information provided was something they already knew.

You cannot un-innovate innovations

Now, after all these fights and arguments, I am still strong in my beliefs. There is a specific reason for that; people can buy Bitcoin, and banks are accepting it now. The cat is out of the bag; the truth about these hashes is real. People will pay money for something you are best placed to judge. Several things make crypto and blockchain a remarkable technology that we have invented, and now it is something that even governments must accept people are using. They try to avoid this reality in some countries; they attempt to tax it hard, or they forbid people from using crypto. For instance, we see this in India, where taxes are up to 30% on transfers, and in China, where they only want you to use their digital crypto renminbi.
But blockchains are here and thus crypto is a real thing. It exceeded over 3 trillion USD market capitalization in 2021 before BTC value declined. Michael Saylor says that, when a company or an innovation exceeds a trillion, it is meant to be. And none of the innovations or companies that exceeded a trillion have disappeared, at least up to now. So crypto is here to stay.

From a tribal to a space odyssey

I have been studying people and how they try to live their lives. I have attempted to find out why people react so differently to the same problems. Furthermore, I found a model that explains some of this in Clare Grave's value levels (LINK,). Using this, he explains the evolution of humankind and how we function from being primitives to tribal individuals, up to level 8. A brief description of a person who has reached this world view, seeing a world in danger of geopolitical collapse because of the adoption of short-term strategies, is that they see life as diverse and paradoxical. So, what happens when we reach these various stages as a society? Why are we on diverse levels as countries? And why have some of the Nordic countries reached level 6, where Individuals operating at this level may have an ineffectual quality. They find it very challenging to accomplish their mission because they're concerned with listening to everyone's perspectives. This is the consensus problem that exists today in countries like Denmark, Sweden, and Norway: too many discussions without results.

Clare W. Graves (1914 – 1986) was a Professor of Psychology at the Union College in New York (USA). In short, the article explains the levels, how we must analyse the Nordic mindset, and why they have not taken the leap to tier two, where level seven and eight are; some people have but most have not. Most people have not entered the ninth level yet but will over time. The average person today has not entered level 7. The prosperity is not there yet across the whole globe to give this option a full stretch.

In most North American countries, people tend to live at level five. On an individual level, this is a 'me-centric' focus. At level five, we discover there is no reason to limit ourselves. Here, our core values are success, creativity, and achievement. So, the North Americans do have a higher living standard and GDP in general than the rest of the world. They strive for themselves. But both levels five and six are far away from tier two the next level, where tribal obsessions disappear. This is core of the leap into levels seven, eight, and nine. The levels indicate what kind of social impact they can have and what kind of products we can expect from a person who thinks less individualistically. What is a society where people try to fit in, and what is a society where people attempt to stand out?
To understand humans, we need a system like this and the Myers-Briggs indicator that can tell individuals how they can fit into a system with others, and who they interact with in the best manner. Compared to others, Graves' understanding of cultural levels is the best tool in the bag. Why is it so important now? For me, it is essential to know why people are laggards or why they think certain things matter, while others do not.

Artificial intelligence, the next frontier

In the film *2001, a Space Odyssey*, HAL 9000, an AI, directs the crew through any difficulties during their journey. Stanley Kubrick had a budget of $10 million to create this marvellous flick. And it was a blockbuster hit, making $146 million. During the period in which the movie was released, this was a lot of money. But the film was a revelation for many people. The film opened the door for a discussion of how our lives would progress and change as the development of AI continues.
The world we are about to enter has artificial intelligence in it. It is already here. Facial recognition has a 99.97% recognition accuracy level as of 2020. Why is this important

to us? First, there will be services where we will have to know those with whom we are speaking. A new example where you can try A.I. out is Midjourney. Here you can write a sentence like, 'A space odyssey spacecraft shaped like a bone', and then the computer will generate a picture based on this (LINK). This is particularly interesting when it comes crypto, as we have opportunities the banks previously did not have. KYC (or knowing your customers) is hard for the old banks to do. Customers will most likely feel strange if they have to suddenly show their passport in a bank, they have been going to for 30 years. But what about now when the chance is here to do it a better way? When crypto can be 100% transparent or 100% anonymous, there are new options to build a trustworthy banking system, both for lenders and for normal credit owners. When A.I. is in the economy, we will have options to use our money in a new way. You do not have to hide your identity if you own it yourself. A non-fungible token can hold it for you on your device. This means that you do not have to worry about GDPR if you do not want to. If you want to sell your identity, meaning making money on it so the large corporations can send marketing to you, that will be an option soon. But the entire system is upside-down. You own your identity; you can hide it, or you can use it when you would like to pay. You can sell it to receive marketing in your inbox; this will also be a part of the new metaverses.

Hal 9000 was a helper, but at the end of the film, things started to go wrong. Though the movie depicts the AI ultimately taking over control of the ship, do we actually have to fear AI? I am uncertain if we must. When it comes to coding, I believe there will and can be an option to make an overall framework for A.I. production within the economy. A.I. can be used in a broader legal frame, whereby A.I. will be restricted to certain criteria to hold the control over the system. But on the other hand, someone who wants to do harm and has access to these systems can build a mean machine. Currently, we see more deepfakes: video clips that mimic a known person, a politician, or a businessperson, done so well that you think you are watching the real person. This can also be used to fake a situation. In war, this can be crucial. Only time will tell if it destroys humankind. Google currently has a library of over three thousand deepfake videos, so an A.I. can theoretically learn to detect deepfake; but it is and will be an ongoing, continuous battle.

Tribal to social economy

Soon, the social economy will be a way that people increasingly interact. A broader term for this is Web3. Decentralized autonomous organizations will bring people together in new ways. DAOs will give you an option to build on a project without having any contact to a person or organisation. You just sign in on the job and, if your proposal fits the needs, you can start building it. When the job is done, you get your money. Simple. We are living in the tribal economy. In Graves' values, the tribal takes us up to level 6, where people are spiritually and environmentally conscious. But still, they think in terms of money and are we-centric. The next tier of thinking is level 7, where people start to create systems leading away from tribal thinking. Socialistic thinking is a thing of the past. Yellow (level 7) can set goals that are unlikely to bear fruit in their lifetime. They can talk to all levels and understand how to set them, so they work together. These are the people who understand the social economy.

Consensus and the waterfall method

In the old economy, the highest levels of Graves' values, are seen in the Scandinavian countries, and the Netherlands and Canada are also on this list. They have the option to work together with the entire world in a joint venture that works across borders. These countries have a high level of trust and build on collaboration. From the outside, it can look complicated, but when there is trust from both sides, the legal logistics are so daunting to navigate. In the old economy, transactions for goods are more common. Transactions involving intellectual property involve things that are easy to steal and hard to prove the ownership of. We do not need this when the collaboration is set in a DAO. The code has been built into the legal contract in all the parts that you create.

Consensus systems, as we see in the Scandinavian countries today, will be outdated in a few years. The public sector works with the waterfall method on most projects. So, we all get a piece of the pie if a person working on a project creates something beneficial. This ends up with a waterfall, the water/ideas that make up the system just keep on producing new needs. Therefore, the project never ends, and it can only end up as a failure and a large budget that the citizens must pay.

With a DAO, you will be able to have people in the organization without knowing who they are. In crypto, the zero-knowledge proof will tell us that the sender and the receiver are who they say they are. They simply just do the job, and the workers leave when it is over. People will say it is not durable, but this is because of yesterday's thinking. This is the reason we need autonomy, so that everything happens in a trusted manner. With the third party out of the way, things become more flexible and even more dependable than we have seen before. This will bring the world an option to thrive even more rapidly.

Tribal thinking

You belong to a certain group and find it hard to be an individual. You require people around you and that makes you feel safe and happy. When it comes to the political systems that are centralized in the tribal systems, with one person set at the top, we have not seen systems yet where everyone has a say. The pyramid power structure is still the status quo. Even the people who think that we should all have a democratic vote and a piece of the power have a centralized mindset in their way of thinking about the system. When I talk to the most extreme believers in this, they often use the word "democracy". But it is a cover-up for a one-leader system; the power structure is still that of one person who must rule at the end of the day.

Space odyssey

Everything around us is based on levels 1 to 6. Socialism is like a lobbyist; its fruits are meant for a specific group of the population. And it is always, "funnily enough", the group you are in. Most socialists say to you that they vote to protect you. It is because they love you that they vote as they do. Trust me, someone said that to me. Most likely though, it is because they believe it is acceptable to take your money and invest it into the public sector, they are a part of. Socialism has changed from being a party for the workers to being a party for the government. Does it happen on the right wing, too? Yes, it does, but not in the same way as in Greece, where the hairdressers go on a pension when they are 42.

"Express Self Now, but Not at the Expense of Others or the World, so that Life May Continue."

The next tier in the Graves' value system is level seven. Such individuals often feel misunderstood and think it is "lonely at the top." They become irritated and frustrated with the rigid thinking of the fours and the lack of regard for nature of the fives. They may also feel uncomfortable with the pointless hugging and emotional expressions of the sixes and crave deeper interpersonal connections. It might be important for you to click this link. If you read the book, the links are all on the website. But to understand a lot of my thinking this link more or less has to be watched, before you read on (Link).

When you're misunderstood, what do you feel? How do you explain things when the only tool you have to resolve problems is a hammer? I regularly find maths professors to be clever people, but they tend to resolve all difficulties in the world with maths. When you know the world as a mason, you try to build a carport with bricks. If you are a carpenter, you would build it out of wood.

There is some hatred between the levels, as people do not understand each other's belief systems. Therefore, there is a considerable gap between levels. They do not understand each other's perspectives. So, if you are a religious person in level four, you think everybody else is stupid because they do not understand that everything is God's work, or that he built the world. Fours explain everything with religion and that is the surrounding philosophy. Even the smallest particles in the world are named god's particle, the Higgs Boson (just to mention how God is mentioned in strange places). When you are a level five you know you can do it yourself and build your own fortune. After this, you know that more resources mean more opportunity to build. Level six is compromised of the consensus-driven collectivists; tribal thinking is still present in the form of a workforce you identify yourself with.

At level seven you feel alone and seek others on all levels in tier one. Those I tier two, that is level seven eight and nine, can have a dialogue with all levels and understand how you can change the world for everyone. Most people in lower levels think of themselves first. In *2001, a Space Odyssey*, there is a clip of some monkeys standing at the edge of a lake. One throws a bone that resolves into a spaceship. This scene shows evolution, from a bone being used to hammer things with or smack someone else's skull, to becoming a space explorer. We are about to go to the next level in the physical form; we have the space station. But do we understand how to reach the next level as a species? Do we still smack each other's skulls, for better or for worse? We even have a telescope in the heavens/space that can tell us about the start of the universe, the Big Bang.

Business networks

The reason I had to write this book was that I went to a business summit. All the people who participated as business angels or VCs were thinking of themselves. A worthwhile investment is one where the money comes back 100-fold. Participants tend to say they will not invest when the tax rate is 42%, as it is in Denmark on investments, unless they are certain it is a promising investment. The investors tend to say, "I am not focusing on this now; crypto, and gaming are not in my scope." This is extremely narrow-minded, and it is the environment that we have in Denmark now in 2022. Investors do not even understand the potential that resides in the blockchain market or in the three billion gamer market. They do not understand our options to help people out of poverty. I know from my years of studying this tribe how they are. Even the government's soft money has a penalty for crypto investments, so they do not look at it. Denmark and other Nordic countries are under 2% in the investments on crypto, even when the world market looks like this.

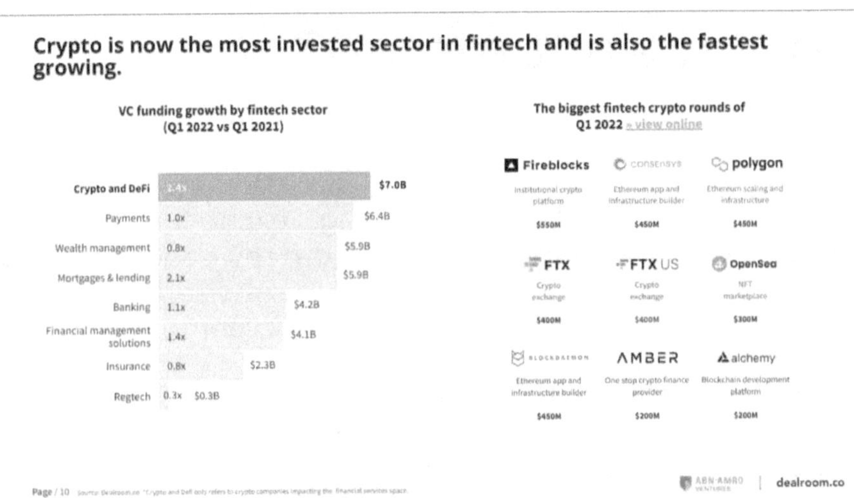

You simply must understand that investors around the world are looking into this area, but not in the Nordics. There is something rotten in the state of Denmark. We are living in one of the world's richest places on paper, but when it comes to innovation and creativity, we do not excel. It is a wasteland. People like me must go elsewhere to find options for investments and growth.

However, it leads me to dive into why it is this way and what the possibilities are for growth in the coming years. Where are the markets, and where will we find the investors?

Chapter 3: Employment

Do you want money?

It seems like a logical way of thinking. I exchange my time for money. I have learned my skills from my education, and now I want to build a family and a life. Likewise, I want a car and a house where I can sit down every evening with my wife and my kids.

People are still exchanging their time for money. The scope of work is only this. You ask people if they wish to be a part of something bigger. First, they speculate what the meaning of it all is and why now? They have mortgages and loans to pay off; they fear you are attempting to scam them by refusing to pay in normal currency.

This is the typical response I receive from people I ask to be part of my company. The way of thinking is tribal; people can't see themselves in something bigger, so they focus on the meal right in front of them.

I know some people will get angry with me for writing this, thinking, "Why are you telling me that this is wrong?" I am not saying that; I'm just suggesting that there is something better for you. The option for a person to become involved in a business and have the upside with the company is a much better option than just getting into the hamster wheel from day one. People who own a part of a company or own stocks are better off than people who don't. People who own their house are also better off than people who rent. These are the facts that I hope more people will understand when we look at the crypto economy that we are facing these days.

Don't steal my plate.

I had a few developers in the company tell me they could build an MVP (minimal viable product) for me. But the first guy told me this for six months and then quit for a job in Norway. The next guy spent two years and produced a demo that allowed you play counterstrike for some test tokens. As it was only a demo, he asked for five BTC for it on the basis it would not be part of the business. Here are some people who look only at what is right in front of them, things they can see like Bitcoin or money. They are both Danes and in Denmark; people tend to be tribal and focus on things that they can see with their eyes. If you move the plate in front of them, they will starve to death rather than move one seat. Level five is related to all of those with no co-operation and an individual-centric focus. We need more people who can understand the larger picture. We require more people who do not suffer from cognitive dissonance.

Network

Building trust with others in a network takes time. You must deal with people every day, so they know and understand what you are talking about. But you also need to have consistency and long-term plans, even ten years ahead. This is the big vision that they do not get, but you must be patient, and you must talk about it, so it becomes real for them. Some people know this from the beginning, but most will simply have to accept that the vision is real. It is difficult to be a messenger with a vision like this. On each level, people fight against each other to be the holder of the right mindset. So, the consensus of lvl6 (we-centric) people with waterfall methods is that this is the right one. They resent the lower levels for not understanding their beliefs. The level five (me-centric) level people who believe 100% in capitalism and becoming rich quickly are focused on the option, for example, of BTC going up in the market. But they do not focus on the technology. The rational people in the (we-centric) blue level, where religion and centralism are rules, believe that there is an omniscient being secretly dictating the direction we take in life. There are still plenty of people who think like this in the world. The clash between these worldviews, even though these people can all be developers who are supposed to understand how blockchain works, leads to troubles with understanding why investing in the company will be mutually beneficial.

Networking between them is also hard as their belief systems are fighting each other, so we must seek individuals who are already enlightened.

Crucially, level seven people can communicate with individuals at their level, to get what they want in a faster and more productive way. They may set and work towards goals that are unlikely to bear fruit in their lifetime.

Battles between truth and doubt

Why all these comments about levels, you may ask. Are levels not a way of discriminating between different belief systems?

For me, understanding these levels is a way to communicate to all levels and not discriminate between them, because I understand where they stand. The fight between the levels is a common dispute amongst the community. People of various levels experience difficulties altering their perceptions and will therefore discuss things from the level they are on.

Most investors are in level five (me-Centric). Their thoughts are predicated around how something benefits them and if it is a sound investment. They come from a life where they have created things with their own hands and knowledge and have done things themselves to become rich and prosperous.

When it comes to the consensus level six individuals, they are we-centric. They often tend to vote for a political party that gives them benefits, but they are unaware of their contradictory thoughts and actions. They think they are helping others, and they think they are doing the right thing, just like all other levels under tier two (starting at level seven). The first six levels are in tier one, the next three levels are in tier two.

The moral discussion between the levels will hopefully bring a larger understanding of the greater good, and the whole purpose of our company. The philosophy around the project is also clear, but some will not understand it, especially those in the lower levels, who will project their negative belief system onto us.

The decisive test here is to give people an option to either choose the salary, or EQT, and a portion of tokens. If they only focus on salary and instant gratification in the short term, you can be quite sure who you are standing in front of.

Autonomy

There are a few things technology can do for us, especially when it comes to automating things.

Autonomy is the capacity of an agent to act in accordance with objective morality rather than under the influence of desires.

We can now use autonomy to supplement formal methods of communication. Task management will perhaps become outdated as a result. However, this is not true yet. Most people who have tried to work with autonomy in their organizations have failed. We know about LEAN, SIXSIGMA PRINCE2 and other tools that optimize the production line, and that even possess credibility certifications for how the production workflow operates. This is set in specific frameworks. ISO is one standard that demonstrates certain standards are being met. Numerous other certifications exist to provide credibility for a company's environmental promises, delivery reliability, and so on. These standards can actually be built on a sublevel in autonomy and in a smart contract. This means that you do not need to have an entire office full of lawyers to do contracts every time a task is executed, or a task fails. The failure will be removed by the smart contract. You cannot do the task if it does not fulfil the requirements.

When it comes to electronic documentation, programming and code is easier to control in smart contracts than in physical structures. You can build contracts around each contract, and an A.I. can be programmed to recognize when a task has been performed properly. Before we let it loose on the smart contract society, humans will still be the final checkpoint to ensure this. Soon we will start to see the real decentralized autonomous organizations work in the right manner. There are still many problems to solve in this kind of "non-human" space, if all tasks are still performed by humans, but, upon the task's completion, A.I. will analyse the quality of work. For instance, humans will still try to cheat the system and set out to avoid doing the job so they can just take the money. But one day we will be able to fully believe in these systems. However, until this point, I have not personally seen one that really works. So Blockchain and DAOs have not yet evolved into what they can become.

Free owner

You are free to own your own company, although you will have to take a stand. You might doubt it, but it will come to fruition if you participate and build it. You as an owner can be free. What will it mean to be free?

If you own your stuff, you can do what you want with it. There is an enormous difference with renting, leasing or having any other kind of contract on the use of a product or a piece of code. When you do not own it, you cannot do anything with it without permission.

So, why is freedom so important to me? It is built into the decentralized way of thinking. You own your cryptocurrencies. You do not own fiat currency like US Dollars, Euros, Renminbi or any other central-bank-produced currencies. That is why so many governments around the globe are trying to stop crypto. This centralization is also the fundamental reason we have inflation because the central banks have been printing new money at a rate never before seen in history.

So, in the system we have today, you do not own the currency you hold in your hand. We all know there is a belief that you do; for instance, when you have one dollar in your hand, you know that you can decide what it can be used for. But you do not own it; you are allowed to spend it, you are forbidden by laws from crumpling it, drawing on it or burning it. More crucially, you are not allowed to try to copy it or make your own version of it. This will get you thrown into jail for a while. Unsurprisingly, the sentences in most countries are rather strict on this, so you won't get out for a long period. The reason why such sentences are high derives from the past. Back in the day, when it was the king who held the money reserve in gold and minted the coins that had a value, it was common for certain types of people to clip a piece of the coin and make a new one out of the collected pieces.

Source: www.finds.org.uk

Money clipping was normal. The newly minted went back into the system and, after a while all coins were bad, so the whole monetary system suffered from inflation. Here is one Roman coin of the sort that was used in England until the pound became the standard. The history is full of attempts to create a stable coinage system that retained the exact value it represented. So, initially, the pound had to retain its value in silver, but what we are witnessing today is the same. People still cannot keep their fingers to themselves. If you can get a hold of other people's cryptocurrencies by phishing or by other fraudulent means, someone will try to do this. There is a need for a better blockchain in the system, one with an ID layer where KYC identification is up front and can help people find discover who the sender and receiver of a specific token were, as well as the date, time and amount.

Anonymity and privacy

Privacy is as important as anonymity in a blockchain, as all transactions will be visible to everyone who searches for a specific blockchain. Only a few blockchains do not have 100% transparency. For clarification, privacy is what you have yourself; anonymity is what the blockchain producer/holder can provide, rather than revealing who you are. This is good when you want to have security but not privacy. Nevertheless, it is wise to have both. So, how can we have this?

One company is producing this Concordium, a blockchain that is built with an ID layer. This means that people must do a KYC up front when they begin buying their coin. This gives the holder of the token anonymity. However, if the holder engages in any fraudulent dealings or is legally incriminated, their blockchains can be revealed to the authorities. When governments decide to invest in crypto over the next few decades, they will be looking at a version of blockchain with this built in. Otherwise, it can be hard to find people on other blockchains. However, if you use a private wallet that has no connection to an online exchange, you can choose full anonymity. This is the prime moment for fraudsters to snatch your money. This will be further discussed under the subject of fraud and bullshit detection. It is no shock that some people have successfully conned thousands of people out of millions of dollars. But what really happened and why did it happen? Well, if you believe in others, you probably should not; if you thought that you could, you still should not. The crypto scene is full of dangerous people who you cannot trust. There are numerous gold-diggers and scammers in this space, mostly due to the fact that it lacks any form of protection, and they can run off with your money if you are a small fish. So here is my advice; do not trust anyone. The question then becomes, what do you do? I met a man at the beginning of 2014 who showed me a hardware wallet (Nano) that incorporated a specific USB made for the purpose of storing Crypto. Today, I recognize that I should have listened to him more carefully and should have invested heavily into this. But that is where it comes down to the doubt and personal beliefs. More on this later.

How to detect a bug

The trap

If it happens to me, it can happen to you. I have been in this crypto space for a long time; however, most people might ask, "How do they get hold of your money?" You might think they can access your wallet, or that they can get your money in the transaction, but that is not what happens for most people. Some exchanges and some NFT portals, like OpenSea.io, have been compromised. Most scammers utilize social media to identify a victim's weak point. In my case, because I'm building a start-up and looking for investors, scammers will often pretend to be investors. Typically, scammers gain a target's trust by insisting they only want to ensure their account and personal information is safe. Once the trust is established, targets unknowingly release crucial information that leads to their account being hacking and passwords changed.

The scammer

In my case, there are a lot of phishing emails. Fake accounts look legitimate as they have appropriate websites linked, social media profiles that fit, the appropriate address, the right phone number, and many pictures of the so-called right people. It all looks right. But when you get in touch with them, they go to WhatsApp, meaning they never show their face. One thing you must do is to remember to use video calls. Their next ploy entails them falsifying the necessity of you contacting particular insurance agencies in order to receive the "investor's" money. As a start-up, you should never pay insurance for investors, particularly if there is an equity deal where they will get percentages of the company.

Then they will tell you that you must go and meet them in a specific destination. In my case, I purchased tickets to meet with someone I believed was an investor. However, when I sent the confirmation of my tickets to them, the person only wanted to know if I had money. Then, one Saturday evening, he proposed sending me some Bitcoin. Do not accept this. Never accept Bitcoin or send Bitcoin to someone you have just met. The scam happens when they "help" you set up the transaction. It works like this. They use a mobile camera to get your code when you are on the page. I tried this, with a small amount of BTC. I knew what was happening, and how to stop future losses. But they can also go in through your browser wallet like MetaMask and place their own wallet in there if you do not shut it down. They also use public sites for NFT´s to create false NFT´s that open up for your MetaMask and rob the account.

Countless scammers will send you emails offering to help you out in every way possible. My best advice is, do not trust any of them, not before you have full KYC on them; this can be passport information, driver's licence, and a copy of an invoice or other document with their real address that matches the address with their online profile. You must know who they are. Some will believe this is an extreme amount of documentation to insist upon receiving. Others will supply it without fussing. Again, this simply boils to doubt and beliefs. You believe in yourself; they therefore play on your ideas of yourself. In the process, they create a set-up where you get scammed because you roll with it.

The high roller and the player

Scammers also target people with a lot of BTC in their wallet. It happened to me in April 2022. I arrived at a fancy

five-star hotel in Copenhagen. A well-dressed man in his 50s was placed in a dining area with his kid and his wife. He had had his agent set up a meeting between us on a Friday afternoon. Before dinner, he had time to sit down with me and discuss the investment for our company. I always enjoy the process of pitching for investors. He purchased drinks for us, so it was a comfortable set-up. Well, after over an hour and a half, we parted ways. As we did so, he said was genuinely interested in this investment. Ten minutes earlier, he had asked me if I could help him with a favour. Of course, I was willing to do so. This particular man was selling his hotel and had 25 Bitcoin staked on it and the rest in DKR. He wanted me to find a seller of BTC so he could make the scam on them. The mobile phone trick did not work, he was caught before this. The sellers I found wanted KYC and deep knowledge on who he was. I advised this to them as well.
Twenty minutes earlier, he had told me this my pitch was a really great idea and he liked this and that about it. For my peace of mind, he wanted to show me that he was the private banker for the family business and that they were in real estate. He took out his mobile phone and showed me some PDFs with their portfolio and investment numbers, their company belongings and what they had to invest. The figure was quite large and rather impressive. The following day, the agent called me to ask how it had gone. Our next meeting was scheduled for 5pm on a Sunday evening. I mentioned the investment and that the potential investor was quite impressed with the idea. However, at the end of the meeting, he discussed the 25 BTC again; this seemed the most important thing to him, even though it was the least essential to me. I preferred not to be a middleman. I was also intrigued that they did not know someone who had their own BTC. He asked me if I had BTC, but I pressed him on why he thought I would possess 25 Bitcoins if I was seeking investors. That would have been enough to start a business, after all.

While scammers may not be the cleverest of individuals, they surely are the laziest. Scamming people into giving you their money is fraudulent but easy and lucrative if done correctly. Unfortunately for these particular scammers, they had to go empty-handed. And I am happy about that.
Let me say it this way, if you have ever got burned, you will know the smell in the kitchen.

Anonymity and privacy

If the crown prince wants to buy underwear with crypto, it does not concern other people. Who should interfere in this? But if he engages in money laundering and buying weapons, Interpol or the FBI will want to know of their activities. However, it is difficult to uncover fraud when using cryptocurrencies. Nevertheless, the example above lends credence to the fact that there is a lot of potential for being scammed with money wallets. Although Bitcoin is 100% transparent in the transactions, unless you exchange Bitcoin online, you are most often unaware of who the sender or receiver is, as ID is not always required. You need a layer of ID built in on the blockchain itself to prevent fraud from happening. If you have this information, you can stop this from happening, and you can also find the crook and any questionable transactions. Nowadays, this can be done with more efficiency and ease than banks show in investigating fraudulent transfers or purchases. Did you know that 80% of all dollar bills have traces of cocaine on them? So, most dollar bills have been in some kind of "transaction". Well, this is how it is: more physical USDs are used for corrupt practices than crypto.

Bug fixing

In programming there are numerous bugs that must be fixed when nearing the end of certain tasks. For instance, a single comma can make or break the function of your entire program. This can be highly frustrating, as you have to look through the code over and over. Thanks to other developers, there are programs today that help you bug-fix, find these small programming mistakes, and tell you where they are. When you find them and the program works, most developers get a small grin on their face. However, when it is a human who is trying to scam you, and you believe in what they are telling you, it is much harder. If they are able to garner support from others, most people will believe what is being said. The structure in a society also correlates to their belief system, as the latter is built around social structures. A social structure can be an education, or it can be a workplace. Within this hierarchy, you either learn how it functions or you do not fit in. So, either you are in or you're out. This simple system works fine for the limbic brain. It is easy to cope with and understand. Most political campaigns work around this, and most socialistic parties work around "believe them or us" rhetoric. The fun part is that socialists always claims that they are on level six (the people who are we-centric and believe in the power of *We*). However, is it related to their We, not yours. Yes, it sounds cryptic describing this using *We* and *Me*, but *We* needs to a group of dynamic thinkers. You might not fit in, so you are out. However, they still believe they are being inclusive if you just accept their orders and give them half of your salary. You can be a part of the club if you invest the required funds. Religion also works in the same way, so they go hand in hand on the same economic level of intelligence. Even the mafia works in the same way. Do you want protection from the extortionists? They will inquire on your behalf. The catch is that they demand you pay 10% of your income in exchange. If someone refuses, they can expect retaliation.

I found a bug

So, to explain it more clearly, countless people don't realize that they are their own worst enemy. The bug is in your level of understanding of the world. You must move to level seven before you see the whole thing and beyond. Socialism always leads to poverty. Pure capitalism only leads to a few rich people. Religion gives the priests the power. In lower levels it is the shamans or the kings who have the power.

If you want to give everybody a decent life, we must decentralize government. Government in its purest form is self-government. Do we need a system for this? Do we require regulations for this? Do we require laws for this?

A bee can be a bug, but it can also be a friendly guy who gives you honey. Bees know their places in the hierarchy from birth it is built into their DNA. When one comes out of the hive, it knows where to fly. If it is a worker bee, it is also female; if it is a male, it becomes ready to do its work at home to make more bees with the queen bee. When a worker bee flies out to find pollen that can become honey in the hive, it knows how to tell the other bees where to go afterwards. Even if it flies over 10 km, it can go back home and tell the bees in the hive where the pollen is. It does this with a dance which has been transcribed by entomologists. The special dance consists of moves in the shape of the number eight and the number of times it is done in a specific direction; this tells other bees which direction to go and how far. Here is a bee dancing to communicate where the pollen is Link.

If you do not understand these specific instructions, you're out. If you question them, you're out too.

Many people have avoided me for questioning their beliefs or their way of extrapolating how the world works. Did I feel sad about this? In the beginning, yes, but I also understood that my questions were legitimate. They might have sounded stupid to these people/disciples who believed in something and treated it as the solemn truth. There's nothing more to it. It seems to be that these findings are the purest of all truths. So, I forged on. I did also have doubt in myself. Was it really the truth they had found? Were they right and I was the one who was wrong? If so, why could they not answer my simple questions? Why did they not have the answer on simple things that coincided with the physics? For these people, it is extremely hard to move between levels and move up a notch. If you believe what your parents taught you based on a specific religion, how can you not see it as a universally accepted truth? My question to them was often: what is the driving factor behind why you believe this? Most often the answers were long and convoluted, but their explanation could never really touch upon the crux of their beliefs. This is most likely due to the fact that, not only are religious beliefs dominant in centralized thinking societies, but religion was also initially created to dominate other cultures or religions.

The bug here is the restraints that people have. If they are in tier one, they are in the tribal way of thinking.

Think of the bees dancing to tell where the pollen is. <u>Link</u> If you need instructions on how to move around, you are probably still in tier one.

If your goal in life is to gain more money to get a better life, you are me-centred, in level five. This is most likely good for you, but not for other people. A huge number of people in the United States believe that this is the only way. As with all levels in tier one, they hate all other levels, and they think their way is correct.

When you are level six, you have a *We*-culture, but this level is dedicated to achieving a life that is prosperous both for yourself and others. You just believe that hiding in a group and makes it okay to prosper on the backs of others. How people function within the various levels is analogous with the bees, because even though bees have their own communication, they are unable to switch between levels. This prompts the question, who is right and who is wrong?

Peer pressure

One of the strongest forces is social construction. When you are born, there are many things that are coded into your DNA. You know how to breathe; you know how to suckle for milk; you start to find out about your body. Both you and the bee are coded to understand basic communication from early on in life. For humans, it takes four years before you truly know that there is a world around you. But this jump from unconsciousness, like a journey from being like an animal to human consciousness, is what makes us human.

Humans tend to learn from their environment. Some tests conducted on human twins show us that, if you grow up with parents who have high income and good manners, you tend to adopt the same stature. However, growing up ay the opposite tax of the income spectrum means you also adopt that way life, and breaking away from it is incredibly difficult.

Twin studies by Hutchings and Mednick looked at the environmental impact on children who were not raised by their biological parents. If the children act in a similar way to their biological parents, then genetics could explain, for instance criminality. However, if they act like the adoptive parents, then environment could be the cause. One study with a test group of 14,000 adopted children found that a high proportion of boys with criminal convictions had biological parents with criminal convictions as well, demonstrating a link between aggression and genetics. There is currently no evidence that suggests a strong correlation between children and their adoptive parents. Therefore, this provides evidence for the genetic transmission theory.

Overall, the twin studies show that there is a larger opportunity for a monozygotic twin separated at birth. If they grow up with a family that has no criminal record, but their biological parent does, they have a higher chance of becoming a criminal themselves. The studies show that the way a child is nurtured stimulates a gene boost if the child is in criminal circumstances. If they grow up in an environment where there are non-criminal parents, the chance of criminal behaviour is still higher. What I conclude from these studies is that it can be hard to change behaviour and to change your social environment to allow you to elevate yourself. Genetics have coded you in a certain way from the moment you were born. This study demonstrates that criminal behaviour is something that is hard to remove from one's genes. Therefore, if you are genetically predisposed to this behaviour, it is even more difficult to ignore.

Let me apply this to socialism, wherein it is acceptable to use other people's money for a "good deed" like the public sector. This, too, is in your genes; you simply have no trouble thinking like this if your parents both have this mindset, or if it is in your DNA. Some people might think that a mindset is not something that can be predetermined by your genes, but twin studies suggests that it can be.

Jumping a level on the Grave's value chain can therefore be hard for people to do.

Peer pressure, as we all know, can be hard to withstand, for instance if you are told you are a wimp if you don't dare to do a bungee jump or dive from more than 10 meters. A well-known study, the Asch conformity experiments - Link shows that people will lie to themselves about something that is clearly untrue, if a group of people around you are saying they believe it is true. It seems extreme, but the study has been run over and over again, and this tells us that we, as a social being, are straightforward to manipulate. Here is the video on the study. Link

As a species, we are able to communicate with words, and the finest of institutions we have in the western world is called the parliament. Professional speakers conduct their speeches in Latin *parlare*. They make a living by speaking, and it is no different from the ancient Greek or ancient Roman Empire where politicians were the first professional speakers. For over 2,000 years, we have heard such representatives speaking so eloquently and persuasively that people believe what they are told.

Family

Some families create an environment which influences their kids to go to school. Some families have nothing of the sort. Most people live in safe families, but some do not. "If you go to school and get a job, you can get the life you dream of." This sentence was said to me when I was a little boy. I did not believe that was the end goal. I thought I could go further; some thought I had megalomania. Others were inspired and thought so too, but they would not travel that road themselves. They had no positive examples of their dreams being fulfilled. For most people, life experiences are crucial for dictating how someone leads their life. This often replicates their parents' choices.
Even as an adult who has lived over half of my life, some people still tend to tell me that getting a job is simply the way life should be lived.

I have always felt like the little creature in this picture; I still do. In my belief, most people tend to use the hammer philosophy so that every problem looks like a nail. If you are a mathematician, you think that all issues have an associated equation. If you are a nurse, you believe that all issues can be solved through care and nurture. We see many people getting the same education as their parents, and they conduct themselves in a similar manner. Families create strong ties that are hard to break out of. But why should you?

DNA

Through your DNA, you are innately coded to certain predispositions. Percentages compiled from a multitude of twin studies performed over the last century demonstrate this. Another reason for the overwhelming consensus among collectivists in the Nordics goes back to individuals who fled to the US in the late 1800s. This was caused by years of famine that also resulted in a large demographic of Irish people fleeing, too.
It is not that a collectivist society can't be productive or that a society will fall apart if there was an imbalance of collectivists to socialists. It is simply much harder to create wealth quickly in a socialist system. If you analyse levels of GDP in the Nordics, it seems like there is a good market. So, how can that be true if there are so many socialists? Well, as I mentioned before, socialists shoot themselves in the foot by taxing themselves and others too harshly. They also have to pay for the welfare themselves. The reason that the Nordics are rich is not because of the taxation, it is because of productivity and the job market. The workplace in general is still individualistic and built by the civil people who own private businesses and vote against the high taxation.
If we look at the people who went to the US, there was also a large demographic who did not want to have a large government like the ones in Europe. That is why there is a law to protect gun rights; guns that can protect them if the government gets too large and too powerful. Some of the people who fled were also pioneers and this is one of the

reasons why the DNA of the Nordic people in the USA is also more innovative. A lot of the innovations that were made in the 20th century came from the US.

If we look at WW2 again, think of the huge number of engineers that were needed by Germany to build the V2 rocket and potentially to use atom bombs. This would have stopped the British from winning the war. They were only six months away from successfully completing their mission. After WW2, who acquired these scientists? The US offered an amnesty to Nazi scientists. On the 16th of July 1945, the US had their first nuclear test, *Trinity* which caused an explosion over New Mexico. The war had ended in Europe in 1945 and the scientist had a bomb a year later. I know that both Albert Einstein (German) and Niels Bohr (Danish) were the masterminds behind the western nuclear bomb.

One of the German scientists served as director of the newly formed Marshall Space Flight Center and as the chief architect of the Saturn V super heavy-lift launch vehicle that propelled the Apollo spacecraft to the Moon. He was a highly ranked in the Nazi party and SS. Wernher von Braun was one of over 13,000 scientists that the allies got their hands on towards the end of the war in Europe. The Russians also got their fair share, and in 1949 they had their first atomic test, too. It was a considerable surprise to the rest of the world that they had progressed so rapidly.

To turn things a bit upside down, the Nazi party was ecological and loved nature. They used this as a propaganda tool to make people believe in their clean spirit and mindset. The eco movement and the clean energy movement we have today are also believers in a centralized system. They are socialistic thinkers who want a one-size-fits-all strategy. This strategy only works in few situations, because there it is true that when we are lifting something in a large group, we can lift more. This is also what brought the war machine in Germany to life. Numerous workers came together and, with the most brilliant minds in the world at the time, created a monster.

However, is the monster in our DNA today? Yes and no. Some people would like to take it to a higher level. Most would not. We collectively agree that world war, and nuclear war in particular should be avoided. The things that happened in the war were awful, and we don't want that to happen again.

So out of war comes a stronger USA, with the pioneers and now also the smartest engineers on the planet as residents. This is another part of the story of the success of the US, and also a reason why growth in Europe is a lot slower but sometimes steadier. When you look at CERN in Switzerland, the budgets afforded to the Large Hadron Collider is huge. In the US, where presidents are elected every 4th year, they sometimes forget to have foresight about future plans for massive projects. So, they halt the former presidents' projects, and the money that has been spent goes to waste. However, in Europe, where the budget is set to build something and it takes 20 years to complete, the profit is still non-existent, and money still goes to waste.

Therefore, the DNA for fast innovation can also be a downside when it comes to long-term projects. If it interests you, investigate the next European mega project, ITER in France. Fission energy reactors take 40 years to plan and build.

One of the reasons that the Nazis failed with the nuclear bomb was because of 12 Norwegians. In the film *The Heavy Water War* on Netflix, the plot is about sabotage and how 12 men planted C4 explosives in the Rjukan heavy water plant in the middle of the winter of 1943; this helped prevent Nazi Germany from completing their mission to control Europe and dominate the world.

Religion

Strong beliefs can make people believe in anything. One study shows that Jews who survived the holocaust had strong beliefs they credit to maintaining their hopes.

Additionally, some crusaders who killed and raped people during their raids were believers in their cause. The individuals from ISIS who drove down streets and killed people by driving into the crowd in large trucks in 2018 were also believers. The believers of Hare Krishna are also devoted to their faith although are pretty much the only followers of a religion without blood on their hands.

Consider the authority of the bible back in the dark ages. It was monks who told people they could not drink beer but who still brewed it themselves. Sex and other human activities were also forbidden for thousands of years, but recent stories and subsequent trials have shown that it still happened within the churches.

Copernicus told the world that the earth orbited the sun, but no one properly acknowledged his last work, *Revolutionibus*, published in 1543. It was Johannes Kepler who proved that he was right. But the church did not really take it seriously. They still believed that the earth was the centre of the universe.

In the film *The Physician*, religious dogma was put aside to focus on science. Why? Because the gift of healing and the power of knowledge was a powerful motivator during a period in which an entire city contracted the plague, and the religion-based knowledge of the time was ineffective. However, the devout Muslims would not allow this to happen. In the early Middle Ages in Europe, people could not keep up with the scientific progress in the Islamic world. Their golden age lasted until the 12th century, when more devout strands of thinking obstructed further progress. Something similar occurred in China to interrupt their scientific evolution because they were superior to most other nations 5,000 years ago. Therefore, nothing really progressed for a number of years. They already had porcelain, ships, and trade. They had fireworks and they had medicine. However, ships intended for exploration were stopped from setting sail by the emperor because they believed there was nothing left to discover. On top of that, they built the greatest wall ever seen on earth a 21.196

km wall that protected the country. See, that is
protectionism. Like the religious people, they had one ruler;
the moral is that centralization and religious dogma lead to
the world coming to a halt.

Money

Remember that the book of Karl Marx and Friedrich Engels
is called *Das Kapital*? Let us dwell on that for a moment.
What is capitalism? And why is socialism superior to
capitalism; or is it?
We are looking for a bug; the system is easy to falsify if
you'd like to. It is easy to cheat other people in capitalism.
This is why some nations are built around lawyers. Lawyers
must then assume responsibility when things go south.
But are lawyers the answer to the world of prosperity and
easy access to wealth?
Centralized thinkers are generally focused on one region of
the world. In present day China, they tend to think that it is
ingenuity that rules the world. There is no one who can
speak against the fact that ingenuity and capitalism have
brought over half a billion people out of poverty. Let us look
at *Das Kapital* and the so-called socialism they have in
China today through the Communist party. It is no longer
hardcore communism. I have spoken to a few Chinese
people, who told me that what happens in China today is
hardcore capitalism, but that they could only see socialism
when discussing the central committee. Marx was born in
the town of Trier in the wonderful Middle East of Germany.
He lived with his wife and kids in the house he was born in
until he was rejected by society and had to move to
London. Now, there is a museum you can visit there; this is
because communism is strongly related to socialism.
Marx's thoughts about how poverty could be redeemed by
circulation of capital to the lower classes have come to be
seen as a prototype of what actually happened in Europe.
The working classes became empowered by democracy
and could then vote for a politician who told them they

would get more money in their pockets if they voted for them. The power structure was clear, just as it was with the monks in the monastery, who also demanded taxation. The kings also asked for their share; that is why it is so funny when socialists perpetuate the idea that we should steal from the rich to give to the poor, like Robin Hood. But Robin was in hiding from the King, who was the oppressor at the time as he took people's money in tax.
Today, it is the socialists who take our money in tax. However, they tell you an opposing story, saying that they will give you money. Nevertheless, every single time a socialist is voted into power, the taxes rise. Here is the bug. If you are a socialist and central thinker, you can't even see it; you can't even understand that you are ruining things for yourself.

Socialism

Morals and double standards.

Environmentally aware people claim that electrical vehicles are one of the saviours of today's societies around the world. However, when it comes to electrical vehicles, you are simply moving pollution from one region to another. That´s it. You do not reduce carbon emissions overall. The whole production of batteries in mines does not meet that goal. Furthermore, when it comes to carbon-neutral electricity, there is also a way to go. We only endorse electrical vehicles to show that we care. It is like the church in the old days where they sold the idea that you can buy a place in heaven. When it comes to cobalt mines, the production is often in rural Africa and the mines there do not have protections against child labour. So, the entire idea is flawed and full of ridiculous notions about doing good. The absurd part is that this is not the actual result. Socialism is advocated by a group of people who vote for other people's money. It does not create greater wealth; instead, it reduces it. The same thing occurs with the green movement, which in most cases is run by socialistic people with centralized thinking. They want the power; that is their only goal when in the end. The kinds of power structures where you get people to believe in a religion or in a green environment are much the same. You get people to believe in an idea, and then you can decide their destiny. For example, schoolteachers often vote for candidates of a socialist party, because they tell them that teachers will receive better materials to teach the children with. Most teachers understand that better resources are a must when it comes to better educated children. They sign up for a specific political party, mostly socialistic ones. They love the idea of solidarity, and they think they can only get it from socialism. This is the situation in Denmark and has been for the last century. So now the candidate gets elected, and they all try to redirect money to the welfare state. Let's say it is a woman and she now can't get all the other socialists to vote for her idea. Some are nurses, some are doctors, and some are workers in the government. Therefore, it is hard to find the money for the new materials for the schools. We all understand the problems which lead to the welfare state, but it does not produce anything, so it does not make us wealthier. It only gives us knowledge. The concern is that most learning materials in schools do not contain information on how business works. The teachers do not have knowledge about it either, so they stick to things they know and can teach about. Therefore, in a society like Denmark, the education will be socialistic, at least for the workers. They believe in this method of finding small areas on the basis of which they vote for candidates, so they can benefit themselves. For example, in schools with old material to teach with, society adopts a slow pace when it comes to renewal of the economy and when it comes to a better and larger economy. The reason Denmark is in the top ten for highest GDP is not because of the teachers in the socialist party, it is due to the people who vote for the right-wing parties, who know how the market works. My point here is that socialism is a narrow form of politics that only focuses on small areas and not the whole picture. If you consider the states that have tried to be completely socialist, they have failed. We now count over 40 states that have tried this, and we will see more in the future with centralistic governments who will fail. Again, it is not easy for a person with a centralized mindset who thinks acquiring better teaching materials for their students will solve all problems to understand the decentralized world of tomorrow. It is also hard for them to believe in anything other than education as the most important thing in the world. This applies to many workers, and this situation leaves them in despair and in a non-progressive situation.

Chapter 5: Doubt and Beliefs

You're not wrong when you're right

Scammers

Seeing is believing. It is an old saying but it is mostly true. Believing in something because you have seen it is reasonable, but it is not true that you will simply believe in everything just because you have seen it. Most people see the world through their own eyes. How could they not? This remains true until they discover books and read about the perspectives of others. On the flip side, you can be fooled even when you have seen something with your eyes. The book *Extraordinary Delusions and the Madness of Crowds* is an enticing read about people who have tried to scam others since the dawn of time. The whole book is full of examples of how people got scammed, when they believed in something with such ferocity, they allowed themselves to be damned. Throughout the centuries, many people have believed that you could make metal into gold whether it be lead, mercury or plain steel. However, it did not work; they were mostly scams. But why would even kings and priests and other highly ranked officials let themselves be fooled by alchemists? And why did the alchemists even exist? Some of these alchemists died during their experiments. After all, it was lead and mercury they experimented with, and this is not healthy for the human body to come into contact within high quantities. Nonetheless, some scammers were able to successfully accomplish their objective, so much so that even kings believed in some of the scammers and began paying them so they could experiment and gather more science-based knowledge. We know today that we can make gold and even diamonds artificially, but the process of making it costs more than the product. Therefore, it does not make economic sense to do it. During this time though, philosophy was closely tied in with science. Sometimes there were no boundaries between them. There was simply not enough knowledge available to understand the complex world of chemistry. It was complex because it was unknown to man. Now it is not as complex anymore because currently we know so much more. We have even developed the technology to view particles smaller than the electron, like quarks. Additionally, we have mapped the quarks in different particles that build the entire universe. We also know about quantum jumps like the ones the Danish physicist Niels Bohr had interpreted in Copenhagen, where he proved that quantum jumps have a quantized angular momentum. This means that the electron's orbits are quantized or separated in space. The electron could go from one to the other either by jumping down and closer to the proton or moving up and farther away.

Physics

Bohr's brilliant insight was to mix concepts from classical physics with the brand-new quantum physics, creating a hybrid model of the atom (Link). This may contradict Einstein's view that physics should look for 'real existing objects', meaning it should be an ontic theory. Quantum physics changed the world over 100 years ago; today it is helping us to build quantum computers, which will in future help use to generate better artificial intelligence. A.I. can help us understand the universe and ourselves. For instance, as a result, many diseases are better understood than before. Cancer pathology is easier to understand when A.I. is in the picture. Innovation is exponential. Innovation is the core to building better societies and better products. It is the core to find better energy resources and to finding better solutions for them to be used. If it had not been for the A-bomb, we probably would have had the third world war already. But the fear from all countries holds them back from enacting a new war. Hiroshima and Nagasaki were the incidents that stopped the Japanese from continuing the war. While some countries have built nuclear power plants, a few plants blew up and this has led to further hesitancy about the method of production. In Denmark, where Niels Bohr, one of the forefathers of nuclear energy, lived, we never had atomic power. The reason was because he provided enough information to the opponents after WWII. He approached the problem of avoiding warfare by releasing enough knowledge to everyone. His reasoning was that, if all countries had access to the same information, they would be more reluctant to engage in warfare as the playing field would be levelled. But the surveillance was so close from the US government, papers show. He did not dare to go further in on how to use this technology to better energy resources. That resulted in the Danes never created nuclear power on Danish soil. Only one test reactor was built, and it is closed today.

The facts are that physics is hard to accept as not being truth. From the devastating disaster that resulted from the explosions Hiroshima and Nagasaki, it was clear to the Japanese government that they had to stop the war. It created the longest period of peace between the larger countries.

But even one of the most brilliant minds had his doubts on quantum physics. Einstein tried to write a thesis against it but abandoned it because he had to accept it. The quantum leap was a reality, but until his death Einstein did not believe in it.

Niels Bohr's debates with Albert Einstein at the Solvay Conferences were some of the most intense and deep exchanges of views on physics and its philosophy in the twentieth century.

Niels *Bohr: If you are not completely confused by quantum mechanics, you do not understand it.*

Again and again, Albert Einstein presented thought experiments that disproved the Copenhagen Interpretation. Each time, Niels Bohr slept on the problem, he could ingeniously contradict Albert Einstein's objections the following day. On one occasion he even used Albert Einstein's own general theory of relativity for the purpose (link).

Again, the philosophy, interpretations and the thoughts of brilliant minds are the prime movers for innovation. Their thoughts and their two ways of seeing the world helped establish a new view of reality, and these findings are what builds the world today. For many years computers were a thing of the future, but people knew they were possible. For many years microwaves were also a thing of the future. One of the funny stories about microwaves is that people thought they were dangerous, so they did not become successful until they had been on the market for 20 years. The microwave oven was invented in the late 50s, but it wasn't until the 80s that they became a widespread kitchen appliance. Today there are still many people around the world who are afraid of nuclear power. They relate it to the Three-Mile Island melt down or to Chernobyl. However, the Chernobyl explosion was caused by poor maintenance from the Russians. The Three-Mile Island accident happened because of a technical error on a shaft that looked to be closed on the panels, when it was actually open; a partial meltdown happened as a result. These events make most people believe in the danger of nuclear power, and for some, it is all they focus on even though there are numerous power plants around the world that work flawlessly. Why is it that some people cannot forget the danger instead of focusing on the possibilities?

You might be afraid of an atomic explosion and the apocalypse it can bring to the world if all the nations go crazy and fight each other. You might also be afraid of nuclear power because you think of Three-Mile Island and Chernobyl. Furthermore, you might also be afraid of it because the press releases news on these topics when experiments are conducted. Maybe we only have the atomic bomb because the press in the 40s could not write negatively about it due to their lack of knowledge regarding the consequences.

The press and the clickbait

There is no doubt the press needs readers. Readers requires news. News is what the reader wants. Readers like to engage with segments on the news that engage the amygdala. The reptile brain is programmed to do two things: flee or fight. The fight or flight scenario is one of the strongest instincts for human beings. As a species, we initially react like reptiles. This part of the brain was what we had first, before we evolved into humans and evolved the frontal lobe. When people have kids, their brain chemistry alerts them to become more focused on their offspring. They become more concerned and more aware of dangers in the environment. It became necessary for society to progress positively, not only for the parent's' benefit, but also for their children. So, you wake up in a way and become aware, aware of the fact you are a part of something bigger than yourself. Your sense of responsibility for another human being emerges. When this happens, you start to read newspapers through a different lens. You go to work for a cause. Your world changes in many ways. It is not only you anymore, but also you and your family. So, news about a nuclear power plant in your backyard is something you understandably receive with great caution. In the film *Erin Brockovich*, we see a woman who finds out that the soil is polluted, which causes families to become more susceptible to developing cancer. She is the only one who sees the dangers in this. She is the only one who reaches out to these families. In the process, she becomes a hero. This film is a clear example of what can happen when someone fights for a cause and uses the legal community in the right way. When it comes to the press, they tend to use hard-line clickbait that attracts people to read their paper. This is how they attract the advertising. Advertising is the agreement that the press makes with the companies to help both of them make money. News is also targeted to a specific part of the public; just as political parties are targeted on voters to vote for them. The different newspapers frame the "news" in a way, pandering to specific political opinions and views. The reader gets a bit scared but interested in reading the whole article and the cliff-hanger, which encourages them to read the newspaper the next day. The press is big business, and countless people who own the media want people to believe that they are free. The free press, they call it. But when you look at the business structure, you will see that the press is not free. When you go deeper into this you will also see that the articles are written to target specific people and segments. This means that the journalist and the editorial staff choose specific topics and angles for the news. The more depth we go into with this, the more we see that the news is biased, and that they tend to run a story even though it is false. President Trump often talked of 'fake news'. But is there anything like fake news? This is precisely why people have doubt; this is undoubtedly why we have factions. If there are people who do not go into the realm of factuality themselves to find out if it is right or wrong, we will always have fake news. Conspiracy theorists are a common problem for the news and for humanity. Some people, as we have mentioned, like to tell stories to gain success in life, or to get other people's money by scamming them. But if you are in the media, your whole business is to get customers to read your pages. Then you are in danger of telling half of the story, just to let them know you know, and if it is not in your favour, you just let them know that you know. The other half of the story is something you don't spend time on. Why is this? This is because readers don't like to hear the full story. In Denmark, there are a lot of people who don't want to know how inflation in the economy works. One reason might be they don't understand the full extent of the problem, and they can't understand the economical explanation due to a lack of education. The other reason is, if they do have it explained, it does not fit with their beliefs about how the world works especially socialists because they are biased. As a result, they tend to reject commonly known economical facts.

You're wrong

In my days as a TV journalist, I thought that the news was a way to tell people what the news was. What was the world about? I came to the TV station with an open mind, as a young person. When you're young, your worldviews can be less fulfilled and less tried. That is a good thing, but it can also mean you are a bit naïve to some extent. The TV station told me what content I would go with in the morning. Every day we had a brief around 6.30 before the sun was up, and the devil had his shoes on. But the news was already running; the day's agenda was painted. The painting was finished. This took me a while to understand. Did the news happen in the night? Some press releases get out during the day and some new stuff occurs throughout the day, but it felt like most news happened through the night, so it was prepared to be reported on the day after in the news. The way our world is perceived through the lens of a camera, or the pen of a journalist, is the way most people understand the world. The mainstream media is a real thing. But most people think this is the real news and this is the way everybody else is seeing the world. The media survive because of viewers, and they live from political perspectives, as I described above. However, when you are working at a TV station, you find out how they package the news, and they essentially paint a picture they already believe in. Just as the carpenter can see all problems as a nail and try to fix them with a hammer, journalists think they can fix the world by producing propaganda with a specific angle, so the world spins in this direction. Many journalists think of themselves as the fourth power after the legislative, executive, and judicial power. They really think they can turn the population in a certain direction, and we know that they can turn some of them, but not all. History gives us a clear understanding of how propaganda works. Countless opinions are minted every day to lobby for a specific person, company, political party, or an organization. The news you see will be framed in a way so that it fits these organizations' specific needs. When you think you know the truth because you have seen it on TV or read about it in a newspaper, you might not be right but wrong. The climate discussion is full of false information, and it divides the world into two groups. Both groups think the other is wearing a tin foil hat and are mad for not knowing the real state of the climate. But one question you must answer to understand the climate situation is, how does the second law of thermodynamics work? There are many more questions that are unanswered by the believers in this discussion. Although this book is not about climate, the discussion is endless because most of my questions remain unanswered by the believers. I just want to say, you're wrong if you believe in this change. When it comes to the new cancel culture, the #metoo movement and Black Lives Matter, the same people who stand behind the left-wing news are behind these organizations. If you watch closely, they are all centralists; they want a unified government. They want to be governed. History tells you that a strong degree of centralization will lead to war at some point. We see it in two large nations in the world; there is strong centralization around one person in both countries where socialism is strong. My hope was that, when the internet was developed in the 90s people would be more enlightened. But understanding is hard, especially when most people are trying to turn your views in their direction.

You're right

Being right takes you to the next tier. The next tier is where you understand that the levels from 1 to 6 in Clare Graves are centralists. Even the individuals who believe in the monetary system and capitalists who believe in themselves believe that this monetary system is their best friend. Central banks govern the monetary system; thus, they govern the whole world. The Bank of England was established back in 1694, so we are talking about an old way of organizing the world. And there is also the ECB, and the Federal Reserve System. Sweden's central bank, Riksbank, was founded in 1668 and is the oldest central bank. We know that Sweden has been holding back on going into other larger organizations like the EU or NATO. They believed in themselves, and they had their own way before others. When it comes to central systems, the world is governed by people placed in these large corporations. But can we trust these people? Are they qualified to be in this powerful position? Is one person capable of having all this power, and if so, why do they make mistakes on behalf of other people?

We live in a world where power is centralized around a few thousand people. They decide from a broad perspective how the money must flow through the system. They decide if the money is not being tracked. Likewise, they decide if the money goes to a certain goal. Some of these goals are not for the benefit of all people. There will always be some money that is channelled into dubious projects even though the whole government agrees. We see governments around the globe frequently doing this, or even tearing down an entire profession as they did in Denmark under the COVID-19 pandemic. Mink, a small animal used for clothing, were destroyed, and the animals were thrown into mass graves as if they were the worst things to ever happen to mankind. Memories of the past occurred in my mind and the way aWith a centralized government with socialists at the end of the table we will always see these kinds of awful ideas where they are power perfect and hold people who have built their companies over hundreds of years to stop immediately. In this case, they thought that the variant from mink was more dangerous than it actually was. The real picture was that the Cluster-5 variant had not been seen for weeks at the time of the decision to totally eradicate this profession. This case demonstrates that you cannot trust them to be righteous, or to not do stupid things just because they have been elected or raised on politics. Most of the politicians on the left wing in Denmark have not had a real job. They might have been students with a Masters' and then worked in a political organization. This means that the politicians are stuffed like geese and in order to produce foie gras. They are placed. Greta Thunberg, the young girl who sat in front of the Swedish parliament for six months after school, became a hero for the left-wing and climate change believers or AGW Anthropogenic Global Warming. She and her family belong to Antifa.

Greta Thunberg and her parents.

Being right is not always what you think it is. Righteous people are people who will fight you in the name of a cause. We saw this with the crusades in the ancient times starting back in 1096. This was to fight Muslims and take land from them that they had conquered years before. Now we see antifascists fighting with fascist methods. Their propaganda, funnily enough, is the same as the centralized fascists. They want you to believe in one cause, just as religious people want you to believe in one God. There can be more gods in some religions, but religious people argue you must believe in them above all others.

Immediately we must raise a flag over the many beliefs and the way they are trying to take over people's minds. What I found out over the years was that many people are level 4 and 5, so their belief systems are easy to run circles around. Level six is also centralized, but they seem to have a stronger tie to their belief system and to herd mentality. The herd mentality was extreme under COVID-19 when most people wore face masks, even though there was the Danish study I mentioned, which had over 6,000 participants; it was published at the beginning of the pandemic and showed there was no evidence face masks worked. Two observed groups, 3000 in each, were counted for having contracted Corona. After one month, twenty-one maskless participants contracted the virus; 19 had it in the group who did wear the cloth. However, the study could not get published in the larger medical papers. Maybe it seems appropriate for you to think that face masks work, but why would you not believe in a study that the medical journals do not dare to publish? Are they suggesting it was rigged? What is the purpose of not reporting on this study in the most renowned papers? The vaccines were given to most people and even then, people still got the virus. Why? The new variants still spread, but people do not die from it, yet we are told we must still spend billions on it.

From my perspective, this instrument of power is used to build a foundation for policies a stronger population previously rejected. Denmark had a long tradition of selectively saying no to EU. One of these instances was to withhold from entering a close military alliance with the other countries. However, the situation with Russia and Ukraine was used to ask the scared Danes if they would remain outside the EU. They did not. They voted yes to remove the restriction against this rule. Politicians who are minted for a specific belief system will always use their power to satisfy the herd of people who voted for them. This contract is often broken, even though it is strange that it happens. As I see it, the politicians who have been given the power will use it for something that they themselves believe in. It is hard for them to actually do what they were voted in for, but in some cases, they must do it so they can be voted in again. This is the contract they sign with the public.

The righteous people

Who are they? They will point at you and say you are the same as them, and that it takes one to know one. If they have dirt on their hands, they will say you do too. Firstly, this is the easy way out of a discussion on beliefs and assumptions with people of lesser intelligence or who have more knowledge than them. Closing the conversation at the start is a simple move for many people, even people who have strong beliefs. In a country like Denmark, where we only have 5.8 million people, we generally try to avoid conflict. The problem here is that subjects that should be discussed do not get discussed. This vice keeps us in a position to be one of the least corrupt countries in the world. The corruption can however be seen in the way the society is set up. It is clear to most innovative and entrepreneurial people that corruption is being inflicted on them. But when there is only 0.1% of the population who are trying to start a new business in a new segment, there is no focus on this, and there are no voters in it at all. So, everybody asks for more innovation, but no one does a thing about it. Many people say others are the same as them. They think you are trying to build a business to become rich, as this is their motive for having a job. They know their salary and therefore what they will get. They are not rich, but average. They don't see what you are really building or attempt to understand why. Back to the hammer problematics where they see all problems as a nail. So, how can we as a society like the Danish be corrupt when we top lists of the least corrupt countries in the world? (Link). Well, if you have municipalities producing a business that kills start-ups, it is not so hard to believe. Who cares? The company that someone tries to start. I tried it myself; we started a business that could go out and help small businesses become better at what they did. However, in Copenhagen, there are a myriad of offices under the government and the municipality "helps" start-ups. Nevertheless, when you want help from them you will find out that they can't actually help start-ups. They might be able to help companies of a larger size, but not the start-ups that have a great idea. It seems as if it is just a project to set someone on the job so they can say that something is happening. There is more to this corruption under the hood than can immediately be seen. It seems fine simply to keep things as they are, rather than producing new things. They want to interfere with all businesses. In the country with the world's highest taxes, they kill new ideas and new companies with exactly this: taxes and formulas to sign.

The self-righteous people who vote for centralized systems and socialism do not see this, and, when it does not involve them, they do not care. If most of the population do not see this, they believe there is no corruption going on. Self-righteous people will not acknowledge this problem, and they will most often tell you that you are the same as them, even though it does not make sense. Discussing levels four, five and six makes no sense to a person in level seven and tier two. What is it like to be on a whole other level? Well, for a person who is innovative and thinks in a holistic way, all the levels must work together so it doesn't become a mess. This is because most discussions can't be held with them. Any understanding of the structural difficulties is misunderstood from their perspective. It can only be understood from a perspective where you take all levels into consideration and aim to create a world where we are thriving together. In tier one, everyone thinks of each other with animosity. If you understand what I'm talking about you have probably seen it with your own eyes. So, there are strong feelings on every level.

You will find self-righteous people at all levels. They are sure they are right. They believe they have found the way of the truth and the way that all things fit together. This is often far from the truth, but it is always really complicated to explain. It might be so complicated that only they can explain it to themselves. If you ask them about this complexity, they won't answer. If you ask them if they can try to be receptive, they won't be. This leads back to the book *Extraordinary Popular Delusions and the Madness of Crowds*, and countless incidents it relates from throughout the last millennia. Numerous fraudsters tried to turn lead into gold. They sometimes managed to be good enough magicians to make even the king and queen believe in their alchemy. However, people today view politicians in the same manner and are unaware they are fraudsters in disguise. There are a few reasons for this. One is that most people will not say that others are fraudsters; indeed, they actively try not to. They will even try to make excuses for them. 95% of the population will not tell you if you are in front of a fraudster. Why is this? Firstly, it is not pleasant to accept, and it feels bad to go into this conflict. So, for many people, they stay in their comfort zone to avoid trouble. At the end of the day, the safe side is now no longer safe when it comes to a war or other humanitarian crisis, or when you confront conflict. We can be happy that there are people with a broader perspective than "normal" people who will accept the conflict and stop catastrophes from happening. However, the self-righteous people are often those who stand back and do nothing when the shit hits the fan. They want a better world but actually create a worse one.

We have also seen other countries like China as a worst-case scenario, because for instance of the way Ran Ma disappeared. He was the head of Alibaba, his creation. He disappeared and the whole organization is now state-owned. In other socialistic/ communistic countries this constantly happens. They want to nationalize businesses as though they belong to the public, like this is a good thing. Why is it not? Because of the rainfall method and the way governments create little to no innovation. They are not market-driven. More about this later.

Holism

Quantum entanglement has been explained by Schrödinger, Bohr, and Einstein. Who was right? This could be described as the cleverest picture ever taken.

Seventeen Nobel Prize winners are in this picture and that is extraordinary. Why did they gather in Copenhagen for the Solvay Conference of 1927? Did they discuss quantum mechanics? Einstein and Bohr had different perspectives on physics. Heisenberg, who was deeply involved in the attempted production of the German atomic bomb under Nazi Germany years later is also there. Europe was moving fast at that time. Philosophical theories about atoms and quantum leaps were a big topic. They already had a theory about this. Bohr's theory has since been proven right. Nonetheless, even Einstein experienced doubt about it that lasted until his death. He was proven wrong on his assumptions more than once in relation to the quantum leap theory. Schrödinger's equation proves that electrons are waves when you do not look at them, but that when you look at them, they act as particles. The Copenhagen interpretation was all about entanglement, whereby two particles affect another, regardless of where they are in space. The quantum theory has been mathematically proven, and today we are even using the superposition in quantum computers.

What does this have to do with holism? The simple answer is that quantum jumps have been proven, but we don't know yet why it happens. We just know that one photon can be in the opposite state of another photon elsewhere in the universe, regardless of distance, and that the theory has been proven right in several experiments throughout the years after Bohr and his co-workers.

As mentioned, Einstein was against this theory until his death. As he said, nothing can travel faster than light, and if an object is in an opposite state 100% of the time in another part of the universe there has to be a connection and a signal to tell the other proton what state it must be in. There is still the question of why it happens, but now we know that it does. Based on this discovery Bohr choose to help the larger countries work out how to build the atomic bomb. The information was leaked in 1949, a few years after the US had used their first bomb and Russia had tested theirs. This led to an investigation of Bohr here in Denmark by the US Secret Service which lasted until the mid-sixties. They were worried about who else he may have provided with the information needed to build these bombs. However, his philosophy on this was that, if they all had it, war would become a chess match. By releasing this information, he thought that nations would be less inclined to use this weapon in the future as they knew it would destroy the whole planet. It was simply a fear tactic. We have not seen this unfold. Therefore, he might have been proven right on this matter, even though the United States government thought him wrong. Holism is also the issue when powers do not fight but thrive together. Holism involves the entire synergy and stopping fighting over spilled milk. Holism, when we work together, will eradicate poverty, and hunger will disappear as a result. If the entire pet food budget in the United States went to hungry mouths in Africa each year, there would be no hunger. If we had holism and worked together, there would be no starvation or poverty. I believe decentralization can make this happen and that means that people must become tier two and move away from levels four and five, and six to seven, eight and even level nine, the highest level described so far.

"To see a World in a grain of sand,
And a Heaven in a wild flower,
Hold Infinity in the palm of your hand,
And Eternity in an hour." - William Blake

In 1992, I was given a book by a dear friend, Theresa, who had some of the same interests as me. One in particular had a strong effect on me: *The Holographic Universe* by Michael Talbot, who died that same year. In the book, he unveiled ideas that were seemed strange at the time. He saw the way that things were bound together. Through his studies of the occult, music, and writing, he became interested in how things were intertwined. We are all one. This was also shown in the holography that was popular at that time (as you could now make holograms relatively easily). If you break a part of a hologram, you will still be able to see the whole picture in one piece. He found out that the brain works in the same way, as studies had shown. Pavlov's dogs were an example of this. The dogs he did his experiments on learned that they got a treat if they did a certain task. They easily learned new tasks due to the incentive. Pigeons were also tested, because the experimenters hypothesised that, if a dog with a larger brain could do this, pigeons would also be able to. They did the same; they learned by incentives. *The Holographic*

Universe told us that if you remove a specific part of the dog's brain, they will relearn this even though the part of the brain that stores this memory had been removed. This was one of the examples that he used to explain the theory that the brain contains small parts of the larger picture as a hologram, which similar to the entanglement that Bohr talked about.

Einstein called this spooky action at a distance. However, we now have proof of superposition, and we have proved quantum leaps and entanglement. But how exactly it works is still a theory, even though the Higgs Boson has been proven to exist in 2012 in CERN.

Einstein and Bohr continued to debate the issue for the rest of their lives. What they really disagreed about was the nature of reality. Bohr believed that nature was fundamentally random. Einstein did not. "God does not play dice with the universe," he declared.

Nevertheless, Einstein knew that quantum theory accurately described the results of actual experiments, rather than thought experiments. Most physicists considered that Bohr had won. They focused on applying quantum theory, and questions about the EPR (Einstein–Podolsky–Rosen) paradox and entanglement became a niche interest. However, in quantum mechanics these two observables are incompatible, and it is therefore impossible to establish values for both simultaneously in any system. Therefore, Einstein, Podolsky, and Rosen concluded that quantum theory did not provide a complete description of reality (Link). As far as I can understand, it is to do with string theory and quantum physics, and it is still being investigated because it not fully understood. We are getting closer, but we are not there yet. We are even talking about multiverses: universes that exist in another dimension, or in the same one, but far away from each other. We don't know yet, but the theories show that this is possible. No one understand why dark matter comprises 85% of the universe or what dark energy is yet, but it has been discovered that there is something there, in between the atoms, the neutrinos and other particles like up-down top-bottom quarks.

-72-

Space and time

It is important to me not to go into too much depth about string theory and other mathematical theories. However, the most significant thing would be when the holographic nature of the universe starts to be proved. Back in 1992, it was hard to find someone who I could talk to about this, mostly because I did not receive an education in which we talked about such things. I was in a study where chemistry was the topic, specifically Ohms' law, and the chemical unit of the mole, which is defined using the number $6.02214076 \times 10^{23}$.

So maybe I was onto something when learning about the basics, but the study of quantum physics was, and still is, up to smarter people than me. The universe is built up of 85% dark matter, and we now know that it is there because of our observations of the way galaxies formed. Dark matter is an unknown form of energy that affects the universe. However, by measuring supernovas, stars that are about to become black holes or neutron stars, we can demonstrate dark energy's existence.

What I know, like most other people, is we are here in time and space time will make us decay. The philosophy is there in the discussions between Bohr and Einstein. It is in the discussions between the smartest physicists alive today. Chaos theory is part of this, and string theory and quantum leaps are being discussed. What we know is that we reveal an increasing amount of information on how things work year after year, even though the theory of everything is not here yet.

$$Z = \int \mathcal{D}(\text{Fields}) \, \exp\left(i \int d^4 x \, \sqrt{-g} (R - F_{\mu\nu}F^{\mu\nu} - G_{\mu\nu}G^{\mu\nu} - W_{\mu\nu}W^{\mu\nu} \right.$$
$$\left. + \sum_i \bar{\psi}_i \, \slashed{D}\psi_i + \mathcal{D}_\mu H^\dagger \mathcal{D}^\mu H - V(H) - \lambda_{ij}\bar{\psi}_i H \psi_j) \right)$$

David Gross explains this equation (which is not fully understood yet), as it is the best equation to explain what we know so far. In this equation, there are still numerous things we don't fully understand.

Space and time are what most people understand, and to live a life, we don't really need to know more than that. We don't need to walk into things all the time or to know that there is a certain time available for us to reach the goal or else it will disappear. Dinner will not wait for us until we reach oblivion; it will decompose. There is a window in time in which we must react before it is no more. Our time is limited. We know this for sure. Think again of *A Space Odyssey*, in which Kubrick tries to describe the evolution of man through a bone being thrown up in the air and transformed into a spacecraft. The scene shows innovation with its depiction of building the necessary tools, and the way that some beings are more advanced than others. But it was the same kind of brainpower that founded both. Curiosity is the bedrock of human evolution; it is when we stop being curious that we stop evolving and the rest of the world will leave us behind. This is why it is known that innovation leads to innovation because you can't un-innovate things. The smartest people say that, if we can do this, we might be able to do that. The philosophical discussions between our scientists about physics are important for us as a species to evolve and become a better version of ourselves.

So EIN ding

The human brain is wired to make us want to find a partner to mate with and extend the lifetime of our genes. This is also the need we must evolve in order to stay on the surface of the globe as a species. This natural process forms a family and builds the next generation. This is in all living organisms. Even a fly or a flower knows how to mature into the next generation. Flowers do it by spreading their pollen to other flowers via bees or the wind. Flies simply mate. But this striving also gives humans a reason to harbour what some will call jealousy. Others, including Darwin, would call it the survival of the fittest. Darwin called it survival of the fittest, whereby the most adaptable species will survive. Adaptation is what make us strive for what others have. Occasionally, the strongest just takes what another person has by force. Or else they create it themselves after looking at what others did. The copy and paste mentality is what makes us go forward. We also try to protect the innovators who have a patent. We attempt to give them a pause to build a business before others take their idea. However, sometimes the others are stronger, and they violate the patent and the holder of the idea to obtain the fortune. In some cases, the owner of the original idea does not get anything. They are wiped away by the people who were stronger because they were in a group, not because they were stronger than the individual. The power of the crowd is something in which cowards hide. But people will look at others and think, ohh so ein ding muss ich auch haben. This maybe they make the product in a way that means it looks smart or it functions better with a strap over the shoulder than with a handle when heavier items need to be carried. We know the refugees living in Denmark settle in neighbourhoods where they copy the Danish way of life, which is beneficial for assimilating and thriving in this kind of society. If they start to live in a neighbourhood where other refugees or immigrants live, ones who have not adopted the Danish lifestyle, they do not learn how the society functions. Sometimes these places become ghettos where a criminal mindset becomes the norm rather than building something from the ground up. Some think it is okay to take what others have because they are the outcasts, the minority that no one likes. Regardless of what they do, they will always be at the bottom of society. There is a huge number of anthropological reports and studies on this phenomenon, and studies find that people must mix to find out how others succeed. The copy and paste mentality that works on all levels. People think, if it works for them to become successful in life, it might work for me to reach the same level. This also applies when it comes to a nice pair of shoes or a dress that you would like to purchase because it is the fashion right now. The innate drive to survive is also activated in the brain; if I buy this, I might find the right mate with whom to build a family. Even when you have a family and have older kids, this behaviour still persists. It might not be as strong though, and for some people it disappears. They feel no need to continue to be fashionable. And so, the cycle continues.

Interview with Lars Tvede

"Supertrends' Lars Tvede is the well-known author, entrepreneur, investor and mastermind behind 17 books on innovation, entrepreneurship, macroeconomics, investing, politics, the future and more, which have been published in 11 languages and more than 70 editions. He is also founder/co-founder of 13 companies, including the venture capital fund Nordic Eye, which is among the most profitable ever in Europe, plus the forecasting company Supertrends AG. Supertrends uses crowdsourcing, A.I., and advanced data visualization techniques to create global innovation dashboards and predict future technology landscapes, in addition to modelling strategies to be used to navigate what lies ahead. The company also offers learning labs and more to assist organizations in their journeys into the future."

Find the link to the interview in the notes.
Here are my takings from the interview in the form of questions and answers.

The Supertrends institute

1. Lars Tvede is a known author, entrepreneur, investor and is behind more than 20 books on innovation and how to trade on the stock exchange. His latest book, Supertrends, is out in Chinese, too. Supertrends institute is a company that makes it easy for investors to look up what the most important technologies are. They use artificial

intelligence to scan news about technology and create summaries of it. They have created a library of exponential laws that you can easily roll forward and use to predict when particular applications will become commercially feasible or possible. They have assembled a board of expert entrepreneurs and scientists who aim to create the future. For them to be on the board they must upload specific predictions about the areas that they work in. They also scan databases and the internet for research from private institutions and from universities. They come up with quite specific predictions that they place in a timeline for the future. They also have science editors who tag all these predictions and research articles. All this information can be found on smartphones and on your laptop. They even have it in their learning labs, too.

The bullshit filters

Lars has extensive knowledge on predictions, but it also takes a lot of knowledge to recognise when something is not the truth. So, when you are from Denmark like me, he states that you are taught to think on your own, which I can confirm that you are. In other countries, the students are looked down upon if they question what the teacher says. You just take it in as if it is the higher truth. But in Denmark, one of the good things is that you learn to doubt and therefore check and ask critical questions. I can confirm that we do learn this in Denmark. People often look up to you if you express doubt and have a say. Lars mentions a billboard at his daughter's start-up company saying, 'Trust but Verify'. Some people have the full willingness to doubt the current consensus. They conclude that it is wrong. But it seems like many other people just go with the consensus. He would like to get involved in a book about how false information gets disseminated. One example of false information that everybody will recognize is that there are many religions in the world. They contradict each other, but they all claim to be the absolute truth. He states that, at maximum, one of them can be the truth. Which means that the vast amounts of religions can't be the truth. You know, if you're born in a certain place, you will almost certainly adhere to the religion that is predominant there.

On a holiday, he read the book from 1846 that is a mantra for financial investors, *Extraordinary Popular Delusions and the Madness of Crowds*, and he has a particular fondness for it. The book is a hilarious record of groupthink, including stock market manias, dress codes and murderers. Lars mentions a clinical experiment whereby truthfully communicating the right number on some dice gets you $1,000 for each dot on the dice, but people lie. If the money goes to a good deed when using a lie detector, it does not even react to the lying. So, people do not feel bad about lying if it is for a good cause. In the Myers-Briggs test, 60% are emotional rather than analytical, and they copy people they like while not fact-checking them. Because of this, and many other reasons, the world is full of bullshit. He finds it surprising and depressing how little fact-checking there is. Occasionally, the bullshit gets to a critical mass where it turns into a fascist movement. The people who go against the bullshit in some places are even killed or ostracized. The new cancel culture is somewhat fascist, as people who have different opinions won't engage with others, financially or socially; they won't hire them, and they won't even let them speak.

My comments: Myers-Briggs is a great tool for identifying personalities and the fine lines based on which people make decisions throughout their life. Is it based on fact checking and down to the minute calculations? Is it impulsive? Or an accurate description of one's current mood? The best filter to avoid being exposed to fraudulent people is to fact-check, if it is possible. The example Lars uses with the dice is a bit depressing. People do try to cheat if they can get away with it. The dice did tell its position to a person outside the room, so they knew that they were lying. Even when they are being checked with a lie detector, they still lie. This example could be one reason not to trust anybody. But this would make the world go mad. We must believe in somebody other than our parents. Occasionally, we even can't trust our parents, and this only adds to the dysfunctionality in this world. The consensus seems to have a strong hold on people. This was proven in the Solomon Asch experiment in 1951 where students were given a test. In a room with eight students, only one did not have instructions. Seven were told to give the wrong length for three lines on a piece of paper. The last student, the real test person at the end of the table, could easily see that the two lines were shorter than B but followed the consensus decision that was untrue. Over the 12 trials, about 75% of participants conformed at least once, and only 25% of participants never conformed.

In the control group, where there was no pressure to conform, less than 1% of participants gave the wrong answer.

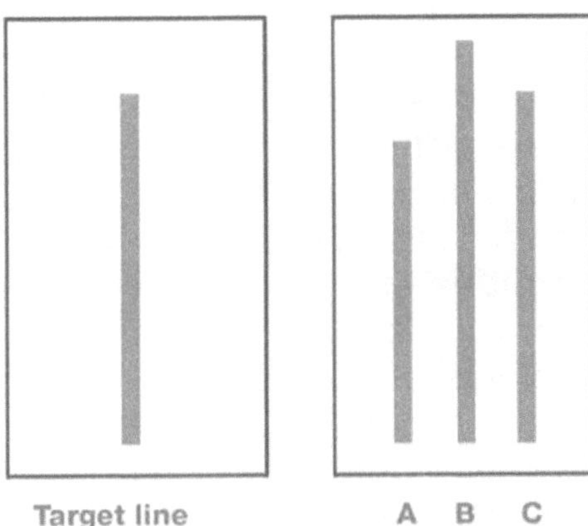

Even in a generally sceptical country like Denmark, there is a lot of trust in the authorities and the system in general. It is often when you become an innovator or self-employed you find out that you are no longer seen as a part of the ecosystem, but a supplier. This shows how hard it is to break through with knowledge, especially when the knowledge is new and not accepted as the consensus. When it comes to innovations like the Wright Brothers' Kitty Hawk experiments, people treated it as though it was only some people who had wild fantasies.

Fraud and psychology

Fraud can be hard to discover because people who commit fraud are exceptionally good at it. They have good social skills but not for a good cause. People who are great entrepreneurs have a different mindset compared to others. You can even test for this in various personality tests. Lars describes entrepreneurs as people who are capable of imagining things that don't exist. They have an enormous, steadfast conviction that they will exist in the future, and that they will create them. They are living in a fantasy, but they can turn it into reality. In his book *Entrepreneur*, there is a chapter about this psychology. Among entrepreneurs, a proportion of people either have personality disorders themselves or have close relatives who have it. There is a difference between clinical personality disorders and the milder versions that can lead to entrepreneurship. This is where you find the geniuses, the great opportunities, and the great companies. This can make them very entertaining, and lead them to find a lot of bullshit, but also plenty of good things.

My comments: The borderline personalities who invent stuff because they see it as a possibility sometimes become the ones who change the world. The one thing you can't do is ignore them because they change things. They push humanity forward. The ones who think they can change the world are the ones who do. Occasionally, they are crazy. Every so often they are geniuses. I've met the fraudulent people, the persuaders, and the ones who light up in a room. Sometimes they show true generosity, other times it is about phantasms or fraud.
In Denmark, where Hans Christian Andersen was born and learned how to write in spite of severe dyslexia, it has been found that he copied some of his fairy tales, from earlier, now forgotten sources. Some fairy tales were known as oral stories and folklore. Some were made up by others but changed a bit as people began to retell them more frequently. Today there is a proud statue of him in the center of Copenhagen. The main street through the city even carries his name. He started his life in Odense, initially trying to become a ballet dancer. He received funding from one of the wealthy families in Copenhagen before he made his own career by telling fairy tales in Europe's castles and palaces. There is also a statue of him in Central Park in New York, and most children in China know about him. Mao gave the fairy tales to all school children because they are not political in any way, but they have a moral. Copying others is not innovative in itself, but copying others and

enhancing it can be innovative. Elon Musk has a disorder called Asperger's Syndrome. He revealed this to the public on *Saturday Night Live* in 2021. We also know that Madonna, Richard Branson, and many other innovative individuals were and are dyslexic. I have mild dyslexia myself. I guess it has something to do with the way our brain works; we see things combined, whereas others see the small differences and can focus on the details. I focus on the next option instead of the here and now. Imagine we are in Newton's Cradle. Most people see themselves as one of the steady metal balls. We see ourselves on the side, having the ride, bouncing back and forth. Even though the energy transferred is the same in each of the chain reaction, it seems like the most active ones are those on the end.

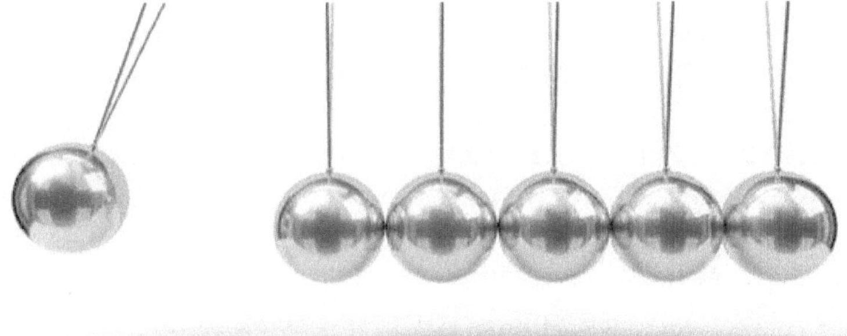

Immigrant in Switzerland

Lars recounts European's mass migration from Europe to the Americas in the 1800s and 1900s because of famine, and that due to this, "there was a special entrepreneurial mindset that moved away". He believes that "this was probably due to genetic selection for people who migrated because it is a big step." Though it might have been preferable too many to remain in their current situation, Lars believes there may have been genetic selection that fundamentally dictated who would be more willing to leave to explore an unknown way of life. This is partly based on his own experience, when he migrated to Switzerland, where he did not feel that he fit in. Therefore, it was relatively easier for him to start his own company. For Lars, this explains why you have so many entrepreneurs in the United States. Switzerland has been the number one country on the global innovation index for several years. Approximately 45% of the population of Switzerland are first- or second-generation immigrants.

My comments: This is one of the interesting things for me because genetic selection is, as we know, something that constantly happens. However, when cultures break down, there can be a shift towards another region. This can even be on the other side of the globe. And this is part of the story of what happened in the United States. People who had no work during the famines and were devoid of a future in Europe had to leave with their belongings. The TV series *1883* showed a story from this period where people tried to find new land in the west before it was settled. One side of the story is about the enormous freedoms the protagonist is exploring. They fight against nature, the animals, the Native American, and the bandits, all of which could kill them. It seems like one big massacre, but it is not far from the truth. They had to go through this to get to the Promised Land. The few that were left were the ones who had the courage, the ones who made it, and the ones who had to start all over. They are built of strong genetic material. In Lars' book, *The Creative Society*, he comes to this conclusion as well. He also mentions how people lived as rednecks in the US. They are people who moved into the mountains to live freely without a town or the local community to interfere with their lifestyle. In addition, the Fifth Amendment allows people to bear arms. This was initially to protect them from the government. Most people had a bad feeling about government in the United States, feeling no one should ever govern them again as they had in the past. And if that tyranny developed, they could defend themselves with arms.

Pattern recognition

Is there a pattern for Lars Tvede? On his own journey, he had a five-year education as a dairy engineer. He sees that as a bad decision, but he really likes to change, and he viewed himself as one of those animals who couldn't see things that do not move. Here we have a person, Lars, who has gone through his trials and errors himself. This means to me that he is a composite personality. He tries to see the pattern and found his path in innovation. It has given him the special gift of continually searching for patterns as he writes his speeches, as he invests and as he predicts future trends. There is a forceful phenomenon called "reversion to the mean" in macroeconomics. Lars explains that when you have a recession or a depression, the economy bounces back not only to where it came from but back to the long-term trend line. If you look at this trend line over 200 years, it continues to hug the line. And it is useful to know that the economy will bounce back in this environment. There are also numerous patterns in how societies function. For instance, when GDP gets to a certain level you have strong pollution. You get deforestation at a certain economic level and reforestation at another level. You can take several phenomena that seem predictable, like economic growth per capita throughout the world, population, and wealth growth. These can be exponential or linear and can be used to predict what will happen with some accuracy. Lars then begins to analyse the economic state during the pandemic. He says by looking at the recession and the inflation that was caused by the pandemic you can use it for investment or commercial decisions. You can learn from this approach, and countless people could benefit from spending more time becoming familiar with such patterns and then reflecting on what they mean. One pattern is the real GDP per capita; the real spending power on this planet is such that it grows 20 percent every 10 years. But not in Italy. This means that by the end of the century we will be 5 to 6 times wealthier than we are today. Lars points out another prevalent pattern within the technological sector, whereby devices are becoming more compact. Your smartphone is an example of that. It rings an alarm bell in Lars when people are focus much on solar and wind because it does the opposite. They take up more space and use a lot more resources. Solar can be integrated into buildings, and then it does not take up any space. However, wind power is probably an interim technology. It is a deviation that will lead us to far more compact technological solutions. Thus, the thought process starts with an alarm that says this is really a violation of a generally good pattern. Then he starts thinking on how we can reverse this.

My comments: One story about animals is that a bull does not attack if the object does not move. It is a good story, but it also refers to bull markets. A well-rounded person like Lars has tried plenty of things. He has also been ahead of the innovation curve with some of his businesses. He has been first with some of his foresight on investments, and he is a considerable inspiration to follow when it comes to innovation and his take on centralism vs. decentralism. Talking to him is always an inspiration for me, just like this interview. His extensive knowledge on the market and market predictions is inspiring to follow and dive into. He shares his knowledge through books and speeches around the world. I think his journey is unique and I know it inspires many people. Wind power is not an option that could service the entire world's energy consumption. Every year wind and solar generate a small part of the energy consumption, around 4%, but the growth in demand exceeds 8% per year. Most energy still comes from coal and gas. The energy source with the least deaths associated with it is nuclear power, next to solar and wind. The EU has just accepted this as a clean energy source in line with gas. But many people who grew up in the 70s and 80s are apprehensive about this, especially those in Denmark, where Bohr was under surveillance from the United States because he gave away trade secrets to countries on how to build an atomic bomb.

Many people thought nuclear power was a bad thing. They did not come to this conclusion by fact-checking but from their emotions. In Denmark the situation on nuclear power was not good for that matter. So, there are no nuclear power plants in Denmark. This is ongoing, even though there is a lot of proof opposing death rates related to environmental pollution and on the recurring energy form that it is. Take wind; it does not blow all the time. Take solar, the sun does not shine all the time. And you can't store the energy generated from them. When it comes to the land masses that you need to have all the windmills or in the ocean, there is not enough space for the energy consumption that is needed in the world. Another thing is that there is not enough copper in the world to produce all these mills and solar panels. It is not that I don't want it, it is just that it is not doable. Nevertheless, politicians who want power over a population feel more than they think. As Lars mentions, this technology does the opposite of what innovation does when it makes things easier; it makes devices smaller; it makes things faster; it makes things easier to carry or transport. None of these are true of renewable energy such as wind and solar. If they were thorium reactors it would start to make sense. If you ask me, logic always wins in the end. It is the same as the people who dream of trains becoming the thing of the future, even though it is a form of transportation from the past. Romantics and have a good heart and strong emotions, but there are politicians who simply manipulate the faint-hearted. I know I'm playing with fire here, but we need to tell the truth. The patterns are a recurring meme that these people are trying to control and manipulate. The pattern is that they got into IPCC and in here we find a climate model made by a man who diluted the heat in the 1940s, so it is presented as a small heat diversion. The same happened when it came the small ice age in the 1800s. The hockey stick has long been debunked but it is still the Holy Grail for plenty of people. To cut a long story short, if you are a feeler, you probably hate me now. Manipulation is thus far still a thing of today. Allow me to point out that there is a widespread fear of thorium, and other related technologies that entrepreneurs are investigating. Nonetheless, in a country like Denmark, there won't be public funding, just like crypto, which governments also fear.

Why are there so many crooks?

When it comes to Bitcoin investments, Lars says he was not in the office that day. People who are immersed in innovation have another personality. They live in fantasies, and occasionally it becomes fraudulent instead. When it comes to short-term gain, there can be out-of-character reasons for going with the short-term gain. He notes that psychopaths or sociopaths technically have a similar personality in this respect. However, you can also go for the short-term gain if you lack conviction in your own ability. If you have great conviction in your own ability, you take your time, and you know that will pay off in the long term. Someone like Warren Buffett, who is unbelievably intelligent, realized very early in his life that the value of shares compounds well. He never deviated at all from this. It is like people who become elite sport people, they first have to suffer a lot. But they have a conviction that they will get a really long way if they just keep on doing it.

My comments: Why do people strive for a thing beyond the unknown? The Wright Brothers wanted to fly, but why? Was it for no reason? If you are innovative, or if you are a person like Warren Buffett, as Lars mentions, you may find early in life, for instance, that value shares compound well. During that time, no one understood the paradigm on this as well as he did. Similarly, no one understood the guys with the bike with wings. I once read a book called *Prima Donna Leadership*. Prima Donnas is often hard to lead because they have their own routine. They have a distant goal in the horizon. They strive for perfection. The extreme sportsmen and women who must suffer are determined. We saw this in the movie *King Richard*. Not only was their father determined, but the girls also had talent and excellent focus on the ball. Determination is a good thing to have in sports. Long-term goals are a must when it comes to innovation, too. However, Prima Donnas can be found in any sector. It is not only people who invent or invest who can be determined or have a higher goal in life than just the monthly paycheck. However, if you only go to work for the paycheck, you are not a Prima Donna. The difference between Prima Donnas and innovators is a narrow one, but you do not necessarily need to innovate new things as a Prima Donna. For the most part, you just have to fine-tune your processes to the extreme extent of becoming the best in the class. We all know of sportspeople who are the best are highly paid and worshipped. Short-term day traders might become rich, but most lose their money. It is often the long run that pays the highest dividends. In my view, the psychopaths and the sociopaths that Lars mentions are going for short-term wins in the innovation space. They do not innovate, but they plaster themselves with borrowed feathers. The types I have met in the space of crypto are typically people who show how much money they have, just to make you believe they can make you rich too. It is a scummy method they use to gain trust and make you jump into the rabbit hole. At the moment when you show them, through your voice and body language, that you think you can be rich like them, the mousetrap hammers down. It is at this moment when you naively think, "Wow this can happen to me. I'm with the rich and famous, they see this." And then they close the deal. The next thing that happens is that you find your pocket empty, and you are on the streets again. The backstage pass had the wrong doorknob on it, so to speak.

It was all an act. It is a well-produced scam that they use to get you to think you have easy money on your hand. Writing this leads me to remember the book that Lars mentions - *Extraordinary Delusions and the Madness of Crowds*. Listen, this has happened for many years. If you think you were the first person who ever got scammed, you can be assured that you are not. Nonetheless, the crocks are not innovative, and they do not have long-term goals. They are sociopaths or psychopaths, and they would sell their grandma if there was any money in it. Can you determine the real innovative people from the crooks? Yes, you can. First, do not go with people who do not have a solid internet presence or a person who does not want you to know their real identity. Do your own ID checking and KYC (know your customer) analysis. Do fact-checks. Even after this, there are crooks who will take your money, so be sure that you are using live contracts. Be sure that, when you pay, the person is in the room and can't escape. Do not use wire transfer if you can't be sure that the product will be delivered. Use a third-party service like PayPal or Fiverr to help you out. This is why we have banks in the first place. Crypto is another story; there are no middlemen. When there are no middlemen, you must find another way, and there is one because a well-known banker, Lars Seier Christensen, invented Concordium.io

To sum up, crook are not innovators; they are low-life scumbags. They can make you think they are investors; for instance, they can come in the form of developers who build something until it is 90% finished and then ask for a large sum of money. Indeed, they come in many forms, shapes and colours.

What is the difference between speculation and investment?

When discussing the difference between speculation and investment, Lars immediately mentioned Tesla Motors, saying, "I went out and said that this would be a terrible investment. After I said that, it went up and up and up, so that was not my proudest moment. However, I think that Elon Musk is one of the greatest entrepreneurs of all time." This is an example of how psychopaths and sociopaths can be both lucrative and prominent within the innovation industry; as Lars say, Musk "has a deviant personality and is extremely impulsive. He sometimes goes out on Twitter and posts things that are shocking, and sporadically, he posts things that are on the edge with the FCC, the financial supervisory authorities, then changes his mind minutes later. He has the kind of personality that makes a great entrepreneur."

Nevertheless, Lars still thinks that the share price on the Tesla stock is now too high. However, Lars is heavily invested in resource companies like metals, mines and energy companies so he is unsure if he would be acting as a speculator rather than an investor if he ever decided to sell. His thoughts on this are as follows: "The average length of the investments I have made is around six years, so it is typical that you have the macroeconomic cycles, which last eight years on average. When things go well, I go in. If I think it is beginning to go down, I sell. I will call that being more of an investor than speculator. I can get into a position but because of something that it does, I can get cold feet, and then I go out. There is an element of the speculator in that."

My comments: Even Lars himself sees some of his investments as speculation when he sells. This book describes a situation where you are on the edge; is it one or is it the other? You will always be in doubt when you are on the edge. "Is there an edge?" Marco Polo asked himself as he sailed out. He did not believe that the earth was flat as the priests claimed. 'Don't sail out and leave us, we are so happy about the tax money you send our way', they seem to be saying. But after the voyage, people found new land and created most of the technologies we know today. Migration can be a good thing. The time horizon is a great tool for seeing if you are investing or speculating. These tools are all described in thick books, and you can take long lessons in this. So, I'm not going to dive deep into this. Lars has a few books in this too, so read those kinds of books if you want expert knowledge. I asked because there is a gap, a chasm. This is important when you are looking at innovations. Is it something that is a real innovation, or is it fine-tuning an already known technology? Let's look at wine labels. Again, crooks will change the labels. Not everything that shines is gold. Wine labels are easy to fiddle with, so you think you are buying an expensive bottle. But in reality, you are buying sprinkler fluid diluted into wine. This happened many years ago in Italy. This is not innovation. Innovation is 12 years on a hill trying to make a bike fly. Innovation is a lot more effort. It can take 20 years, which is how long it took to build the James Webb Space Telescope. But is it just fine-tuning already known technologies? For me, as an outsider, it is hard to tell, but let's just conclude that the JWST was an innovation, based on the following aspects of it.

1. Measuring Eyes: New Wavefront Optical Measurement Devices Lead to Medical Spinoffs
2. Laser Interferometers: High Speed Optical Sensors Lead to Commercial Applications
3. Restoring Hubble: Integrated Circuits Used in Camera Repair
4. Astronomical Detectors: Webb Detector Technology is the Universal Choice

Innovations of this scale often have spinoffs for other industries. The amount of money, time and knowledge put into this innovation was humongous, but it will bring humankind new knowledge on how the Big Bang happened and thus take us closer to understanding what we came from. In innovation, there are cycles for investors, and there are some patterns that have been seen before. But do we have a pattern for innovations like JWST? How frequently do they occur? This is another thing Lars Tvede is working on with his Supertrends Institute, a knowledge base where you can look up innovations and get an insight into what is coming, what is new and what is right here, right now. This tool will be a goldmine for investors, no doubt. With the Tesla stock, he did not invest and still believes it is overrated; this is one example of what this tool might be able to help with, not only when he invests in the future, but for many more investors to come. I will follow this innovation of the Supertrends Institute. Tools like this are what we need.

What is your take on crypto?

As he moved our discussion along to crypto, Lars gave an interesting perspective, because his view on crypto is not entirely one-sided. He "recently read a report on crypto from Alpine Macro... or was it Credit Suisse? That said it is not an inflation hedge because it just dropped a lot during inflation. It is not a store of value because it just dropped seventy percent. It is not an efficient payment vehicle because you cannot do enough transactions and they are too little and too low." The conclusion of this report was that crypto was simply a Ponzi scheme. While, on the other hand, the report also said that crypto possessed no inherent value, Lars points out that paper money also has no inherent value. "The value of USD or Euro is a network effect. It is a fact that we have just come to believe that this is a valid means of payment. You are not paying for the money; you exchange it for money. However, if you have a well-entrenched network effect in crypto, then I think there will be a value because it can also have a network effect. It seems to me that it is so entrenched it won't go away. It can go up, it can go down, and you can have more and more currencies."

My comments: - The gold standard was discarded in 1971, the year I was born. Money no longer needed to be backed with real gold in a vault. Fort Knox was now reduced in status. By FIAT, it shall be done. Fiat currencies only have value because the government maintains them. There is no utility to fiat money itself anymore; no collateral pledge as a security for repayment of a loan, to be forfeited in the event of default. "Real" paper money was invented, and bonds were now only backed by the government and not the amount of gold in the bank. The whole FIAT economy is based on trust, and the dark side of this is the doubt cast on other currencies. Why do you not trust other currencies? The reason for this is inflation. The governments in countries where you would not trust the currency have hyperinflation. This can happen when you print all the money you want and send it out of the system and into the pockets of the workers, who are mainly working for the same government. Recently, both China and USA have been minting paper money like never before. It seems like a war based on printing money; if one nation flushes their market, the others are ready to do the same. But it has not happened yet. The money has been posted to the bank as a source from which to lend money to the public. However, if they do this too much, they will be responsible for the decline in the currency's value. Banks have no reason to want less value in the money supply; they make money when people have debt. The market must be strong, so that people will trust the currencies. It is a catch 22 situation. Inflation is one thing a nation can do; it is a tool in the box for a central bank. In crypto, it is the opposite way around. There will be a certain amount of money in the vault, but no new pressing and devaluation. You have the opposite type of inflation, not deflation. This makes it more like gold; the price of gold inflates approximately 2% per year; this is the amount that comes out of the mines that "produce" mined gold. It appears to me that the inflation on normal terms follows this pattern too. A small amount of inflation is good for the economy, as it means it does not stagnate. But after a pandemic, during which people could not go out for around two years, all prices and all systems must adjust to this situation. My take on this if that, it had been pure Bitcoin that was in the system. I simply cannot say. This situation is one of the scenarios I will look at later in this book.

Decentralization?

Concluding our interview with a discussion of decentralization Lars discusses his book, *Super Trends*, the inspiration behind writing it and the message he wished to communicate. And ultimately this leads to his thoughts on decentralization. "I try to make a distinction between technologies that are clearly supporting centralization and others that clearly support decentralization. I am a fan of decentralization; it makes institutions more efficient and people happier. I also have the numbers to back me in that. Great companies and great civilizations need to have quite high levels of decentralization." While he notes the necessity of decentralization for great companies and great civilizations of decentralization, he is quick to also mention that this system does not work for every company. "There are exceptions; for example, McDonald's needs to be centralized and software companies decentralized." Nevertheless, he is a firm believer of the benefits of decentralization and brings evidence to back his beliefs. "The Internet has been a fantastic technology for decentralization because it removes the monopoly of information. It also opens funnels, so you can have people sitting in areas where there is no great business environment, but they can still work for companies in Silicon Valley." Lars then says that it is his great hope that strong new technologies will also support decentralization.

"For instance, you are deep into blockchain, so you also know that cryptocurrencies have been the killer app where you can have smart contracts, self-executing contracts, and plenty of other things. I hope that this part of it will really thrive."

My comments: It is funny. I don't know where to start on this and the reason is the millions of thoughts that I have. Here Lars kicks it right in the bum, the killer app. What can you do with crypto? The millions of thoughts on what you can do fluctuate around in my frontal lobe. So, let me start with the basics that Lars touches upon here. Decentralization and centralization work together; they both have strengths and weaknesses. I understand why he might have his money on the horse that is running in the old system. I understand that the whole scene looks speculative and not like old-world investments. In the crypto world, economic fluctuations are more extreme. This is a new pattern; people must fight more because there are only a few people in the market space, just like in the Wild West. *1883* is a good place to start if you have no understanding of how it was back then. The settlers who went away from the old Europe had to fight things we can't imagine today. And they did so successfully. That must have been decentralization on steroids to be a part of this, in the middle of nowhere. It wasn't just something that was said, it was real. Build whatever you want in the scenario that is right in front of you. Beautiful mountains, rivers, forests, and the wide vistas you see in front of you. It must have been spectacular. The funnel that opens for people to function also works around the globe, from the poorest shed in countries with no running water or sanitation, to the companies in Silicon Valley. Across the globe there is something that the internet made accessible. The next frontier is crypto. The reason for this is that the central banks are limited when it comes transferring money around the globe. PayPal does not have the access to carry out money transfers to all banks around the globe. This is because the central banks and the central governments in the United States still have their say when it comes to transfers for a private business. This will change with crypto because it is decentralized.

Who are the sharks and who are the whales?

A small fish

How did the world's largest instance pf money laundering, involving 1500 billion kroner happen through one bank? Who let this happen? This case has not been closed, yet it is still under investigation. One of the smaller fish has been caught, but nothing comparable to the large amount we are talking about here. They might never be caught because the information disappears in Russia where the oligarchs can hide. The clues end there for most cases. The smaller fish had an office I previously worked in, a few years before COVID-19. I was privy to the bank statements of the small fish who took the fall. She did not live in any extreme luxury. She got eight years in prison, I'm happy that, when the police came to my door 7.30 in the morning and had a "meeting" with me for two hours they did not arrest me. Thanks to the legal system in Denmark, I'm not behind bars. I think if we had a more corrupt system in Denmark, someone would have had the idea of just throwing people behind bars to look like they were acting accordingly to threats. This is why movies like *The Shawshank Redemption* are produced; it is still one of the best movies out there. The two policemen who came into my apartment were armed, though they were in civilian clothes. When they announced who they were, and verified their identity with a badge, they paused for some time to analyse my reaction. Although it is not frightening if you live in an uncorrupted society, the situation was bound to be serious. I'm just happy that I'm not in jail for something others did. The contract I sent to the small fish did not get

a return. I had a line in there about the responsibilities, explaining that I, Steffen Kirkegaard, could not be responsible for purchases or money transactions if they had not been seen by a third-party accountant if the amounts were above a certain size. It ended up with me being right; there was something rotten in the state of Denmark. At court, I found out that the government uses the Broken Windows fallacy here too. The court was full of police; one for each of the prosecuted, and one for each of the prosecutors. There were five judges, one main one and four in reserve, or whatever they did there. It was an absurd scene I was witnessing. I went to a chair in the middle of a room the size of a basketball field. I took my coat off and remained in the room for about two hours, being questioned about any possible illegal association to the small fish. The office I had been in for the last four months had been bugged with recorders and microphones. But one good thing I got out of the meeting with the small fish was that she agreed to my idea that we were building on two megatrends. Now, after three years, she was handed her sentence and she said to them, "Why are you placing all the responsibility on me? The Danish Bank had helped Russian oligarchs with over 1500 billion kroner money laundering through an affiliation in Estonia."
So, can we agree that it is wrong to launder money? We agree that there are people in other countries who have large amounts of money they want to keep hidden from the general public. They have taken this money into custody, and now it will belong to them for good. I was involved in this business because the set-up was that I should help start-ups of innovative companies with funding. But looking back, I can see that the set-up was all designed to whitewash dirty money from oligarchs so they could buy multibillion euro yachts the size of ferries and palaces across Western Europe. They wanted me to have a holding company so the money could flow through with my name and signature on it. If that had happened, I would have been behind bars. This would have applied

even if I had thought it was for a good deed, like investing in a company with a great idea. This case is still under investigation in the USA, France, and Estonia and has deep roots into Moscow. As a person who was close to all this, my faith in the good nature of humanity has not been swayed. I will clearly need a better bullshit filter in the future. But, as you can see, even the authorities have a hard time with cases like this. Even when they have a massive office in Copenhagen with hundreds of police officers working on this case, they still can't find everyone responsible and stop the fraud.

A big fish

In this case, the small fish got a sentence of eight years in prison while the large bank is too large to fail. We already know that there is no one in the bank who will be personally imprisoned. The court´s judgement was a fine of under a thousandth of what had been transferred through the bank. This means that it is the bank itself that will be prosecuted in this case, for 15 billion. Even the bank had set more money aside for this. But they got around this. And they are already setting aside large amounts of money for the bill to be paid. They know that this will not simply disappear. It will be one of the largest corruption cases in modern history. But is there really only one person responsible for money laundering at the bank? No, probably not. It was a mistake in the whole set-up. It was also an IT failure; the specific bank affiliate office in Estonia worked with the old system while the rest of the affiliate offices around Europe had already implemented a newer system. However, at the end of the day, we can't blame it on the non-transparent IT department or the lag of implementation. The money did flow through the affiliate office, after all. I believe that the Bank will carry the weight of the sentence and pay the bill to the EU commission and the other countries involved. On numerous occasions throughout history, we have seen money with no traceable owner getting into the wrong pockets. It sounds like we don't know what is going on. The truth is that we have no KYC, no customer ID or any knowledge about who is who because the old banking system is based on trust. Trust is present when we think that these people can't be bribed, and that they will follow their hearts and do what they think is right. What will the consequences be of following a system in which no one can investigate monetary transactions? What will happen in a system where everything is based on trust? This is where we are today. But it will change in the future with decentralized tokens. The token economy can be 100% transparent and the ID layer and KYC can be something that we do up front, not when things have already gone awry. The cryptosystem will be most beneficial at the start of a relationship between the blockchain and the holder of the money (tokens), but don't delude yourself into thinking we will have a fraud-free world. We will have less fraud than now, and we will have a freer world. With transparency in the monetary system, we do not need the same level of trust. Therefore, we can begin to live in a world with reliable transactions and strict rules that are implemented. When it comes to blockchain technology, the world functions completely different to how it does today. This is because it is decentralized, and the tokens rule themselves. Smart contracts can honour a contract, even when it comes to the rights of an author or a musician. You pay for the music and the music is yours. A non-fungible token can then be worth billions because of its uniqueness. And a token can be worth billions because of its scarcity.

Chapter 8: Breaking the Barriers

Tier two; crossing the chasm, and tipping points.

Crossing

What kind of world are you living in? Are you a peasant jumping into the hamster wheel every day? Are you living a rich and happy life? Do you think *I want that* when you see someone else wearing a nice dress or fancy shoes, driving a nice car, or living in a big house? Do you measure your success against the successes of others, or by your own standards? Are you an early adopter or are you a laggard? Do you see yourself as an individual? Do you try to help others in the same situation as you by voting for a better future for your business segment? Do you understand what innovation is? Do you buy the climate set-up? Are you angry at people who vote for a specific politician? Will you change anything in the world? Is family the cradle of your life? Numerous questions such as these can and will tell us who you are, what you live for, why you live and how you live. The first level in the theory of spiral dynamics is easy to see for most people that we have surpassed. Here is a brief description of the tiers.

1. Do what you must just to stay alive.
2. Keep the spirits happy and the tribe's nest warm and safe.
3. Be what you are and do what you want.

4. Life has meaning, direction, and purpose with predetermined outcomes.
5. Act in your own self-interest by playing the game to win.
6. Seek peace within the inner self and explore, with others, the caring dimensions of community.

Most people today are in level four, five and six. Some countries have more of their population in four, others more in five and then some countries like the Netherlands, Canada and Scandinavian countries have more in level six, where community is important to them. All of these levels hate each other. There is a constant war on beliefs and political observations, as can be seen in current debates about the current climate. Democracy has a difficult time managing these different ways of life. A few years ago, my girlfriend and I went to Trier in the Mosel district of Germany, where the wine is good and bike trips even better. This is also the place where Karl Marx wrote his book about capitalism and how capital could be distributed to other parts of the society. The main intention of writing his manifesto was to reduce the severity of poverty. The working population was being exploited, as they said. There was a big difference in the world when most people were only on level four and five. Back then, these two groups fought against each other, and the church was losing. Religion became a factor that defined beliefs, not the economical factor as it had been for thousands of years. Now, with the Freemasons in power, the merchants and the entrepreneurs changed the economy. But Marx got his foot in the door. As a young man, he was prone to drunkenness and duels; he was a man without a country. Once, his wife pawned his pants to buy food. He died broke and just 11 people attended his funeral. He was run out of Prussia in 1842, expelled from France in 1845, rejected from Belgium in 1848 and forced to leave Prussia again in 1848. He then moved to England in 1849. All in all, communism had a hard time taking hold. But this was also the start of socialism, too. In the Karl Marx Museum in Trier, there is a description of how this philosophy and political system is still a strong trait in the Social-Democrats and other parties with the social stamp on it. The left wing in the US also tends to hold some of these principles. In later years, we start to see that the Democrats are flirting with healthcare and more public controlled welfare systems rather than privately held hospitals where insurance gives you the privilege to go there. In a country like Denmark, people will not give up on the welfare state for anything in the world. A majority swear it is the best thing that ever happened to them, and they are willing to give half or more of their salary in taxes to keep this system up and running. The lack of services compared to a private health system can be huge, even when you compare the pricing for both models. This comes into perspective, especially in countries like Denmark where the taxpayer's money has been given in large amounts without being targeted on specific benefits or better services. This is what happens when socialism takes over. People in Denmark say that they are happy to pay a high tax. That is not entirely the truth, but that is what they say. Mostly the people who are in the welfare sector themselves are the ones who benefit from this.

The hamster-wheel

Some people go to work to make money. Some people go to work because they are driven and passionate about it. Others work as a lifestyle. Some do not work and stay away from this life as much as possible. What is work after all? It is a contract you make with a company that you will give your time in exchange for money. What is it if you are being paid but just love the job and feel freer when you are working and not at home? We live in a world where the older generation think that work is the way to freedom at least the way to economic freedom. However, is it a life worth living if you hate the job and the lifestyle associated with it? Is it worth it to simply live every day anticipating the weekend or vacation time? To many people, this question is non-negotiable; it is set in stone. You cannot discuss this. Alternative ways of living are not on the table. This is where the haters come in. The different levels must also be taken into consideration when I look at why some people can be of a specific orientation. In the fourth level, there is a widespread idea that women are obligated to be homemakers and take care of the kids while the male goes to work and makes the money. Those associated with level 5 know that there is freedom in money; it provides options to do what you want. Their entire understanding of this world is rooted in the economy. The US is a good example of this. Countless people live and breathe purely to make money. I believe that is also the reason they have the strongest economy in the world. When it comes to self-proclaimed socialist China, the citizens also profess a different lifestyle to the government's, one that is also deeply rooted in the need to make money in order to survive. People tell me that China is one of the most capitalistic countries in the world. Well, if we analyse the way they have grown into the world's second largest economy in about four decades, we can speculate that there must be citizens whose inmate desire is to make a profit. People will work for money; the communism and the socialism are thus more of a government philosophy than reality.

The collective economy of Scandinavia is also one of the strongest in the world. These five countries have a strong workforce and a strong business side. The battle between the workers and the companies is also proving that there are people who believe that socialism is for their own benefit. However, if we did not have the conservatives and the liberals (in Scandinavia, liberals are right-wing; socialism is left-wing), we would probably not have a strong mercantile side. Most of the Scandinavian countries have half and half; liberalism and socialism go hand in hand. The trade-off is that the socialists pay for their own benefits out of the taxes. This can be helpful for businesses, as they don't have to pay for everything out of pocket. For everyone else who is not a socialist, they are expected to overpay in taxes. This is the beginning of the problem of being forced into doing something you may or may not find right. The majority vote to get other people's money, but in a world where 99% of a population strive to invest in innovations they did not create, the remaining 1% have a hard time being understood. This is not due to the marketing of the innovations, but due to the process of creating it. If you live in a socialistic society, everyone most likely believes all work done in the same sector is equivalent. This means that the wealthy are often despised. All people in Denmark know about the Law of Jante. But is the workers job behind the assembly line worth the same as the one who invented the assembly line? Let's turn it around. If no one had invented the assembly line, would the worker be manning the farmers' fields but at a lower wage? Are the workers not just looking to get a better piece of the pie by asking for higher wages? That is also why conversations often cease when I mention the fact that being the one who hires, rather than being hired, is more lucrative. They believe they are suddenly less than someone, and are being exploited, even though it is the opposite of what happens in real life. Maybe the hammer issue is present again, whereby all problems look like a nail. Many people want to understand others and have charitable instincts. Socialists do not do this. They put themselves into their own place not others' even though they say that they do. Too much socialism kills innovation. However, if you look at San Francisco, too much capitalism leads to 48,000 people who are homeless. That is a high number in a city with approximately 870,000 people. However, both forms are built up by centralism. It is the same mindset that creates poor people lying around in cardboard boxes, living on scraps, that also creates some of the wealthiest people in the world, like Gates, Jobs,

Zuckerberg, Page, Brin, Dell and many others. Centralism around a strong state and centralism are built around a strong financial sector with the central bank as the main ruler.

The chasm and the hype

Early adopters' and visionaries' buyers of the first microwave oven in the 60s in US were probably not apprehensive, or they did not worry if things were going to blow up. The first people who bought the iPod; were they visionaries? The first people who downloaded content from a torrent site; did they have a clue about copyrights and that they were engaging in something illegal? In my opinion, people are not visionaries simply because they use things early, but early adopters are. Visionaries are people who bring an invention to life. Gardener (see notes) explains the hype surrounding marketing cycles for products and innovations; how do they go to market, what is the go-to market strategy, and what can you use a hype cycle for? This tool was built to show us the phases that a product goes through. Whether a product dies out or a new one is invented is also reliant on us. The hype cycle can tell us about emerging technology within the context of an industry and individual appetite for risk. This is an accurate depiction of what crossing the chasm is all about. Do you dare to cross it? Or will you stand back and tell the others that it is fine where you are? Do you dare to use the microwave oven before everyone else, despite the rumours and urban legends? Why do people believe it is their unique belief system that is right? When in doubt, they either read a chapter from the Bible, Quran or Torah. Others turn to their community for help on certain matters. Yet others will ask the spirits of the shamans for enlightenment. You should possess so much knowledge that you could ask yourself and find out if it is right for you, and if it is right for your civilisation. When it comes to fraudsters, 95% of people want to avoid calling them out as cheaters. This is due to self-doubt and a defence mechanism to avoid getting involved. Common knowledge is built from the community that surrounds us; it is even possible that the community and public opinion can be wrong, especially when it comes to new innovations like the microwave oven. People also thought shares on gas would blow up back in the 80s, not considering the fact that gasoline is also combustible. That is the entire idea of a combustion engine, but the public are easily deceived. They often go with the flow of bubbles like the Tulipmania in the Netherlands. There was also the housing bubble in the US in 2008 that burst; and the IT bubble in 2001 that burst. After the 1929 market crash based on people's belief that the bond market would make everybody rich, it took decades to restore the balance. If you have seen the series *Babylon Berlin*, you will know that the Krupp family predicted this crash. From their prediction and pre-emptive planning, they received massive funding, allowing them to build an army. Innovation is not always good, but that depends on which side you're on, too. However, after the war, many scientists were deported to the US and the USSR, not in equal amount. Over 13,000 scientists with profound knowledge from their experiments in the camps and in weapon factories emigrated with a new life and salary. You can read more about this in *Operation Paperclip*, a book by Annie Jacobsen. For example, NASA got Wernher von Braun, a leading rocket scientist for Nazi Germany, who became the leading scientist of the Marshall Space Flight Center in Alabama. He led the innovation of the Saturn V rockets. During the war, Werner Karl Heisenberg, who had discovered quantum theory with Bohr, stayed in Germany. This worried the allies because Germany also had Heisenberg, who knew how to build atomic bombs and had the materials to do so. We know now that he didn't.

The barriers

When I was young and went to school, I often tried to understand why things were as they were. I hated to be told what to do, and that is not a positive characteristic when it comes to learning. Nevertheless, I was curious enough to find out that some things there were exciting. When afforded the opportunity to work with the things that excited me, what stopped me from learning? What is a barrier to learning something, and what is a belief system built on? As a child, I did not subscribe to a particular belief system; I was merely a spoiled brat. What does it mean when we want to learn and are curious? Why do plenty of people stop learning after the first years of education? Why do we sometimes have a concrete understanding of things, as if they are carved in stone? In the comfort zone where we do not feel any fear, the limbic system is in no stress. But if someone asks us a specific question, we feel uncomfortable. We sometimes even feel threatened. The amygdala tells us to fight or flee, and the smarter part of the brain, frontal lobes, will usually not get any room to negotiate or to think things through. Only through learning can we change this behaviour that is inspired by the primitive limbic reptile brain. It takes a lot of training in the military to find out that it might not be the best decision just to go head-to-head with an opponent. As George Washington said, the worst decision is to do nothing at all. But what should you do if you know that innovation can't be un-innovated? It is like time: it can't go back. When someone has died, they will not be resurrected. When we first had the atomic bomb, we had to deal with it, no matter how frightening it was and still is. Still, we must think, will we use it? And if we do use it, what will the consequences be?

This is the philosophy of war; you will think things through one more time before you just go out there and fight them with the biggest bomb that you have in your arsenal.
Steffen Kirkegaard

The tipping points

When you see or hear someone yawn, you often tend to yawn too. This effect is easy for us to relate to, but when it comes to buying shoes, it is difficult to feel or see yourself doing something similar. It is not a phenomenon that elicits as clear a feeling as when someone yawns. But what is it that makes you buy the same shoes as others? What is it that makes you think they look good on someone else but not you? What is it that makes you buy a jacket to look like someone in an advertisement? Abandoned houses get graffitied. Why do criminals work in certain areas and not in others? Why are stones thrown through glass in some neighbourhoods and not in others? Authorities learned that, if they paint over graffiti, it will not get painted so often. You must buy some more paint for your walls if you want to keep the graffiti away. And if the walls are kept in order and up to date, they will not get tagged. I live in the middle of Copenhagen, where the houses are from the 1790s, not really the ideal target; however, occasionally when the old houses stand idle and vacation for too long, graffiti will grace its walls. So, there is a clear symptom of this phenomena can see from my own window. When it comes to a virus, it spreads under specific circumstances. The criminal mind works in this manner too. If there is already graffiti decorating a building, you feel you are also allowed to tag it. Young men have this urge to go and paint; I was once friends with a crowd who were attracted to this lifestyle. I even tried myself but was not good at it. The thrill that you get from doing it, the adrenaline that rushes through your body, is a part of human behaviour. I'm not saying it is smart or well considered or in any way something to strive for. I just found out that the adrenaline kick was a way for these youngsters to get something out of life. Later, they started to smoke hash; that was not for me either. But I realized that these guys shared a similar mentality, regardless of social status or the occupations of their parents. The only consistent variable amongst these kids was that their parents were not present. They did not come from close families where they had a mom or a dad, or both, who cared for them. They were often the latch-key kids, who had to unlock the door themselves after school until their parent came home. There are a lot of tragic stories following such disheartening starts; some made it, most did not. One thing is for sure, love is what moves us forward. A lack of love and care is what makes people turn into someone who exploits others; those who do not see the fine line in what is yours and what is mine. Somehow, they take instead of creating. It cannot be said for everyone, but for some, they develop a dependency on such things. If your parents never taught you right from wrong, the same lack of education follows you into adulthood. If your parents exhibited negative behaviours but were still successful because of it, a child associates these traits with opportunity and recognition. While some upbringings teach children there is success in vandalism or breaking the law, other upbringings teach children there is success in being an entrepreneur or innovator. These parents excite their children with new ideas. They talk to them of the fantastical things that they can achieve through innovation. In short, kids are taught to have a completely different mindset, thus altering their approach to life.

Are you born in a country where poverty thrives? Or are you from a family where you have what you want and there is no specific reason to venture far from what you already know, as you have what you need. What drives a person to be a part of society that contributes positive things rather than negative ones? What drives a person to be someone who constantly thinks of how to improve situations for the better? Why are some people thinkers whereas others are not? Some innovations are driven by an urge to improve, some simply by a need, and some by poverty and the desire to escape such environments. But some innovations happen because others have come to life. Some innovations happen in a group, others come from one person. But for most innovators, it is one person who makes it happen with a team to assist them in bringing such a vision to life. One such example is of the Wright brothers who invented the first aeroplane simply out of their desire to fly. While going through the process of creating of a plane safe enough to fly, although they were the brains behind the operation, they enlisted a reliable team of people to help construct their vision. Some innovations happen out of a good heart. The LifeStraw was an innovation that happened in the West, but it helped people who did not have clean water. It can clean polluted water; you just filter the water in the straw before you drink it. The pivot for life straw made inventor's focus more on hikers and people who like to explore the wilderness. Innovations often come from positive tipping points. But when we study tipping points, there is also a dark side to them. This is what Malcolm Gladwell writes about in his book *The Tipping Point*. Even viruses have their tipping point; this is when they start to spread. When does a viral video begin to go viral, and can you increase its chances of going viral by using marketing and other channels? This mechanism has been well researched over the past 20 years due to increased demand and accessibility for people with an internet connection.

The tipping ideas

My favourite pastime is undoubtedly having many discussions with a company advisor on this very matter, exploring new, untapped ideas. How many ideas were conjured up from nothing but a crazy aspiration two young men who wanted to fly manifested through their imagination on Kitty Hawk hill? Think of Tesla, who spent many tireless nights striving to deliver accessible electricity; or the ingenious team of scientists who experimented until they created the ultimate weapon, the atomic bomb, forever changing modern warfare. There are also seemingly simple inventions created by happenstance for which people of the time did not fully understand the consequences, the potential, though we now know how they shaped the world. These products may very well not have been here had there not been access to previous discoveries that allowed modern scientists to ride on their coat tails. One example is the curved stick for skiing "innovated" or redesigned by Swedish and Norwegian skiers, Ole Einar Björndalen and Fredrik Lindström. Innovation is sometimes also the GoPro camera, that was built in a way so everyone could have it with them when they went skiing, diving any other activity in which they wanted to document their life and new experiences. GoPro staked its claim as a sought-after invention after vloggers uploaded their videos to YouTube. YouTube was an innovation that Google bought after a year of trying with their own Google Video service. They simply saw that the video service they had made did not attract the same number of viewers as YouTube, so they acquired it. I will dive deeper into this in the next chapter on Tipping Ideas and why ideas and innovation matter. The list of trials before YT.

Some innovations come to life because politicians want them to happen. The moon landing could be said to have sprung out of John F. Kennedy's head, but he was not alone. His government knew it could be done with the technology available back then. They had to build it bigger and spend more money, but it was within reach. Out of the moon landing and the Saturn V rockets came plenty of further innovations: solar panels, heart monitors, shock absorption for footwear, chlorine-free pools, quartz watches for precise time, liquid methane, vacuum-sealed food, the insulin pump, water filtration, wireless headsets, CAT-scans, memory foam, the battery-driven drill and many more. Nevertheless, many inventions require such massive funding, they can only be achievable with government aid. An example is the ITER in Europe that explores ways to utilise fusion energy as a feasible alternative to modern energy sources. Although ITER is planned to start production around 2035, it seems it may already be surpassed by the SPARC project, created to produce fusion energy through their tokamak. To make fusion work, the fuel must be heated to temperatures above 100 million degrees Fahrenheit. Matter in that state is called plasma – where the particles have a net electric charge. To be kept hot, this plasma must be completely insulated from ordinary matter. While we have not yet begun to meddle in such things, Denmark aspires to utilise fusion through an energy island in the northern sea to bring accessible energy to half of Europe by 2070. These large projects are expensive, and they are innovations on a massive scale. For instance, the new windmill from Vesta can produce 15 Mega Watts of power from just one mill. The diameter of the rotor is 236 meters V236-15.0 MW™ (vestas.com). These enormous mills would allow enough initial energy to be produced to make the construction of such an energy island possible. However, smaller energy fields already exist under private ownership, such as Seaborg's Molten Salt Reactor. They will have a commercial prototype by 2024, years ahead of the large TOKAMAK productions from the US and EU. These innovations are being built at the same time, but also with different perspectives and funding streams. The privately held energy companies innovate on a smaller scale. As of now, it is unknown if small thorium reactors will be a thing of tomorrow and every man's own home reactor, or whether the large-scale continental fusion reactors will produce the energy of tomorrow. One thing is for sure, fusion is coming to a home near you soon. And it will be the countries that have the money and the talent to do so who achieve it. Will the centralized innovations built by governments win or will the privatised companies?

Tier two

As humans, we face a constant struggle to escape from our comfort zones. We are slaves of the known, and haunted by the pleasant belief that the past was superior. While it is definitely not a new phenomenon, romanticizing the past can be problematic.
Tier two involves a shift away from the silos in tier one. Level seven is the first type of people who are able to combine and benefit from all the levels that come before. It is Me-centric. Holism is now an option. Level seven thinks systematically in multiple perspectives and with great abstraction skills. Rank and status are unimportant; the focus is on competence and knowledge. It is also within the capability of those within this level to understand the global flow, the geopolitical structures and what we can do with universal networks. People who understand how the mainframe works and the basic computer networks understand the systems for level seven but moving there on a social level is different from having a computer network understanding. In this level you are already systems-oriented; this also counts applies to self within an education system. You already use the internet system to expand knowledge, something which is done on a regular basis. You self-educate, you gain new insights, you follow all your friends and family on social media as you know systems better than the tribal people who need others to tell them how to use them. Personal autonomy for education and occupation are within your system.

Level eight is we-centric.

Now that we grasp the big picture of global flows and universal networks, we can discover personal freedom without causing harm to others or having an excess of self-interest.

We now understand fully automated systems and processes, all of which can be optimized and monetized. They also know when to apply all levels of thinking with a deep intuition. We currently see this with Amazon, Facebook, Twitter, Google, and all other companies that are highly systems oriented. You have probably seen a commercial in your social media feed a few moments after you had talked to someone about the same subject. You know they are listening in because it is the first time you mentioned it. On a personal level, you understand that global workers are people who you can get involved via the internet through a variety of services that give you an option to work with both your country fellow men but also around the globe.

Level nine is once again Me-centric. This level starts to understand entanglement and the way in which everything interacts with each other. Quantum entanglement and the big questions around Schrodinger's cat are accepted as something that you know has a big potential for humankind. A.I. is also something you want to understand and wish to implement in your organization. On this level you understand what a decentralized autonomous organization can do for your society and for humanity in general. You also understand why blockchain has massive potential for the economy and the international economical realm.

Level ten is me-centric and can use femtotechnology. This means that we can upload our entire consciousness into a computer. Femtotechnology is a millionth of the size of nanotechnology. Uploading our consciousness will bring humankind to a new level. We will be able to have multiple copies of our consciousness and they will work for us as a single individual or, holistically, all together. The collective intelligence I will describe later will be implemented in all decisions. The higher power and the digital God figurehead will advance the world into another dimension. Quantum technology on this level will also unlock new understanding and potential for atoms. On level ten we will already have people/minds on other planets. Quantum transport, and so-called entanglement, will be used for this.

Commitment is voluntary

To take the jump into the next tier, people must understand voluntary decisions. Force has been used for too long. The tribal way of thinking has to stop; however, this will occur naturally, as it is a fundamental step towards achieving total freedom of the mind. When people first discover the tools, they start to use them. A wooden axe became a stone axe; a stone axe became an iron axe. No one will go back to Windows 95 because it crashes all the time. Well, it is the same way with freedom when you first obtain it; after that, you will not let others decide for you. The power structures of today will be given to the people, as a result of the new technologies. And autonomous organizations will be the new way to get the most out of things.

Innovation ideas – where do they come from? How and why? Why can't innovation be revoked?

Being innovative

Since I was young, I have wondered about innovation. The question in my head was, and is always, how can we do this better? There must be a way we can combine innovations to make things even better. One of the most iconic videos is *Think Different* from 1997, the year when Apple launched their Macintosh.

"Here's to the crazy ones. The misfits. The rebels. The troublemakers. The round pegs in the square holes. The ones who see things differently. They're not fond of rules, and they have no respect for the status quo. You can quote them, disagree with them, glorify, or vilify them. About the only thing you can't do is ignore them. Because they change things. They push the human race forward. And while some may see them as the crazy ones, we see genius. Because the people who are crazy enough to think they can change the world are the ones who do."

The advertisement was designed to save the company from going bankrupt. Steve Jobs came back to the company after a few years when he had been working on other companies like PIXAR and Next. Microsoft invested 150 million in Apple shares but sold them after five years and acquired a 260% gain from this investment. If they had kept the stocks until today, it would have been 850 times

this money and a 5.9% share of Apple: a total $127.5 billion stake in the company. But that is all history now. Gates regrets the fact that he did not buy into the company to be part of the smartphone wave. The iPhone was one of Apple's biggest drivers for success.
The advertisement is still great, and when you are an innovative person like me, you see yourself in this small text. If you have read *Crossing the Chasm* by Geoffrey Moore you will understand that innovators come before the early adopters.

Crossing the chasm

Moore shows that in the Technology Adoption Life Cycle, which starts with innovators and moves to early adopters, early majority, late majority, and laggards, there is a vast chasm between the early adopters and the early majority. While early adopters are willing to make sacrifices for the advantage of being first, the early majority wait until they know that the technology offers improvements in productivity. The challenge for innovators and marketers is to narrow this chasm and ultimately accelerate adoption across every segment. There is also the problem of cognitive dissonance that makes people disbelieve in what they are about to buy. For example, colour TV was expensive compared to black and white television. For some people, it was not necessary to have colour on the screen. But today we are looking at pixel density; is it necessary to have 4K? Yet, some will spend the last of their money on an 8K resolution.

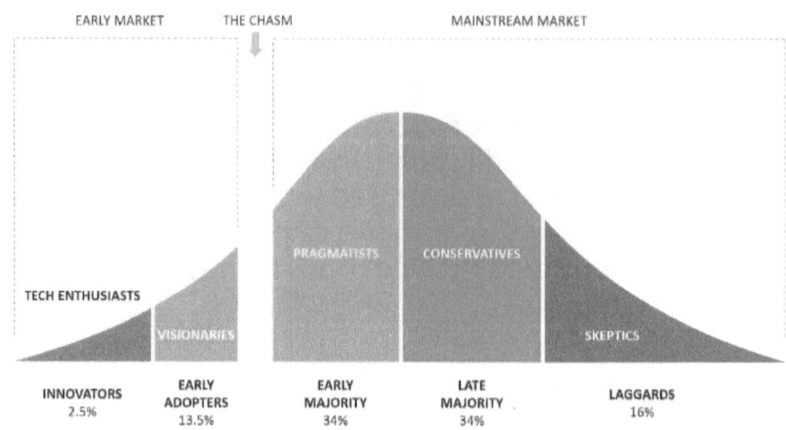

Moore discusses marketing and aiming advertising towards the early majority, and why it is important for a company. However, the tipping point of crossing the chasm occurs when people adopt an innovation or an idea and buy it or own it as it is theirs. There is a strategy for marketing to get them in on this idea. Steve Jobs didn't like the idea of a marketing concept called "Apple is back" because in 1997 it was not true. The slogan "Think different" was a smarter idea; it encompassed an entirely new platform for Apple. He was back, but the company had to start over. The person who had kicked him out as a CEO was gone, so now the company could return to its former glory. This story is interesting to me, because we see a man who brought his own idea to life, got kicked out of his own company, and managed to retain it. Bill Gates invested in them, so they could financially recover the company, which was days from going under. In the movie *The Pirates of Silicon Valley*, Bill Gates steals some ideas from Jobs at a podium show. It might not be true, but the premise is verifiable, as they were each other's muses. Gary Kildall was the programmer who invented CP/M which was the first real operating systems for PCs. IBM tried to buy the OS and offered Gary a one-time offer. However, he refused. Seattle

Computers had a clone of Gary's CP/M OS called Q-DOS, shorthand for *Quick and Dirty Operating System*. IBM then approached Gary with the idea that both systems could be on their PC's, and they would let the market decide which one to use. But Bill Gates was smart; he priced his version at $40 while Gary Kildall's version was $240, a massive 6-1 chasm.

They attended the same conference in 1982 where Gary announced there was room for more companies. However, Bill clarified that there was only room for one. The fact is, Gary had an OS before Bill, and Bill obtained a copy of the OS from a company who had cloned Gary's OS. If Gary had been tougher, and had taken Bill to court, he would have been the billionaire. Unfortunately, Gary died a tragic death due to alcoholism. He was broken. Here is a great documentary on the story Link. This story reminds me of the facts that not all people are honest; not all people are fair; and not all people think of others before themselves. It is also a proof of the nature of level 5, that most people strive to be in the US. Level 5 is known for being self-centred. The levels change from self to group thinking. 1 level is self-survival, 2 is the clan, 3 is self, 4 is the religious collective, 5 is me and the money, and 6 is the collective and the community. But all the levels in tier one is about centralization. They all focus on either the monetary system, as in level 5, or what I can get by being part of a community as in level 6; the community is also centralistic. Socialism is one system that supports a group, not the whole. One worst case is fully fledged communism is the other is when national socialism is tried. Both always go wrong. The reason is that they depend on leaving someone out. There is no Holism in tier one. Crossing the chasm comes with a price tag, for most people. They choose between two options, that are relatively similar. So, the majority collectively decided to save $200 and go with the lesser expense. Who wouldn't? IBM effectively killed a man because they wanted a cheaper product. They ended up with another company who had not been the inventor of the OS.

Trial and error

Countless innovations are built from ideas that others failed with. One of them is what initially made the Apple computer something special compared to its competitors, namely the mouse. Nevertheless, it had to go through multiple innovations in order for it to become what it is today. A student called Engelbart observed that the way we used the PC with a keyboard, or a joystick, was inefficient. Subsequently, in 1966 after a trial period, NASA confirmed that the cursor was most effective and efficient way. Two years later, he and Bill English Douglas showcased the mouse. However, after five years, they ran out of funding. They both began working for XEROX, and in 1979 Steve Jobs offered XEROX shares in Apple for inventions they did not use. That is why the first Macintosh had a mouse that worked so well with the cursor on the screen. Again, just another minute thing that made Apple what it is today. Convenience was always what Steve was striving for. It is much more effective and convenient to use a mouse than the arrow keys on a keyboard. The mouse has not evolved much since then, except it is now equipped with an infrared sensor, it is faster, and it has a scroll wheel and more buttons. However, it falls under the category of optimisation, not innovation. Nonetheless, this invention given to Apple through shares created thousands of jobs for Apple. The difference in using this PC compared to others was huge. And you know by now that innovation can't be un-innovated. You will not go back to using only a keyboard and a screen using text and syntax. Occasionally, innovators lose their lives in the pursuit to make a change. They can sporadically run out of money, resulting in their innovations being acquired by a third party. Then there are certain times during a crisis when a government will step in, to provide funding and overtake the process. Tesla's first car was built on top of a Lotus Elise; it took 4.6 seconds to reach 60 mph - 100 km/t. Only around 2,450 models were made, and I had the pleasure of testing a prototype in 2008 when it was brought to

Denmark. But if it had not been for a $465.5 million loan

granted to Musk in 2010, we would not have had this car manufacturer today Link. My motivation for mentioning this is that it highlights the occasional necessity for government intervention and subsequent biases and favouritism. A government can push innovation, but it can also push other innovations away when governments use taxpayers' money to fund a specific brand. More on this later.

Metallurgy, the nail, the printing press, optical lenses, the chronograph, the sexton, modern sanitation, steam power, the tractor, the spinner, the combustion engine, electricity, refrigeration, the semiconductor, telecommunication, space travel, flight, the processor, and advanced medicine are all innovations we take for granted today. But in some parts of the world, they do not even have these.

The world is going in the right direction. Hans Rosling, who is one of my heroes, died a few years back, but we can all view his videos on how the world is thriving, providing us insight into the way that some people do what others think is wrong. He wrote the book, *Factfullness*, which demonstrates the false conceptions amongst most doomsayers. The world population will stop growing around 2050; this is one prediction you can make when you look at statistics covering birth-rates in poorer countries. But one of his YouTube videos, called *The Magical Washing Machine*, highlights inconveniences women face when they lack a washing machine, and thus spend more than four hours a day washing clothes preventing them from pursuing something that would improve their lives. The opportunity for employment affords the family some surplus and some money they can spend on better food, better clothing, or a vehicle to cut down on the transportation time forth and back from work. Overall, the washing machine is a great innovation for most people in poor countries. And again, once you have one, you will never voluntarily go back to the river to wash clothing. For many people, recent innovations have been the reason why the world is a better place to live in today when compared to just 30 years ago. One of the initial catastrophes that human innovations caused was the refrigerator. Sure, refrigerators make storing ice cream and long-lasting food possible, and we take this for granted but it had to be cooled by Freon. Freon is a fluid that changes into a gas through evaporation. When compressed with a simple pump, it becomes hot. When it cools off, it regulates the temperature, keeping it cool. Once, I met a man on a flight to London. He was on his way to sell containers full of refrigerators. I asked him why and how he could sell these. He simply explained to me that the ozone layer that we now know must remain intact was not something they cared about in the Middle East or in Africa. All the effort we made to save the ozone layer in Europe was a waste because these refrigerators were still in use, albeit only in the poorer parts of the globe. I still wonder why discussions concerning the ozone layer disappeared from the newspapers, when the Freon pollution was still ongoing. Out of sight out of mind? Another innovation came from a Polish immigrant Stephanie Kwolek, who worked at Dupont for 40 years, and experimented with aromatic polyamides, making a type of polymer that can be made into strong, stiff, and flame-resistant fibres. When I first heard of Kevlar, I was astounded that a fibre could be stronger than steel. But did you know that it was first rejected by a co-worker because, internally, they thought it would clog the spinneret? Nevertheless, she persisted, thus Kevlar was born. It is five times stronger than steel by weight. She also registered 28 patents for Dupont, among them Spandex, Lycra, Nomex, Kapton and others. Occasionally you just have to try something and go for it. Therefore, it is so important not to go for full centralisation on innovation. How politicians acquire votes and power is unclear to them. They make laws to minimize failure; they want to exactly control a population through micromanagement. They typically try to get funding during the early stages of their rule, by any means in order to rule and manage. This interferes with innovations more than it aids them. I will go into why this is true in a later chapter. In short, the public sector tries to manage innovation as if it is something you can control. Innovation must be beneficial for all the voters in a demographic segment for the politicians to have enough power to push it through. This is the opposite of what innovation is. For instance, the market has a demand for transportation. The Wright brothers tried to invent a suitable machine capable of flying but each for a different reason. One brother wanted to be first to successfully invent an aircraft. The other wanted to understand the physics behind it. Rumour has it that the former brother lost interest in his pursuit once he became aware someone else had already achieved his goal. The desire to innovate stems from various motivations, and not everyone maintains the motivation to complete their task. It is said that the brother who wanted to be first who found out that another group of people had flown before them, lost interest and stopped advancing in this field. Innovation has different drivers too.

You won't change the world, walking in others' footsteps. If you stay in the same paradigm, you will not find a new way. We cannot solve our problems with the same thinking we used when we created them. –Albert Einstein

If you stay in the same paradigm, you will not find a new way.

Innovation drivers

"The true sign of intelligence is not knowledge but imagination." – Albert Einstein

It was believed that the earth was the center of the universe until the 16th century. In 1563, Tycho Brahe Copernican and Ptolemaic table to predict the conjunction were discovered to be inaccurate. He invented The Tychonic cosmological model that gained traction after Rome declared the heliocentric model was contrary to both philosophy and scripture in 1616. At that time, Kepler and other scientists were trying to convince Tycho of the heliocentric model of the solar system.

In 1565, Denmark was at war with Sweden, and as vice-admiral of the Danish fleet,Tycho's father, Jørgen Brahe, became a national hero for having participated in the sinking of the Swedish warship Mars during the First battle of Öland (1564). Shortly after Tycho's arrival in Denmark, Jørgen Brahe was defeated in battle on 4 June 1565, and shortly afterwards died of a fever. It is said that he contracted pneumonia after a night of drinking with the Danish King Frederick II, which resulted in the king falling into a Copenhagen canal and Brahe jumping in after him. Brahe's possessions were passed on to his wife Inger Oxe, who treated Tycho with special fondness. Tycho had to flee from Denmark when King Christian IV didn't want him to stay. He practiced medicine and alchemy, of which the church did not approve. The King curbed the power of the nobility by confiscating their estates to minimize their income bases, thereby also removing their belongings. Christian was known for his palaces, his observatory the Round Tower in Copenhagen and many other landmarks. He was keen on maintaining his power. The support that Tycho received from the Crown was substantial, amounting to 1% of the kingdom's annual total revenue at one point in the 1580s. At that time Denmark nearly went bankrupt due to the wars, the palaces and all the other extravagances. In Tycho's most famous poem, "Elegy to Dania", he chided Denmark for not appreciating his genius. The mixture of hostility from the nobility, the churches and others made Tycho move to Prague and build a new observatory with funding from the emperor and Oldrich Desiderius Pruskowsky von Pruskow, to whom he dedicated his famous *Mechanica*. Tycho even lost a bit of his nose in a duel because of a dispute over who was best at mathematics. He had a prosthetic silver and gold nose glued to his head for the rest of his life.

Contrary to popular belief, science, at the time, was taken so seriously that it was not uncommon for violence to arise in an effort to protect a scientist's credibility or ego. Furthermore, it is my belief that science was something, and perhaps still is today, that you literally fought for. The perspectives of philosophy and alchemy were the driving forces for science. Back then, Scania was a part of Denmark (having been won by the king), and Tycho had his observatory on Hven. While countries fought for land, the scientist had sword fights over disputes when he was drunk. Once, even a muse was drunk and died of this in one of his parties. It must have been a wild period for science. Tycho attempted to develop the narrative that the earth was the center of the universe. In Prague, Tycho worked closely with Kepler, his assistant. Kepler was a devout Copernican who considered Tycho's model to be mistaken and derived from simple "inversion" of the Sun's and Earth's positions in the Copernican model. But things changed in the next century. The Dutch perspective glass helped Galileo Galilei (1564-1642) to build a telescope in 1609 that could magnify the objects of the sky up to 20 times. Why is this important in a book that is about doubt and innovations? The innovation behind this is clear; it was the most ground-breaking tool with which to observe the sky, and, subsequently, the earth's placement in the galaxy. At this time, the religious level four people had the upper hand when it came to science. Science pertaining to the location of planets and stars belonged to the church. Therefore, it was the priest and later the pope in Rome who dictated how the earth was placed in the universe. But remember that, at this time, common people also believed that if they sailed over the edge of what was known to the human eye in the horizon, they would fall off. People believed that the earth was flat. In 1543, *On the Revolutions of the Heavenly Spheres* was the last written words of Nicolaus Copernicus, arguing that the earth was not the center of the universe. He described the heliocentric system, but it was ignored by the priests and the Holy Roman Empire. All this was hard to reject when you could see it with your own eyes, as Galileo made it possible to do. Around 1676, a Danish scientist, Ole Rømer, was born in Aarhus. He discovered the speed of light, through observations of Cassini, a moon of Jupiter. Rømer never made a public announcement of this discovery, but many others calculated the speed from his data. Christian Huygens deduced that light travelled 16+2/3 Earth diameters per second, which is approximately 212,000 km/s.

I find it quite amazing that perspective glass and the speed of light, were discovered a mere sixty years apart. In addition to this, and perhaps much more amusingly, the church had no choice but to accept these. Science had successfully replaced the power structure. Now people started to listen to the scientists and the modern era began. The world was still highly centralised, and people knew who was in power. The kings around Europe were still fighting over land in hundreds of small wars. The small wars were fought between the nobility, though kings often settled the disputes, and they also fought against each other every now and then. Sometimes this was to gain land, sometimes to steal what the others had.

Philosophy, alchemy, and science were not always exclusive as they were sometimes the same. However today, philosophy has once again become an essential part of science pertaining to quantum physics, something which we still do not fully understand. Alchemy is a thing of the past. We know how to make gold out of a chemical process, but the process is too expensive compared to the price of labour.

A triangular sextant and other similar instruments were all they had at that time, but the telescope made the difference. Any doubts regarding the way the planets and the stars were positioned were now settled. We are still in the early stages of the modern world. The early drivers for innovation have triggered further innovation as we understand it today, where scientists have a say. We are now out of the religious dark ages.

Imagination is what drives innovation. Imagination is somewhat close to alchemy. Imagination is also philosophy. We know that alchemy was also used fraudulently on numerous occasions. People used it as a scam. Some nobles believed in it, and exhausted their fortunes, leaving them bankrupt. Imagination is still the driver for innovation, but you must be strong in your belief and your ideas to bridge the gap from idea to reality. Today we have the James Webb Space Telescope that has just launched. The United States has spent $10 billion on this project. It will give us the option to look further into space than ever before. And who knows, we might find out something that we did not know before. Our worldview is expanding, but people have spent decades trying to debunk the big bang theory, and now they are attempting to utilize data coming from JWST to substantiate their claims.

Innovation structural drivers

Personal reasons, research and development, educational, public service, or coincidence: these are all structures that help innovation become real.

A. The person is one person who sits with a problem and tries to solve it. It does not even have to be a scientist or a professional within the field. Occasionally, it is just a person who thinks they can innovate and find an easier way. Periodically, altruism is the leading motivator. It can be based on a daily obstacle. It can be the desire to invent something first. Sometimes it is a person who just can't stop thinking of new ways of doing something, like me. Some people go for it, whereas others suppress the idea and leave it at that.

B. Research and development are often carried out in companies with a specific department allocated to researching new innovations. Every so often they refine the products they already have. This process could be based on updated surveys they conduct with their buyers and customers. Occasionally, it is in an effort to push products forward ahead of their competitors. We see this in the electronic business all the time. Even though it has been proven that the human eye can only see 4K, after which we don't have an ability to differentiate the pixels, the development of 8K televisions is progressing. On the other hand, I believe that the early full cinematic experience, where smell and movements are a part of the scene will be feasible on the 8K screens, so your eyes will see all the details in the distance too. There is a possibility that it will thus engage our cinematic experience and will give us the sensation of dreaming while we are awake.

C. In education, we have seen some improvements like Duolingo, Khan Academy, and many others that help people learn from any age. We even see efforts like Ameelio, which is helping the incarcerated get an education and aim for a better life after prison. But these products were built by people who saw a problem, not the educational system itself. Typically, we see entrepreneurs build these products because they see an issue. However, education needs to improve in many ways. Education helps us become entrepreneurs, but it is a recent development that people with Bachelor's or Master' degrees are offered courses specifically based on entrepreneurship. I believe that education can be much more when decentralization becomes a normal standard for paid content. Paid education, sponsored education, and the new genre Play to Earn are becoming educational to learn; you earn money every time you open a book read a sentence or, most of all, finish an exam.

D. Public service is one of a kind because the money involved can be enormous. If the money is being spent wisely, they can sponsor some of the largest breakthroughs in history. But sometimes public innovation fails when it is 100% public. Now a gigantic telescope is orbiting the earth. It was sent out there in December 2021. James Webb had a price tag of $10 billion. But if everything goes right, it will be able to see so far into the universe that we will be able to look at the start of it. The infrared light that we see will be from the birth of the universe and this will give us answers to questions not even asked yet. The public sector created the internet framework. It also created central administration for banks, which has been the standard so far. But will crypto surpass this with its decentralized form?

E. Coincidence can also play a role - John Pemberton was a pharmacist who tried to find a cure for headaches. He came up with a simple recipe where he combined Coca leaves and Cola Nuts. In 1883, a seller mixed the syrup with soda by accident, creating Coca-Cola. The first antidepressants were made for tuberculosis; the creators noticed that it did not do much for the disease, but it helped the mood of the patients. Wilson Greatbatch was trying to invent a device that recorded the heartbeat, but by mistake added the wrong electronic component, which made the product recreate the heart's rhythm. This is now known as a pacemaker. This mistake has created a device that allows people many more years of life. Another great scientist, Alexander Fleming, had a mess of petri dishes around his desk with different kinds of bacteria. One day, he found mold in one of them containing staphylococci bacteria. In 1945, he received a Nobel

Prize for discovering penicillin. Even Teflon was to a degree invented by mistake. An experiment was underway in the DuPont labs for trials to find another substance instead of Freon for refrigeration, which ruins our Ozone layer; it took years before something else was found to surpass Freon, but Teflon was invented in the process.

What is not understood

Reverse engineering, or plagiarism, is often used by people who do not innovate, or it can be part of the original process. For example, there have been stores in larger cities in China that were entire copies of Apple stores. Even cities like Paris and adventure parks like Legoland or Disneyland have been copied. If you see a Chinese person in your country taking pictures in a store for more than just a selfie, you might see it come to life in full scale in China. We are back to the mindset of a person who would say, "You would do the same". But no, innovative people, engineers or scientists would not; they create new things and innovations. However, in China the rules are different; it is an honor to do better than others, but copying their concept is not protected by Intellectual Property Rights. The western world's standards do not count here. When the market increases rapidly for an extended period of time, and you have money invested in this, everyone looks like a genius. Everybody can financially contribute to a project and claim they have invested in it. Unfortunately, this occasionally results in crises like the tulip bubble, the market bubble in 1929, the IT bubble in 2001, the housing bubble in 2009, or the current bubble that has occurred post-pandemic. It seems like people who go with the short-term investments will always be the losers. Maybe people who do not understand innovation will lose over time. The economy might go up, but it will always benefit the few who understand the trendlines, and who can analyze the market, and especially those who understand what the next big thing is. However, that is harder to understand and easy to copy. The world will become more and more complex; the innovation curve is exponential. One innovation leads to another, and these two innovations lead to four new ones; this is how it works. Innovation is thereby expanding faster and faster, just as in Moore's Law.

Exponential growth

There is a Chinese proverb: "You have an egg and I have an egg, we exchange, and we both have an egg." You have an idea and I have an idea, we exchange, and we both have two ideas. Maybe it thus seems logical to you that everybody should just exchange ideas, but this is not how the world works. Many people can exchange ideas, as they already do. However, the work behind an innovation is larger and more complex than that. The Wright Brothers knew this. They spent around 12 years on that hill to make something fly. Well, there were more than just the brothers out there; there were engineers, the people who were driven and explorers who thought it could be done. Some came and helped for a while and left, not thinking it would work. There is always the human aspect involved in great innovations. Does the innovation occur because there is a demand for it? Sometimes innovation is stopped by religion due to doctrine. Sometimes innovation is stopped because a geographical region thought they had invented something that shouldn't exist.

There are roughly 1.6 billion Muslims in the world, but only two scientists from Muslim countries have won Nobel Prizes in science. Today, the spirit of science in the Muslim world is as dry as the desert. Pakistani physicist Pervez Amirali Hoodbhoy laid out the grim statistics in a 2007 Physics Today article; Muslim countries have nine scientists, engineers, and technicians per thousand people, compared with a world average of 41. In these nations, there are approximately 1,800 universities, but only 312 of those universities have scholars who have published journal articles. Of the 50 most published of these universities, 26 are in Turkey, nine are in Iran, three each are in Malaysia and Egypt; Pakistan has two, and Uganda, the U.A.E., Saudi Arabia, Lebanon, Kuwait, Jordan, and Azerbaijan each have one. Over the last 1,000 years, scientists have been struggling with religion in Europe and in many other regions of the world. Level four is one of the strongest forces for us as a species that means we are held back by ourselves. If it had not been for people who despised this and went beyond the thoughts of others, we would not have travelled to the moon. We would not have had penicillin. And all the things we see in the world today would not have been here: TV, cars, planes, trains, and computers. Up until the thirteenth century, the Arab world was leading the world in science and then it went back to a more regressive doctrine. This will never happen again. Most people around the globe are living a better life today than they did just 30 years ago. Most people are in the middle classes today. If you do not believe this, please look up the video with Hans Rosling on YouTube called, *How to End Poverty in 15 Years*. The video shows how the entire globe can be without poverty in the next decade and how the population will stop growing because of this. This is another driver for exponential growth in innovation, because the more we build, prosper and innovate, the more innovation there will be. If you do not see the logic in this, you should start over with this book. Exponential growth is a fact because, due to various factors we are becoming smarter; there are more innovations that back other innovations; there will be more people on the globe who will find new observations. The best thing is that religions will fade out when we start to move into level 7 as more people will naturally leave religion behind. Evolution shows that we move between the levels when economic innovation moves us to. When we then observe what is written in the old books, the old doctrine will also be a thing of the past. This is because, as a species, we do not need these hard rules to make the species move forward. Another fact is that people will accept that religions were developed in the regions where they were born. If they live elsewhere, they see another religion who also claims to be the only and righteous one. The reason I bind this to level four is because we are already on our way to tier two and level seven. Central politics like communism and socialism will also disappear, to be replaced by decentralized economies and people who anchor their thoughts around factual knowledge instead of beliefs. The more people who leave this regime, the more innovation arises. Centralization is not good for innovation. We know that people turn to religion in hard times. We know that beliefs can hold you up for a longer time than a lack of such beliefs, but beliefs are not built on facts.

Crushing innovation

Centralization has not been shown to be perfect for innovation. However, the market has shown it is at least good for innovation. What you do not need is one person who believes that they know the truth or how things should be. We often see this when politicians are in full power, like with dictators and others who have the population's full support or have got it through fearmongering. The pandemic was notable for politicians who could feel their power and used it to the full extent in order to do what they wanted, rather than merely doing what was necessary, but was good for the population. We witnessed a scenario in Denmark where an entire business sector was abolished; mink is now gone in Denmark. I don't believe this decision was necessary, but it was done in the way dictators have done things in the past. But it was a good time for politicians to flaunt their power and let others understand that it could happen to them too. Even the farmers in the Netherlands have been put under a lot of pressure lately, due to the climate taxes they have to pay. The Netherlands is one of the largest agricultural producers in Europe because of innovations there after the Second World War. The Netherlands has a third of the country under sea level, so dikes were built, and the country was then able to prosper without fear of flooding. A multitude of greenhouses were funded, and more young people became farmers. Now it is possible to farm year-round by warming up the greenhouses and filling them with extra CO_2 so vegetables can grow even faster. They made large farms and mass production on top of new machinery like tractors, fertilizers, and harvesters, resulting in a massive yield difference. Today, the Netherland has an export market of €65 billion of crops. The same thing has happened in Denmark; the overall number of livestock has doubled, and more than five times the amount when it comes to chicken farming. The point is that farming has grown in all sectors. Some countries have understood they need to do this to the full extent. The proportion of landmass for farming is a sixth as large in China as in the US. This means that 1.4 billion people compared to 375 million farm a sixth of the land area, while there are more than four times as many people. Therefore, China has to import a lot of food. In addition, in the last 20 years the earth has become around 20% greener because countries, particularly China, began creating farmland in rural areas and deserts. Nevertheless, they still have to import vast amounts of agricultural products. However, they have been innovating as they come to understand how this production works. They first copy the production facilities, then after a while they expand the knowledge while utilizing larger farming methods. Even when it comes to dairy and milk production, they have a huge export of necessary machinery around the world. I recently got involved in this during my trip to Dubai, but the NDA I was asked to sign was not to my advantage, so I passed. Crushing innovation can also happen when salespeople only have their own pockets in focus. The centralization is good in China when it helps growth, but I'm not sure it will be good for the country when the people start to insist on being the sole profiteers from their own land. But why would they? In the Netherlands, the farmers are given a piece of land on which they can prosper. The machines and the equipment were not provided but the whole country had to prosper, so the loans and the options for building large farms were pushed with subsidiaries. The farmers had a reason to invest as the profit was a good motivator for them to increase production. We know that China can use all the products themselves and that they also have a large import market. A population that becomes wealthier and has more to spend will also buy better products. I believe that much production will soon move into vertical farming. Vertical farming uses up to 99% less water with aeroponics used for watering and less than 2 percent of the area that conventional farming occupies. I'm not sure if it makes sense to ask why China didn't do this 20 years ago when the LED light was invented. I'm sure they will start vertical farming now that others have invented it and they can see how it works. There are a lot of innovations that have been imported through universities. China is also well-known for innovating apps to make them better and more accessible, as they did with TikTok. The same thing happened to Jack Ma, who was the front man of Alibaba and Alipay, but Jack Ma recently left the company after years of innovation. Specific details of why he has left are unknown; we just know that he is no longer present.

My point is to stress that centralization still holds back innovation in the world's largest country. Someone wants to keep the power to themselves instead of letting business people obtain the power over the companies they have built themselves. A similar thing happened to our mink in Denmark; someone in the government (the prime minister) did not like that others wore expensive mink fur coats, so she took advantage of the fact that cluster-5 was present in the mink herd. Why is this possible? Well, central governments always think about the next election cycle. They know their voters have the same envy towards expensive fur that they can't afford. Removing a business was a strategy pursued without sufficient thought about the money and the many jobs that were lost. After all, Denmark was the best provider of mink fur in the world. Well, you might ask me what mink has to do with innovation. First of all, doubt is one thing people had during the last pandemic. Was it actually this bad? Was it so dangerous? Did the politicians do the right thing? We also know that centralized decisions are not always right. Compare Denmark to Sweden. Sweden did not use facemasks and did not close down shopping in the two years of the Covid 19 situation. Sweden administered vaccines, but all the other countries enforcing lockdowns did not. Now we know from reports that they did more or less follow the same pattern; the same number of people became sick, so my conclusion is again that the facemasks and hygiene guidelines did not help. We also know that even among vaccinated people, some still get sick. There are other variants, I know, but after two vaccines I still got sick again myself. Centralized decisions about mink were also wrong. Breeding of the animals had been going on for years, and this form of evolution had made the finest furs in the world. Breeding animals is another kind of finetuning; in this process we have discovered that we can change animals. If we can change animals, we can also change as humans. Removing envy from people would be a start of a better world. That would also change some of the power structures that are stopping us as a species from innovating and prospering. It is my prediction that vertical farming will change the world's supplies of agricultural products and lead us into a situation where hunger will be a thing of the past. Another great example of crushing innovation comes from the first moon landing. Parker the pen company were asked to make one that the astronauts could use in space. It took them some time, but a pen was eventually invented that cost $1 million. They asked the Russians, who also had people in space after a few years what they used. The answer was, "We use pencils". The point is that overthinking is a problem; using the finest tech that fits the needs of a situation is not always what we should do in a new environment like space. Other times, the market crushes the best technology. That happened to Betamax, the video tape that surpassed VHS in quality. VHS not only dominated adult cinemas, but it also crushed Betamax, because people wanted to watch adult films at home. Blu-ray was said to be the next big thing, but it got surpassed by the internet before it had a chance to fully take off. Even Netflix had its video era, where it sent DVDs to people in envelopes before it came to the internet. The internet market crushed Blockbuster in bringing streaming services to market. Often, the market can't be held responsible because it is you and me who go for something more comfortable or convenient and it is therefore a decentralized process. The big difference here is that you can adapt as a company; you have time to adjust and find out what your competitors are doing, and then do it better. But centralized decisions from one government are often crucial and devastating for a business or sector. Consider the farmers or forestation; what is next in this crazy world of climate-enthusiasts? There are those who glue themselves onto the road in front of our parliament, or get in front of the Tour De France riders, just to get attention to a cause that probably won't be heard in the countries who are polluting the most. When it comes to this case, they lean on someone who has fiddled with the numbers, but it ends in the same centralized thinking as the socialists who believe in one leader and one big state that governs us all. As a decentralist, I see them all over the place. They probably see those of us with a free mind as the means to all evil. One thing is for sure; they do not innovate; they work more like the Luddites who smashed the new agricultural machinery. They break things for their cause. If you mention thorium to them, they don't truly know what it is but think of it as traditional atomic power, and therefore ban it. Society is for them a fight for classes. They do not see that we have moved on and that that fight was won long time ago. Now we should work together but frightened people are often in lockdown, their minds are not able to see the future. Mostly because they are thinking this is mine instead of thinking how can we progress with what we have. Class thinking people will not see the future as bright.

DAO. Decentralized Autonomous Organization

Why DAOs?

Why would you want less people working in your organization and more contracts to be handled by computers? Why would you want less administration and why would you want it to be autonomous? First of all, DAO's can be more efficient than other organizations because the contract is already made, so when the job is done the paycheck will roll out automatically. You will be able to have less meetings, less tasks, and fewer lawsuits. When the world becomes decentralized, the DAOs will be one of many options we will have with crypto. However, most jobs can be done autonomously with DAOs. Therefore, let's look into what they are and what they can do for society compared to the challenges we have in society today.

We will not see fully automated care facilities because human contact in hospitals and in elder care is what makes it unique. But it will allow the hospitals and the elder care sector to concentrate on what the main focus should be, namely care and not administration. Therefore, it makes sense to have a DAO in the hospitals and all other public service functions for the administration so the personnel can do what they are best at. When it comes to commercial business the DAO can also take care of the more routine tasks in the administration and even A.I. This will help us make the world an even more efficient place for the benefit of everyone.

The two unique models for DAOs are token-based and share-based memberships; both have team-centric motives not a sign of a superiority complex.

This way, the concept of bringing decentralization into private and public governance has been birthed. Decentralized autonomous organizations have been used in projects like Dash, Digix, and even BitShares. We have even seen torrents operating similar models and seeking to integrate blockchain into their future upgrades. As Vitalik Buterin, co-founder of Ethereum, said, most companies are likely to buy into the DAO system as it helps to reduce operational costs and improve the bottom line of these companies' finances.

What is a DAO?

The acronym stands for digital autonomous organization. It can be best understood through the idea of a vending machine. You want a chocolate bar and insert a coin on the top; you press a button and out comes the chocolate bar at the bottom. To keep this machine running and the customers coming back, we need to fill it with new chocolate bars and other stuff we need to restock. This can be done by sending the necessary information to a server. Then, when the stock arrives, a robot can insert the new product. This can even happen in fully automatic grocery stores. The money inserted follows a smart contract, where the royalties and the tax are automatically paid, if need be. In addition, board meetings are unnecessary and there are no stakeholders involved who want to tell you how to run your business, although there can be anonymous, silent investors who don't have any legal power to guide the running of your business. How else could this happen if the code could not be improved? Today it seems like you must update your PC on a regular basis. You must update firmware on your coffee machine, your watch, and your headphones. But in a DAO, shareholders can actually vote for changes in the software. So, if all smartwatch owners with a DAO watch wanted to have a new turquoise color for the watch, they could vote for it and the software would apply the color to the next batch produced in the factory. This would account for the amounts of fertilizers dumped on fields by DAOs, as well as methods used by car manufacturers. It is not hard to see the endless possibilities with DAOs. The rules for change can be written into the DAO, so it never changes. These changes don't have to be permanent, though. Votes can be recast on one, or all, of the options the possibilities are endless. A DAO can also be ruled by one leader allotted admin rights. However, when this happens, it becomes a semi-functional DAO, because the decentralized option and the autonomy are gone. Nevertheless, the option will remain; it will be up to those who want to repossess some control to enact their desired changes. The perfect DAO has yet to come, but I think we will see some DAOs include a backdoor safety net to allow administrators access in case they need to regain control. On the other hand, when the first real DAOs hit the market, we will start to see autonomy in a form that we did not know was possible. Even when it comes to complex systems, we will see A.I. combining different DAOs so they work together to benefit each other. In addition, we will see A.I. learning from different DAOs and implementing new advances. In short, A.I. will be used to build software to create the most efficient system.

A DAO can even hire developers, then vote on what salary they should have, and employ them if it is already permissible in the contract they signed. Small tasks will first be allocated to DAOs when simple programmable workloads must be accomplished. By doing this, we will come to understand what works best and what needs to be scrapped.

Decentralization in the public sector

Buurtzorg is a success in the Netherlands, where around 10,000 nurses are working together with no more than two overseers, the CEO and CFO. 900 independent teams take care of more than 70,000 patients. 60% of community nurses work for Buurtzorg in the Netherlands. This has inspired many home care companies to follow the same model. Patient satisfaction is 30% higher than the national average and their client base awards them 9.1 out of 10 for the service provided. The nurses are also on 50% less sick leave than their competitors.
Jos de Blok quit his nursing job out of frustration with the existing system of care delivery. He started in 2006 with three former nurses and set up the social enterprise Buurtzorg, which is Dutch for "neighbourhood care".
The system is built up of teams of ten to twelve nurses who provide both medical and supportive home care services. The IT allows teams to monitor their own performance, and regional coaches promote the best practice and offer advice but without their own performance goals.
The numbers indicate that this process works much better with decentralized organisations than centralized. The product that comes out of this to help the customers is better. Even the patients consume less of the care they are entitled to compared to the sector standard 40% compared to the normal 70% and the hospital admissions are reduced by a third. At the same time, the average hospital stay is shorter. The stakeholders in the company are nurses, patients and relatives who represent the local and national government. The self-management was built out of a trial-and-error strategy.
Again, it is one person who came up with such an innovation, and it seems like it could save a lot of money in the world. But more importantly, it could save a lot of lives and make people happier. Jos de Blok, his wife and a few other nurses began the operation themselves as a trial-and-error team. The system also relies on a high rate of

higher educated nurses; 65% have a bachelor's degree compared to 10% in the normal care system. This means that the nurses are capable of controlling the IT system and their own time. The nurses are self-driven individuals. It also reduces the number of care workers assigned to each client. As a result, client satisfaction is higher as well as the health of the clients.

Buurtzorg is an example from the real world of people who manage the IT, rather than it is managing the IT. It is proven that this makes the work more meaningful for everyone involved. It makes more sense for all when it comes to resources used and time spent, and it makes more sense for the overall economy. Is there anything we can learn from this when it comes to bureaucracy?

Smart contracts in the Healthcare management

Are we on the brink of something bigger, smarter, and better? Will the world evolve into a better version soon? We know that blockchain is a secure database that can be used for different purposes. Management, money wiring, distribution, infrastructure, and the zero-knowledge proof give us autonomy, so we do not need bureaucrats to confirm and validate our work.

Bureaucracy changed the world when the farmers in the western world went from the fields to the assembly lines. They had higher wages, their quality of living increased, and management was controlled by bureaucrats overseeing individual documentation. Before this happened, we had royalty around Europe controlling the peasants and the workers. Occasionally a few people tried to change this system, but unsuccessfully. One was the now forgotten Dane who tried to change the system, Jacob Jacobsen Dampe. He wanted democracy. He was a philosopher and a theologian who analyzed democracies as they unfolded in other countries. However, the Danish king was bullheaded and had him sentenced for treason. He was sentenced to 15 years on a small island the size of two football fields, closer to Russia than any place in Denmark. This happened around 1820, about 150 years before Nelson Mandela. We know that Mandela was imprisoned for 18 years for his campaigns, but the Danes warped Mr. Dampe's character into insanity. This may have had something to do with the minds of the Danes or others trying to take credit for his efforts. In fact, if it had not been for the international focus on Mandela, he might have been forgotten too. Both examples are proof that change can be implemented. Currently, the western world believes democracy is the route to a fair and honest world. We know that the world is not like this yet; there are still large countries that do not even have democracy. However, from democracy comes a large amount of bureaucracy. Furthermore, the factories that sprung out of the industrial ages have moved to other parts of the world. The companies and the public sector get more and more bureaucratic; more and more people are hired to do paperwork and administration. It sometimes seems like they are doing administration to administrate the administration. But as we have seen with the Buurtzorg example, we know that decentralized organizations do perform better on most parameters while having less layers of administration.

Blockchain technology provides numerous benefits to medical health care providers and individuals. This has not been rolled out yet, but if we take a look at the options, we can see the potential for it to be revolutionary in this sector as well. With a blockchain it will be optional to have data on apps. All information from a patient will be stored in smart contracts and will be easily distributed between the doctor, the hospital, and the patient. Smart contracts will comply with the safety and management regulations. Because it is based on blockchain, the process will be done with 100% security and anonymity. Only the system knows the names of the patients, but the insurance companies will know that they must pay for the treatment. The doctor knows that the patient has a record and even the laboratory will be made aware that they have to deliver medication to the patient; it can all be done on the blockchain. It will reduce costs dramatically and it will reduce the time and effort currently required from all parties. On top of this, legislative work will be easier when the whole process is already written into the blockchain, and the smart contracts take care of the signing. Before this can happen, we might see another Dampe or a Mandela. The healthcare system in most of the western world is in a state of controversy. The whole system is politicized and in a bad state. Politicians try to gain popularity from reforms, but the reforms often do not work, and the healthcare system becomes less patient-focused. Thus, it becomes more and more impersonal and bureaucratic. The systems they use have not been updated for years, and even the doctors spend over half of their time typing in timestamps, journals, and other administrative actions that a blockchain would do automatically. Data sharing would be better; the supply chain management would reduce or eliminate claims returned due to insufficient information; it will bring proper data requirements because it is stored on the blockchain specific to each patient in a secure and private manner that only the patient can access and share.

A shared ledger with the patient's full record will be supplied along with a smart contract with business terms for the insurance with a secure authenticated and verifiable journal where all of these functions will work autonomously. It means that the way we work on this today will be eradicated. The verification and the distribution will be taken care of when the money from the healthcare or insurance is paid. And even the money will be paid in an autonomous way because the contracts authenticate the process.

DAO projects

Aave is a lending protocol that allows borrowers and lenders to interact without a centralized intermediary.

Uniswap is a DeFI protocol with over $5.5 billion in TVL, which is a decentralized swap for crypto. There is a huge ecosystem behind this swap. It is all peer to peer meaning that people exchange directly with each other.

Tamadoge is a play-to-earn Metaverse where you build up your pets to make them competitive to earn points on a monthly basis.

ApeCoin is strongly tied to the Bored Ape Yacht Club NFTs and seems like a meme coin. But as with all other meme tokens, the fluctuations can be hard to follow.

Illuvium is an upcoming NFT gaming Project with DAO Governance. It holds play-to-earn and looks incredibly promising.

Decentraland was started in 2017 and raised $26 million for its Initial Coin offering. Some of the parcels have been sold for up to $100,000

The Sandbox from 2011 is a DAO fused with NFTs to create the ideal gaming platform featuring a metaverse with playable characters of Snoop Dogg, Deadmau5 and many other artists.

Meta DAO is a yield on gaming assets. The income form, P2E, can be more than the average salary for people in developing countries, although they often can't afford the expensive NFT purchase for the game. The solution can be to rent out your assets to other players and secure transactions for both sides.

Crypto has given a lot of people money from speculative exchanges. These are just a few examples of DAOs. The reason we have not seen DAO's in large organizations yet is probably because of the lag in the legislation and regulation of them. While the EU and US are in the process of producing the legislation, we have not seen anything yet. It is like having a racecar in the garage but outside there is only gravel road. Another problem with these DAOs is that people do not fully understand them yet and do not trust them. I believe that we will see more of these in the near future, especially when the banks, corporates and public sector know how to handle these options and how to use them. We know that compliance is key for a lot of organizations, as well as how to implement it and how to handle it afterwards. Even though it seems like everything is going to be easier this way, it will take some time before it is compliant with old systems. One of the big old players in the crypto field is IBM, who have an entire division dedicated to it. We know that META is working on crypto for their metaverse and that will affect 3 billion people. However, we don't know if it is going to be autonomous. However, let me have the freedom to say that Web3 thinkers will use the options that already exist. Autonomy is built into the blockchain because of zero-proof knowledge. You do not need to know who sends the money or who receives it, you just need to know that it happened. When large corporations like the Danish shipping company Maersk, the second largest in the world, fully integrates a blockchain to follow all the goods in their system to reduce cost, it will inherently have some autonomy built into it. In addition, the organization will benefit from this. If they go full DAO, they will also benefit from all the other options that blockchain technology has to offer.

Collective intelligence

In the blockchain sphere, we are able to vote for the most intelligent solution. We know that people in groups can often predict trends better than the experts. Between 2006 and 2013, Intel ran 959 prediction experiments, and in nearly two-thirds of the cases, the crowd beat the experts. In a typical case, researchers found that the US presidential election predictions made by the Iowa Electronic Market beat professional pollsters 74% of the time. So, what will happen when it comes to voting for the next big thing? You buy into it. By doing this it will ensure that it is not just your opinion that counts. Over the past 50 years, the New York Stock Exchange, as a whole, has outperformed each of its constituent companies. This means that ordinary investors, in the millions, have made smarter investments than pro investors. Why? Well, the market is smarter than the hierarchies at allocation resources. No wonder start-ups often get to the future first. In the last decade, Silicon Valley has poured $350 billion in as venture money. This has built half of America's 122 unicorns (venture backed companies worth at least $1 billion). There is no CEO of Silicon Valley and no central authority. Turning these thoughts into DAOs will make the world prosper in a new way. The power of the crowd, both in taking risks and also in knowledge, is crucial. In Silicon Valley, it is not unusual for a would-be entrepreneur to get turned down a dozen times before finding a willing backer. In most bureaucratic organizations, a single nay is enough to kill a new idea. But markets are capable of extraordinary coordination. Imagine you live in Copenhagen and are setting up a dinner party. You go online and order spaghetti from Italy, potatoes from an exotic Danish Island, wine from France, chocolate from Kenya and strawberries from Spain. We know this is an option today. The infrastructure is here. Imagine how this will work in a DAO when people vote with their money for the best outcome. This coupled with autonomous smart contracts makes it all stick together like a picture on Midjourny. The money flows to the right people, the tax goes to the right authority, the contracts are signed, and you get to eat a wonderful dinner with your friends in no time. We can even build in sustainability and ask that the products are ordered from the farmer, so they get the money directly without middlemen (excluding the transport company).

If you now take this thought into consideration for a new company and use the crowdfunding model and the collective intelligence, it is then a logical expectation that we are about to enter another era, the time of the collective mind, collective money, and collective income. This, but without bureaucracy and without consensus-driven slowness. If people do not need it, they do not vote for it in fact, they probably do not even know it exists. This, hopefully, will also eliminate politicians who take money from existing goals and use them for their own sake, to entice voters to elect them. Political systems are the opposite of autonomy and digitization. Politics attracts humans that will spew any lies that will get them elected. Once elected, they misuse public funding and break the people's trust. In a DAO, crowds form around the idea that must be fixed. The right amount of money and resources will also gather the digital network and the blockchain will be the infrastructure that make this work, so you do not have to think about the risks, or how the money will come because the smart contracts are written in your favor. Take the energy crisis that has emerged after the war broke out in Ukraine. Now Germany feeds the Russians with billions of euros with around €150 billion. However, the Germany government did not outright confess to the way they were supporting Russian citizens. It had to take half a year. I would speculate that if it had been a DAO decision the energy would already have been flowing from thorium power plants that we know just need more funding to work. Seaborg has a commercial mini version that can fire up a whole city, set to launch in 2024. So why do we still see all the green windmill projects that only produce electricity half of the time and solar panels taking up fertile land? Because it has become a sign of green politics, and most of the population vote for something that feels good.

Furthermore, it is unlikely that they know there is not enough copper in the ground or how it is produced. They do not care about how cobalt mines use child labor, so they can drive around in electrical vehicles. There is no collective intelligence in using a scarce resource. There is no collective intelligence in reducing CO_2 with the least productive method. These decisions are only made by politicians who ae trying to look good. However, a DAO contract can be written so that the money flows to the right people. There are no politicians who can help a person in need with a job or launder money from a project for other means. Corruption is present in the political system, but even though it is there, people do not know about the quantity of money that is channeled to other people within the system. It is funny how consensus-driven people think that consensus is collective intelligence when consensus is not. It is more like a promise that is never executed in the agreed upon manner. This is why the public sector always has a deficit on their balance sheet, requiring them to seek further public assistance by asking for more votes, not the opposite way around. There should be a surplus so people can benefit from this, as they do from a stock in the private sector. But the deficit just grows and grows and grows; the bureaucracy will never end. In a perfect world, influence would correlate with expertise rather than positional power, and would be contingent on the topic at hand. The naivety pertaining to a program circulates around a few ministers' thoughts, which are propelled by the desire to get more voters, by manipulating them to believe the politician will do them good. Voters then fully believe in the potential good thing a politician has influenced them into believing they can achieve if voted into office. But it has nothing to do with collective decision-making, it is only about gaining power. After getting elected, they can cause terrible harm in the four years they are in power. The press thinks they are the fourth power of the state and can hold them accountable, but in actuality, the truth unfolds only when the people are in power as opposed to the collective. This is how things work in Switzerland, where 2,800 regional councils rule for all 8 million people, you do not hear much from the 7 ministers in the country. This is because they have voted in very different ways in different areas, so the lws fit the people in the region. If you happen to like the idea better in another council, you can move there and find out that you probably fit in better with them. One collective mindset does not have to fit the whole country; it can fit into smaller groups. This is also the best time to let smaller groups decide what fits their needs better. This is not like being tribal, because tribes have one ruler. Collective councils have taken all in on the voting. And, in tier two the money also follows the decisions.

Chapter 11: An Entrepreneurial Mindset

Why do you do this? Do you want to be rich, or do you want to change the world?

I'm often asked why I'm doing what I do. In a country like Denmark, where 96% of the population is hired as employees, it is hard to understand someone who does not want simply to be an employee. Look what we have – why do you not get the same? Why do you make things harder for yourself? One thing I am certain of is that technological progress is an incredibly difficult sector to succeed in, especially when you have the government on your back. They simply do not want extra competition. This creates an incredibly difficult predicament, in which there is no easy explanation to provide to outsiders. For example, blockchain technology is never the issue – even though it is not hard to understand, as Lars Seier Christensen states in his interview. The conundrum arises when you are faced with difficulties due to government intervention. We must ask ourselves: why do we do this when it is so difficult? All start-ups are hard. It is arduous, especially when the lay population mock you for inventions yet to come. If you are anything like me, however, you remove yourself from the negativity and happily drink beer while watching football. Ideology is strong in a consensus-driven collectivistic society like the Danish one. One thing is for sure, innovation can't be un-innovated; we do not regress. We will get DAOs, but why must it always be the people of Silicon Valley who create them? Why does Denmark not have the desire to invest in these fields? This question does not go to the 96% who are minted into the workforce. I know they can think on their own, but most decisions are not made by them. There is not even a way to hide, as recent events illuminate the hard truth: 60% of employed citizens are not happy with their work and would rather do something else. However, this controversy is not something we will discuss. Furthermore, when it comes to the public sector, we can't discuss that either. It is a monster of bureaucracy, but it is what it is. You can vote every fourth year, even though we all know this won't change a thing. I will reiterate, in a consensus-driven collectivistic society, there are a lot of dogmas, a lot of stigmatizing and a lot of fear – fear of being dispelled by rules. Even the Law of Jante is ever present. You mustn't inflate your ego; you mustn't challenge the laws. This, unfortunately, is done to the people, by the people. Group dynamics and group thinking are so strong that the thought of becoming self-employed is far from the realm of possibilities for many. This is why I do what I do. I don't want dogmas. I hate not to have freedom, and I don't want others to tell me what to do. Why should I? Most level five and six individuals in this country would rather forget themselves than assess what it is they are actually consuming.

The mind

I'm different. I try not to conform. I try to find the best way to improve with new technologies. I constantly ruminate on what I can do better and how feasible it is with the current materials.
Why do I have these thoughts? I actually do not know why I can't stop thinking about what we could do and how we can utilize new technology. If you have a free mind, it is hard to force it back into the box. But the pace of society

does not move at the same pace of the mind. Lars Tvede told us that he sees innovative people as being like someone living in a dream. Sometimes it seems like they are a bit crazy compared to what others see as the normal way of doing things. The mind of a person who can see combinations is creative, whether they are philosophers, or they are scientists. They work on the edge on what is possible today. Some even get locked up. Others waste away, unfulfilled and misunderstood.

Manipulation and change

As a child, you most likely manipulated your parents in hopes of receiving what you want. You tried to make them give you food earlier or more times than they initially planned. You spent money on different clothing so you could find your own style. So, thinking as a changing mind is not new to you; it is something you have already tried. But somehow it stops when you go into the large organizations with bureaucracies that are ruled by accountants, not by builders and administrators. Only a fraction of employees are members of what Phelps calls the "Imaginarium", and it is a problem when entrepreneurship is a part of the business. I have seen many people make fun of the innovation department and tell me that nothing will ever come from trial and error. Stay with what you know, they tend to say. It is such a common occurrence that most small businesses do not last longer than a year. In Denmark, it appears the entrepreneurial spirit is something which is only experienced on TV. At the same time, large corporations have grown. Decades and centuries of consolidation along with the winner-take-all dynamics of the digital age have left us with an economy that is dominated by politically connected oligopolies. This centralistic mindset seems to be what the confirmative people in level six like, as they do not want to change. It is easy living; it is not especially interesting to people like me to step into an organization where the hard knockers and the infighters reach the top. That kind of attitude is unnerving and shouldn't be rewarded, but it so often is. If someone interfered, it would impede their ability to reach the heights and make enough money to buy a nicer car, larger house, or anything else they may desire. But it is easy for them to let you down. They just say "We have tried that before" and don't want to know. Yes, even when a company was ignorant about Decentralized Autonomous Organizations, it has been tried if you ask these infighters. But if we want to change anything this mindset has to disappear. We must provide space for the more creative, albeit eccentric, entrepreneurs. It will happen anyway, so why not just go with it and assist in speeding up the process?

Ownership

A lot of people dream of starting their own business. However, it is so much more comfortable to stay within the organization that is paying you. Before they make the break even, it requires a lot of planning and more thought. Much of the time, those opening a new company will take clients they have an established rapport with. These types of entrepreneurs do not stand for innovation; most of the time they are accountants who copied a concept from someone else. It might push society in the right direction, but it is not rocket science and it is not something that changes society. Yet, the freedom they experience by being self-employed is often something that sticks with them for the rest of their life. This is the same thing that happens when you invent something. You will strive to accomplish more when it is your idea in jeopardy. It is your baby, as you say. In larger corporations there are sometimes new factions or businesses being built stimulated by a new idea. This is called intrapreneurship and it can influence new concepts. It is also smart for new businesses because the new unit can now serve the old business while benefiting businesses with a similar approach. Sometimes they become a self-governed entity without ties to the old company.

Faith

There is a lack of faith in others when it comes to innovation, especially when the companies are centralized hierarchies that have most of the political influence, along with a few other centralistic oligopolies that steer the economy. What happened to the small businesses around the corner? Did they all become 7-11 kiosks? Yes, most of them did. The corporations took over. Top management with huge piles of bureaucracy took over. When they first come into power it is difficult to predict how things will unfold or how it will all tie together. But it will. On the other hand, the entrepreneurial mindset needs to have faith, not only in the entrepreneur themselves but also faith from others. Conformity, centralism, and bureaucracy have ruled for a long time. But there are a few larger corporations that have had success by giving their employers more self-governance, so much so that they make a lot more money than the companies that don't. Why do we not give the 77 percent of millennials who dream of becoming self-employed this option in the new century? Why must we be in this one-size-fits-all society?

Government

The Chinese government organizes about three quarters of all business in China, but this only produces about 20% of the revenue. This shows us that privately held companies outperform publicly held ones. In addition, top-down management is inefficient compared to decentralized companies.

When we look at management in a country like Denmark where each and every year looks the same, we do not see new innovations. In fact, the companies attempting to bridge the gap between the private and public sector, the so-called growth houses that are built to help small companies, are unlikely to succeed. You know that the country is doomed to die, unless something drastic happens, and it wakes up to the world that has changed around it. Otherwise, it will die in the same way as it is doing now, if nothing happens, it just follows along. It is like a company that suddenly feels as though everyone has surpassed them. Even when it comes to crypto, the EU decides what has to happen in Denmark. PSD2 legislation is nearly finished and will be rolled out soon; the payment services directive will be rolled out over the next decade. However, when all countries accept the same top-down approach, we will end up with a whole continent where things progress slowly. Once more, this is not what innovation is about. This is another way people avoid changing their way of thinking. I think like this because the way the system currently functions is obviously incorrect. Furthermore, what interest does a government have in entrepreneurs other than as a source of tax money? If the entrepreneurs are never likely to vote for the socialists in office, and half of them are socialists, there will be constant pushback. This will create difficulties for the more effective, more agile, and better performing individuals in start-ups. Therefore, there is a mismatch between self-employment and the centralistic governments in the EU, the US, and similar countries around the world.

Private corporations

Some countries have attempted to cultivate a more autonomous and agile innovative structure, but it looks like they hit the same barriers as society. When it comes to the accountants and middle managers who all like the bureaucracy, they are hired into management. We end up with the same problem innovation faces all over the place. Intel has tried for years, and IBM have tried to increase innovation in their company due to low employee satisfaction levels. Sometimes it works, other times it does not. A surprising difference exists between the budget for a company like SpaceX, who send rockets out into space on a monthly basis, and NASA. SpaceX has an annual budget of around $1.95 billion compared to the $93 billion budget that NASA must make work in order to successfully create the Artemis 1 rocket, which has already had its launch date postponed multiple times. At SpaceX, they save millions on each rocket they send out because of the reuse. The thought of reusing is far from the minds of an employee at NASA.

When we look at innovation in the most innovative companies around the world, tech companies dominate the list. Forbes keeps track of such innovative companies Link. However, how do they measure innovation? Some reports look at the number of patents that have been filed, which is laid out in the country report Link. Fun fact, Denmark charts in 9th place, which sounds pretty impressive; the patents that have been filed from this country are numerous, but it does not necessarily depict an accurate picture. When we look at the number of engaged people in companies, there are further inconsistencies. Innovation does not correlate with more engaged people. Why should it? I believe that, if countries had more start-ups, there would be an increase in innovation and public engagement. Fortunately, the number of start-ups has surged in recent years. Current statistical analysis of innovation may not be calculated in an inclusive or representative manner. For example, it is stated that it is difficult to map out innovation and calculate engagement. It is also hard to map out which country is the most innovative when it depends on specific measurements and methods. There is another list provided by the World Economic Forum based on data on the most innovative cities in the world. Link It does look like there is a correlation between the countries and talent. One particular observation that struck me is that the religious countries in the Middle East and north Africa do not enter the list. I wonder if this has to do with the old Islamic tradition where innovation is viewed negatively. If we look at the Graves model, there is not a lot of innovation in the level four segment. Therefore, it might have something to do with their state of mind too. The U.S. is still the world leader with their model and the ecosystem that they have built in Silicon Valley. I have been there, and they have a lot of centers for innovative companies. People travel from around the globe to get there to showcase their ideas. Two thirds of all venture capital in the U.S. originates from this region. That movement is hard to copy, but we are beginning to see that the European region is inspired by them, with its pursuit of building more and more growth hubs and accelerators, like the many co-working spaces where people learn from each other, and employee interaction is high. Knowledge shared is knowledge owned. In this way, the entrepreneurial mindset hardens. It takes a lot of trials and tribulations to build businesses. In my mind, it boils down to building the right product. Also, the market must fit the price of your services; for instance, consider the first DOS operation system produced by Gary Kildall, which he priced too high. It is not beneficial to have your products stolen in way his was as a small start-up I have experienced it myself. Such a disaster can cause many sleepless nights and a lot of speculation. However, that is also a part of the start-up scene. It is not all about who is truly innovative. But let me remind you that some of the best ideas were not popularized by the first company to think of them. Some of these were second or third movers. They tweaked the concept and, *BAM!* Success. The mindset of an entrepreneur and an innovator can look like they are living in a dream, but they simply see things others don't. But why do they try so hard if it does not work? Some of these entrepreneurs get it right the first time, but most of them do not. The investors know that, if they invest in 100 companies, one or two will become the blockbuster of the start-up scene. It is not easy. The investors have to throw a lot of money into a lot of companies that only cause headaches and empty pockets. Nonetheless, compared to the public sector, it is the trial-and-error process that challenges some of these companies into succeeding.

Chapter 12: Lars Seier Christensen

Interview with Lars Seier Christensen

You can find the link to this interview in the notes.

Lars Seier Christensen is a Danish entrepreneur and investor who is the founder and chairman of Concordium, a Swiss non-profit foundation that develops a permissionless layer 1, science-backed blockchain platform1. He has over 30 years of experience in the banking and financial sector, and co-founded Saxo Bank in 1992, an online trading and investment platform1. He is also an advocate for Web3 and crypto communities, and has taken an expanded role in Concordium to raise awareness of its innovative and useful blockchain technology

Why is innovation important?

During our discussion regarding innovation, it became quite apparent that doubt is also something that occurs throughout the process. Therefore, while discussing his background, Lars also touches upon how he overcomes any adverse doubtful thoughts.

Lars Answer
With his experience as an account manager in London, Lars assisted clients in gaining access to foreign exchange markets as well as future options. Throughout his career, there was a common theme. A high percentage of clients referenced the 80s and early 90s when discussing how things were to be done. However, Lars noted that the efficiency with which things were done in London was not

very concentric. Unimpressed with the inner workings of the financial sector, Lars and one of his clients, Kim Fournais, decided to start their own firm in 1992. As a result, Lars spent the majority of his time in Berlin, until about 1995; he was not directly involved on location, but he did assist with accessibility to training, assets etc. on a daily basis. In 1995, he decided to join what was to become Saxo Bank, though at the time it was called Midas. After that, he was co-CEO of Saxo Bank until the end of 2015. Saxo Bank was originally created as a program, but it was also an early example of embryonic attempts to bring in training, particularly in e-stocks. As it was an early adopter, it was spotted. Street trading stocks on the internet seemed quite efficient. So, Lars began to wonder why it was not also possible to trade foreign and exchange on the Internet. He thought, why not also see if they could trade foreign exchange on the internet. In conducting his research, he discovered that it was indeed possible, and so his firm built a very simple platform. Though it was basic, it was one of the first in the world. The original platform was updated in 1997, although Lars was unimpressed with it and reworked the platform into a better version in 1998. At the time, there were only about 25 to 50 million global users of the Internet. Lars recognized that it was by no means extending to everybody that the program had the potential to reach, which also meant that it was not reaching people who also thought that this program could be the next big thing. Numerous talks with financial executives concluded with the decision that it was unwise and silly to attempt to trade online. While Lars was dubious of this advice, he recognized that foreign exchange was very much a sector dominated by and for big investors. His practical experience led him to becoming an expert with assisting clients that he had direct access to, meaning those he could help were those he could converse with in person. But through the internet, the firm was able to offer quotes to many people simultaneously. It began with a dozen, then a few 100, then a few thousand and then hundreds of thousands of people, and then smaller investors took an interest in the program once they realized they could market it in such a way that was beneficial to them. The view of this program swiftly changed, and it soon became recognized as one of the most efficient markets in the world. It also just so happened that it was one of the few markets that was comprised of a majority of people who were not experts in the sector. This is because companies hire people who follow the markets closely. But in foreign exchange, the playing field is more equal because there are less bankers involved. Even when they recognized trends, the bankers remained quiet and did not trade on that basis. Therefore, it is a great market with great liquidity. While the original platform had a number of assets, the program today is multi-asset, containing about 40,000 instruments that provide brilliant surprises every second. Because this turned out to be a success and wasn't going away like many people had believed, Lars then found a way to share the program with other financial institutions, through what is called a white label process. This became a crucial part of Saxo Bank and allowed them to acquire about 100 other institutions who used their software. Lars now had access to a larger group of people than would have been accessible with only the resources at Saxo Bank, and this played a major role in central banks. Lars slowly sold his shares and finally sold the remainder of them in 2018 in order to focus on other areas. He became a full-time investor after finishing his CEO work around the end of 2015, culminating in his full withdrawal in 2018. During this period, Lars had been following crypto currency and first became aware of Bitcoin around 2011. He followed the market for more than 10 years, initially just observing it for investment potential, but became quite excited about the general opportunity in the blockchain space. Lars also noted that some of the problems in the blockchain space didn't fully correlate to what he had been noticing as the CEO of a retail bank during the same period. Though, while being a quite enthusiastic ambassador for Bitcoin and subsequently Ethereum, he also saw problems with anonymity, lack of scalability, and relatively poor tech in many cases. This is what eventually led him to create his own project, Concordium, where the focus is on distributing permission-less blockchain but in cohesion with the reasonable requirements of society and what corporations are seeking. This is most evident in what Concordium does with the anonymity through their ID layer, which just so happens to align with the entry points of the blockchain. Lars and his team work on scalability and making sure that the fees are predictable and low, which is a problem in many blockchains. After this was achieved, the foundation for a very solid cryptography and more corporate checking processes was built. Lars thanks that this detail is what corporations would really need to get placed in this market. While Concordium doesn't have a lot of corporate adoption currently, this is still an essential feature that needs to be present, making them a great option. In the meantime, Lars invested in various other blockchain- and crypto-related businesses, both for observation purposes and for building up new benefits for blockchain from his perspective. This brings us to the present day. The majority of his current investments are in blockchain, though he can still be tempted by other things.

My comments
Innovation in Saxo Bank has been enabled by the internet. Most of the time there is some uplift for new markets with the options of a new technology. Internet was a new technology at the time, but it was also an infrastructure. The way it was built created a lot of options that could be seen by a few at that time. Lars and Kim saw that the time to get in and work on it was now. The old organisations with the deep brain power and huge amounts of clever people would not be the way they had to do things. It had to be smarter. The smarter part here is what we see in a blue ocean strategy, in which often you move away from the "normal" way of doing things. Think of Cirque du Soleil,

the circus where the animals have been taken out, and the focus is more on small acts in a play at a theatre. Here in Saxo Bank, it was the agile organisation, distributing software instead of heavy consulting. They got in on millions of PCs around the globe with a smarter piece of software than the companies could build themselves. They even built white label solutions. They had access to information at a speed not seen before. They could trade from "home", more or less. And latency was thus a thing of the past. Speed was the key to worldwide success for Lars and Kim. They took on the heavy lifting and made an agile organisation. Lars learned that scale is one of the success drivers for companies. And it can be done if you have the right version of a piece of software that people need. It takes some trial and error, and this is a phase that all startups must go through. There is also the pivot where you have to change the software to another version. The learnings from his years being a banker gave him insights on knowing your customers. And startups that succeed do exactly that; they look into what the customer needs. It's not about what they think the customer wants. But talk to them for a long time and maybe even over the phone to know what kind of problems they are bumping into along the way.

What is bleeding edge innovation?

[You] are an investor and have had a long career based around innovation. When we're talking bleeding edge, a lot of people have a hard time understanding crypto; it goes up and down it's very volatile. But there's also the technology behind it that I prefer to focus on. For example, I think we should focus on understanding why it's volatile. The 'bleeding edge' is something we know exists and sometimes pivots. During your career, have you developed a red line so as to know when to invest and when to back off?

As Lars begins his answer, he admits that, while Saxo Bank did at one time have a red line, the bank was a small player amongst very large investment banks, with even larger funds. "For us to do exactly the same as them wouldn't necessarily make that much sense because [we] potentially couldn't do it as well." Acknowledging the challenges Saxo Bank faced from its competitors, Lars explored options to do things in a better, smarter way, as it was their way to gain an edge against the multibillion-dollar corporation. This is when they turned towards the internet.

"It is for the products that you [can] deliver [and] create an environment where people are allowed to try out things and also fail sometimes." He continues to highlight the bank's propensity for trying new things and allocating the necessary funds to support it. However, if things didn't work as anticipated, they would not hesitate to back out and move on. While this could be disconcerting to some firms, Saxo Bank understood that with consistency and experimentation, a few good things would stick and be profitable. However, Lars admits the reality of risk taking. "[Things] may even be a good idea, [but] nobody else thinks [the same]. Nobody wants to use them, [so] you need to back off, you know, and focus on what actually works." In order to do this, the banks need to be amenable to mandating the responsibility to the smart people. They are there to assist in creating your overall vision for progress. Lars explains how imperative it is to formulate a value and to strictly operate from that, so as to allow it to dictate your interactions. However, Lars notes that, as a CEO, particularly in a relatively large firm, you can't micromanage everything, especially when a problem arises.

"One thing I liked in Saxo was, occasionally, someone would knock on the door and come in and show me something I didn't even know we were working on. As Lars reminisced about his time as CEO as Saxo Bank, it became apparent he held the firm in high regard. He appreciated this particular example because he noted that it set a positive example for the other employees. They were able to explore new and potentially great ideas, on their own if need be. The reason behind this was that Lars thought by giving people more freedom, you allow them to develop themselves, and subsequently their work. Nevertheless, Lars mentions that it is still advisable to curate a space for others to bring their honest feedback to and allow them to help bring your idea into fruition. For him, being the CEO meant that he viewed his position as inherently involving mentoring his colleagues by providing frequent feedback on whether or not he believed they were on the right track. By doing this, Lars cultivated an environment in which they had resources at their disposal and a group of people willing to help. On the flip side, he points out that it is equally as important to say when you don't think a proposal is a good idea, while also providing possible alternatives.

He speculates that it wasn't quite as obvious in the mid-90s, but that everything centred on technology, smart handling of it, its solidity, and critical mass usage. "Combining innovation with followed processes, I think is pretty key, and you don't necessarily have to be the very first in everything. Monitor what other people are doing and make your own assessments of whether you think you can add to that or do it better." Brilliant and new ideas no one has ever thought of are not necessarily the most important thing to focus on, he explains. It has more to do with projected trends and how people will respond to solving certain issues. Some important questions to ask yourself when evaluating these situations are: Do I agree with the way that was solved? Are there aspects you could add to that solution that would make it better? These are things that Lars thinks the blockchain does well. He considers the blockchain to be a database of sorts. It's really about securing data completely, knowing who owns what data, who controls it and registering data to various people and organisations accordingly. "I think that could add a lot of value to existing processes."

While other people would know more about particular business domains, Lars believes the blockchain adds something to the businesses' processes to make them more secure, more scalable, and safer for people to use. "I think the infrastructure is good." After having described the process at Saxo Bank, Lars points out that this way of delivering information to 100 other organizations is much easier than building 100 other organisations. He further elaborates that he believes that this is exactly what they're doing with Concordium. They're trying to create a platform that can help other people build great products that they have a deeper knowledge about than the people at Concordium but still may have the need for. A platform which completely secures the data that they need to identify their users and for scalability.

My Comments – Organisations like Saxo Bank where the employees can come in on the CEO´s office and talk with him directly on ideas are key to innovation in large-scale companies. This requires an extremely flat organisation without the same level of hierarchy. The flat structures as we have in Scandinavia and Denmark in particular give us a step ahead compared to other nations. It is a small country where we have seen over the history that talking directly with each other gives us an advantage. It solves many small things that will become large over time. At Saxo Bank, Lars was surprised over things that people were autonomously working on that fit the needs in the organisation. This shows it was a true self-driving organisation; that can and probably will be the way things work when decentralized autonomous organisations are built in the future. Talking to Lars gives me an insight into his perception that things are not a lot different from what they used to be. But he sees the small changes, and this is where he finds a niche. As he explains it, a blockchain is only a database. In fact, it is even a slower database than an SQL. But here we can have safety, we can have an ID layer, and that is what will make if successful, as he builds infrastructure for the future. And in my opinion KYC, AML and ID are key to success. If you identify people, and this has been done with passport, drivers' licence, a bill from your home to verify your address and your phone number for two-way authentication and on top of that the credit card number, you know that this person is who they are. This gives you a lot of options for autonomy; they can't cheat, and if they do, you know where to go. That infrastructure is not built into any other blockchain out there, just Concordium. I guess this comes down to the fact that Lars has been in banking for many years; he knows that this is one of the problems that has to be solved and now we can do that.

What has been your biggest doubt in your life?

After listening and coming to understand his approach in both Saxo Bank and Concordium, I found myself in total agreement with Lars. The ID layer that they're building is unlike any other because it prevents any fraudulent activity, scams and relies on there being KYC. This led me to my next set of questions: Was there ever a time in which you doubted these ideas? If so, how did you deal with these doubts, especially considering the great deal of knowledge you have pertaining to this sector?

 "I don't really have a lot of doubt about my overall vision for blockchain, which is five, or six years old," Lars answers honestly. He was 100% sure that at some point there would be regulation in this sector. This is because, naturally, there will always be processes in place to regulate how people's money is handled while adhering to the company's values. However, Lars notes that this was a particular issue during the early years because people had less experience with working with this new format. So, while sympathetic, Lars criticises the fact that, due to this mentality, some companies create something that they believe is nice and something nobody should interfere with, even though it is not necessarily how the world operates. Nevertheless, Lars notes that He was privileged enough to have the benefit of initially exploring this new sector as a hobby in his free time. While being CEO and dealing with regulations on a daily basis, he was able to observe the somewhat chaotic view of the people working within the crypto sector. Lars noted that these guys sought to have all of the freedom in the world with no responsibility and no accountability while remaining anonymous. But because other people's money is involved, Lars understands that this is an impractical perspective. "When you want other people's money to be involved you will have some rules. And that's really the underlying vision for Concordium."

While Lars firmly believes that distributed blockchains and permissionless blockchains have a lot of ways in which they can improve, he equally believes that regulators, lawmakers, and society at large will have expectations on how to do so. However, he admits that this aspect of blockchain is still something he does not fully understand, but it is still something that is being proven every day. He also believes that most people are coming around to understanding that this is how the future will be even if they don't like it or wish it to be another way. He notes that we saw the same attitude many years ago with traditional financial markets. "You can either accept that and adopt it, or you can try to circumvent it and see if [you] can get away [with] not adopting it." Although this approach is possible, it is most likely a very bad solution. In Lars' opinion, if you want a happy life, this reality will catch up with you sooner or later. Most certainly, you aren't likely to get a mainstream adoption of this platform if you don't adhere to it. Furthermore, you may also find yourself in serious trouble if you deliberately avoid the legislation and regulations. Very simply, Lars states, "you need to accept it."

The public must see it for the good that it brings, which is a framework that allows people to use the space with confidence. While discussing this, Lars reminisces about how a lot of people didn't want to use the internet in the early days because [it was] seen as unsecure, and [corporations] knew it [would be] very hard to get people to use a credit card on internet in the early days." Obviously today those concerns are no longer relevant because regulations were put in place to ensure people couldn't just steal your card information. Nevertheless, these things do happen, although at least the law is on your side which results in more people being willing to embrace this innovation. Because of this, and what blockchain has to offer, Lars "firmly believes that blockchain will only gain mainstream adoption." At some point, there will be a relatively clear legal status established along with relatively clear regulation. Unfortunately, this has been slow to happen in many countries today, which is why big corporations and even smaller companies cannot really adopt this platform. It is simply too unclear what they're getting into. Currently, the benefit of good regulation is poor. It also dramatically increases the number of people who are happy to participate in it. Nevertheless, Lars touches upon the abundance of good for this regulation. Also, Lars encourages readers to analyse themselves, to think if you are a reasonable person. If so, he says, "you can understand why, for example, you want to protect the weak access in the market, amateurs, retail investors [to whom] you should give a degree of protection." He says we should see that, behind anti–laundering legislations is the fact that something needs to be done to prove there is no criminal activity involve. Lastly, Lars insists the capital should there be to support the activities that you do, as well as main pillars of regulation, protection of particular retail segments, and prevention of criminality. Understandably, Christensen claims that "if you end up owing people money, you should be able to pay it."

My comments - doubt is not in Lars vocabulary when it comes to crypto and what they do at Concordium. He is building it based on the years of knowledge he has as a banker and as an entrepreneur. He knows that, in a world of money, there has to be rules. Otherwise, you can't hold other people's money. And when there are rules, there is regulation. In a world where every driver could go on whatever side of the road they want, the insurance companies would probably have a hard time making money. We need to know who was on the wrong side of the road. We need to know who ordered, and who bought the goods. We need to know who lent the money and who spent it. We also need to know who wants to lend you money, when it comes to the many fraudulent people in the crypto space, so we have to have rules and regulation. But when it comes down to a framework where governments set the rules, we are not quite there yet. This is what Concordium can solve in the future of finance using blockchain. Regulation is not bad; it is only bad when it becomes too fussy and bureaucratic: when stacks of paper and red tape are made by stupid rules and regulations by bureaucrats who are hired to make rules and regulations for their own sake, in order to have a job. This is what happens when the welfare state grows too large as it is in Denmark today. The regulation will also protect people who are amateurs, the normal people who should not have to deal with criminals every time they buy something. But also, when it comes to a mistake made by a person, such as an incorrectly fulfilled order, you have to know who is. Another good thing about regulation, as Lars points out, is that the corporations and the public sector know how to act in this space. What is legal and what is not: before this is fixed, we will not see the larger corporations or public sectors in this space.

Is there a formula for success in building companies?

Taking the history of it in advance here, the PayPal Mafia was trying everything out in the early days with the money on the internet, just like you were as well. But is there any kind of formula for success when you are building on the bleeding edge?

Lars answers.
"Hard work, I think. Persistence, if you have a good idea." Although it is normally the opposite of what people want to want to hear. When developing new programs, Lars emphasizes that it is important to be incredibly intellectually honest with yourself. Nevertheless, there will be much spilled tea in the future. Perhaps people will understand your vision years down the road, but because you don't know this, remaining consistent is essential. In further explaining this, Christensen uses a great example. When people work out, they understand the results of the dedication won't be immediate. However, unlike exercising, blockchains can actually provide a space for quicker returns, which creates a mentality that everything can lead to instant gratification.
"But not everything can be done in an afternoon by five guys in a garage, right? If you want something solid, it's a lot more complicated than that, which is why we have 30 to 40 scientists attached to this project. We have professional tech-building operations; we have people that understand what big businesses are out there, and precisely what boxes they need to tick." While providing a breakdown of manpower to explain the in-depth, technical reality of creating a successfully innovation, Christensen concludes that good products don't succeed overnight, something he believes is crucial for the reader to understand.

My comments - persistence is key, knowledge and insights in a business are key for having success. Building on solid ground, known technologies and on top of this making the new innovation is also one of the key pillars for success. The Crypto Space has given some millionaires and billionaires overnight success stories, more or less. And that gives people an overenthusiastic view of this space. Because speculation and getting lucky on a few tokens is not the same as building a company on a blockchain. Building a company is still the same hard work. Getting lucky with a crypto purchase is not, hard.

What is the success story for Y Combinator?

When pertaining to Y Combinator, I quickly learned that they do not follow the next red ocean idea that may simply be a copy of another company. And this may also lead them to entering a dangerous zone, as they actually go out and find what is cutting edge as well as finding investors.

"There's a lot on Y Combinator because I have a little bit of insight in that. These numbers are directly from one company's data: from one of the senior guys. 88 out of 100of their companies go bankrupt. Only about 10-12 of them became okay businesses, and then they have a homerun of one or two per 100." Through Christensen's example of how many companies go bankrupt and how many companies succeed, it becomes quite apparent that the odds are not in your favour. When we apply this to crypto, there are roughly 20,000 crypto projects currently on the market. Furthermore, there may be about 10,000 listed tokens on the centralized exchanges, and he speculates that the majority of these are going nowhere.

How did you get the idea on the ID layer and the KYC for blockchains?

Moving on to the ECB, The Fed, the ID layer and the KYC, why are these important, particularly with the technology behind the KYC and the added ID layer? How can the added ID layer protect against fraud and scams? Furthermore, where are we currently with the new legislation with the bigger banks?

"I think they're still trying to find their way. There's no question that they want identification of people that interact in the space, and it is clear in most of the messaging out there that they don't want their name to be seen. I think that's a given right. In terms of broader regulation, they're also finding their way. Regulation by definition has to be [relative to] the real world because you need to identify what's out there; you need to understand it, and then most of the time, you need to regulate it. They will always be a little bit behind, but one thing you can be sure about is that people in this space probably think, 'Oh, now we got this this law, it's right'. But it's not. Regulators will continue to bring out new rules, as they understand the space better and as they identify new problems. This is an everlasting process; it has been happening for the last 40 to 60 years in trading with finance." Christensen further says that we shouldn't expect this simply because we begin to comply with the new set of rules. There will continuously be a new set of rules put in place because that is simply how regulation works. They are by no means finished with this process. They are most likely simply in the beginning stages. He also believes that people will think that because we're different, we will get a different set of rules and be regulated accordingly. He doesn't agree with this mindset. In fact, he believes that because we spent "30 to 40 years, building the boxes that kind of work for traditional finance, it took a long time to get there. And they're going to try to put this into roughly the same boxes, because they're not going to invent two separate layers of regulation. I think it's very [likely] that regulation will come. It is very likely that it will look a lot like what we know from other markets. I think that should be your assumption, that you're going to have to comply with the parameters of traditional finance. I think that's pretty clear that the aspect that people also focus a lot on is, how do you raise money for your products? Are they security for the utility? [Are] they investable assets? Are you a pure utility." Christensen explains that people can argue that not many of the current regulations are strictly necessary, but the fact is that most of the projects on the market portray themselves as a good investment, which sways people's opinions of them. This is because people are less likely to see these investments as a utility. He then asks, "If you raise money for a project, if you go out with a broad offering, is that the same as an IPO? Does that mean you should have a full prospectus and have a registration with a regulator before you do it? That certainly seems be the SEC view, that most of these risks were things that should be registered, and that should follow a similar process to an IPO or something like that." However, Christensen points out the fact that many of these projects in fact didn't operate like this. While there may not be any laws or regulations currently in place, regulators are still susceptible to having a backwards mentality.

"I don't think you're in the clear because you think you did it many years ago. In Concordium, we sell to a limited number of people that understand risk and understand the project and retail offering. This approach is contrary to other business models in which they sell to hundreds of thousands of people, not requiring proper perspectives or proper processes for doing so: where you just sell to hundreds of thousands of people you do need to have proper perspectives and a proper process for doing that... I think the main focus at the moment is on getting rid of anonymity. Establishing what types of assets these tokens are and what types of assets are NFT's, what types of assets or holdings and what degree of regulation do they require? Is this computed? And then, of course, there's a focus on not making it easy for... potentially criminal activities." Christensen concludes that while this may be the current focus, it is definitely not the end of the line. It is more accurate to say this is simply the beginning.

My comments – regulation will come; this is a fact that Lars points out here. The two sides of regulations are that we hope to live freely without it, but we can't live with criminals around us. We know that if there are no rules of law, society would be like the Wild West, where everybody had to have a gun in his belt. But too much regulation makes the society rigid and unresponsive. In this vein, I had an experience with the municipality of Copenhagen over a parking ticket. It took 10 weeks before I could get an answer. It shows it can be a crazy system we have. In the crypto space as it is right now, the lack of regulation is the reason why governments and corporations simply do not touch this space. If we had some kind of acceptance of it, we could move forward. But we know that the new technology is so much faster and smarter than the old, and that is why smart money like crypto will be a thing of the future.

Why is crypto important?

While we take a break from conversing like crypto nerds, I would like to ask what you think the big shift for people and civilization will be compared to the traditional economy.

"I think we should distinguish a little bit between crypto and blockchain. Crypto means all the tokens that people like to trade; I'm not terribly interested in that [because] if a crypto coin doesn't have some kind of function, I don't think they're sustainable. I don't think they're very interesting, you know, meme coins and that kind of thing." The value they will have in a few years' time is highly speculative. He says that "blockchain and cryptos [are] just something because the normal payment system doesn't work properly. If you could make micro payments instantly in US dollars, everybody [would] use the US dollar, right? But we can't because of the way the system is put together, as the transfers are too slow. Too many fees. Too many complications. So that's why crypto exists; to be like a maybe a temporary solution for that."

Though critical of crypto, Christensen believes both types of currency will exist one day. He doesn't think we should rule out the idea that there could be CBDC's, no central bank and digital currencies that could fulfil most of those roles, but they're just not here yet. Nevertheless, he believes what is truly important is how blockchain can benefit you. But how people could be incentivised to keep the blockchain is a different question. Nevertheless, he says it can be done in many ways.

"For example, Concordium has a China only version, where tokens are not allowed, and hence, people are paying licencing to use it. So, it can be done in multiple ways. But blockchain itself, when you cut away all the buzzwords and all the hype, is a database; that's what it is, end of story. [However], because of the nature of the distribution of knowledge and that database, it is safer because you don't have the single points of failure that most databases have today...

If you will, the bank sits on the data. In theory, if a bank goes under, or it's fraudulent, it can change the data. In any context, you typically have very few factors that actually have control over the data. And that lends itself to possible manipulation or suspicions of manipulation. You have to have a lot of trust in somebody that sits on a database that is of importance for you. Remove that and you have 1,000 nodes running in a database, which makes it very difficult for any single participant to manipulate it. That's what this is about. The blockchain is just a database where your data is 100% immutable [and] once it's been placed there, it is easy to register who owns it. You can move that data around in various ways between the participants on the network. That's what a blockchain is." In Christensen's opinion, blockchain is not very complicated. However, people like to view it as a convoluted approach to data security and ease of use as well as, perhaps, a lot of consultants and middlemen. Though, for Lars, these players have an interest in making things very complicated or seemingly very complicated. "Trust me, the function of the internet is far more complicated to understand than a blockchain. Any process where you have data, which is most processes in the world today, that you want to make more secure, where you want to be more certain about who owns what could benefit from a blockchain." Nevertheless, he cautions that areas where the monetary value is so small that the subsequent security means very little, blockchains are unnecessary. However, if you are working with something that you feel is of high importance, a blockchain is pretty much the only player in town.

"I see what we're building as a piece of infrastructure to help other people make their business models and processes safer and more efficient than they are right now. That's all there is to it."

My comments - security is one of the key pillars of crypto. But also, the autonomy and the speed will give us a different life. Blockchain is like the internet, it is also an infrastructure, and it is a framework where new business will be built in a different way to today. Some will have self-executing contracts, others will have self-destructing contracts, and others will be fully autonomous. A car that drives on its own, that has to pass a station to get juiced up for some time, has to have a payment system that uses a contract for this if you want to get a discount and maybe even be a part of a point system to save more money on other purchases. Just like humans do today, it can be built into the tokens that are transferred. And you know the owner and the sender because it is zero proof knowledge. The two tokens know their owner, they know their purpose, and they also know the time and place of any transactions, so there is a lot more information in autonomy than there is in a normal money transaction. The contract that is minted in on the digital document that follows the token, which also holds information on royalties and how to distribute these. Zero proof knowledge lets them know that it is legit, without revealing who they are. This is the smart thing about the public and private key that is baked into the blockchain.

Decentralization versus centralization - what kind of society are we building right now?

Our central banks today prioritize monetisation above all else. And that's one of the things that's going to change the speed of money transfer and the security behind it. And yeah, that's how I see it for the blockchain as well. But then the next question is about the question of decentralisation versus centralization. Because today, we have the central banks, we have a monitorisation above everything else. And if we continue in these terms, saying that we are all having a blockchain and that using them will create a new world, then what will decentralisation mean for society?

In Switzerland, Lars says that less centralized things work better. As I mentioned, less centralised things are, the better you know, I'm sitting here in Switzerland, one of the reasons that Switzerland works well is that you have 2,800 local authorities. In Denmark, for example, we have 98, but the countries are roughly the same size. "So, there's much more direct responsibility in my little village for the mayor here. Everybody can go up and say we don't agree with what you do. Everybody can even ask for a vote. If they can get 100 neighbours to sign up, they can ask for a vote on anything, which means that you have a much closer democracy than at a national level or in very large communities. That's one form of decentralisation. But of course, it's not full decentralisation because there's still somebody in those smaller units that has central control. But it's a step in the right direction." As Christensen provides his answer, he begins to discuss his discrepancies with the EU, stating that he never liked the EU much because, in his opinion, it goes the opposite way. For instance, it's travelling down a path of popularizing very large organizations that have absolutely no possibility of fully understanding everything that it deals with. He quickly pauses the conversation to revisit the initial point. "I think we should focus on the fact that the blockchain is decentralised, and hence ensure its properly built. But if you build it properly, your data is secure and the registration of ownership of that data is secure. I think that most use cases on top have to have some kind of centralised accountability." He says this is done because most cases are owned by a group of shareholders or a group of token holders. In this regard, he says we're much more decentralized with more secure data. However, returning to DAOs, he doesn't think that in the short term they would have much of an impact because they are typically used as a way to avoid promoting accountability. As this is the case, he wonders who a regulator would go to implement change when there is something they don't approve of. He says that this is one way of protesting pushback and regulation rather than accepting it.

"In the long run, I have hope because it does seem that it goes that way. The more affluent people get, the more they want control of their own lives. I'm actually a positivist; I'm a technology optimist. I think 100 years from now, the average person will be much, much wealthier and have many more opportunities and options than they have today." Lars says that he believes once the government reaches the point where they want the people to decide just as much as the people want to, they will have the ability to decide for themselves and it would create an overflow of distributed wealth between many people.

"...We're already far richer than five generations back in history. Our great grandfathers and mothers were working in the fields." This, he says, is an obvious example of how they had very little say outside of their immediate domain, whereas, on the other hand, affluent people with more power in society began to push back against those who wanted to govern their own lives. He says that if we could all imagine a world in which we were all millionaires, in practical terms, we would all be able to have access to similar resources. There wouldn't be any days where we would worry about food, shelter or providing for our loved ones. If we achieved a society like this, Christensen believes we would reduce our dependency on centralized political systems.

"If you have everything that you want, then you [only] have to worry about corporations that might be abusing the [current] technological situation at that point. But I'm quite optimistic that, in the long run, wealth will continue to accrue and be reasonably fairly distributed. In a society where, as I said, we [are] all millionaires, people will want to run their lives because they won't have to worry about the government giving them a check or because the gas price goes up or things like that. So that's where I see more freedom and genuine help from the people around you."

My comments - Wealth will be distributed to all people because energy will be free for all. This will happen when thorium and fusion are used to generate energy. There will simply not be troubles which justify anyone having power. This means that we will all be millionaires as Lars points out. We know that we are really close to this scenario; the first commercial thorium reactors will be on the market from 2024. We also know that crypto is here to distribute wealth in a more direct, controlled and autonomous way than we know today. A lot of people seem to have cognitive dissonance when I start to talk like this, but if you have read this book up to this point, you know that a lot of people are working on this, and it is not just talk. It is how it is going to be; this is where the money is. And to understand something, always follow the money. The less centralized things are, the better things are, as Lars states, that he lives in Switzerland where they have 2800 regions, for 8 million people. That means that you can get downtown and make a difference to the mayor if you have only 100 other people who thing that this should be debated. When it comes to crypto and blockchain, the tokens can achieve this for you. It can have a specific purpose, or the autonomy tell the token that it can only be used for a specific reason. Or that it will send the royalties to a specific organisation. The options are endless.

What is your take on Decentralized Autonomous Organizations?

Throughout this interview, you discussed decentralised, autonomous organizations (DAOs). First of all, what is a DAO? And what is the culture that we need to have for them? Are we there yet or is it premature to speculate about the real DAOs? They would allow for people to have more of us be a part of the creative process and the innovation of creating a DAO. So, my final question is, what is your take on DAOs?

"I think a DAO is a decentralised, autonomous organisation. You have some stakeholders [that] make decisions and, in a funny way, that's not so different from a listed company. I mean, you have shareholders, they make decisions and build businesses. You have concentrations of people that have more shares than others, just like you have in a DAO. Most likely [some] people [will] have more tokens than others, unless you ascribe one vote to one owner, or something like that. I don't think it's that different." During Christensen's explanation of what he believes a DAO is, he takes an intermittent break to point out that we like to view this space as hugely different to everything else. However, he thinks the only real difference is that we're dealing with secure data. He expounds on this by saying a DAO is like a membership of an organization that we already have to some extent, a listed company with a broad spread of their shares. As Lars deepens the conversation about DAOs, he highlights the potential problem that there is a lack of security for holding someone accountable, which he doesn't think will sit well with regulators. This is because, if you don't have protections in place that inhibit people from doing or saying what they like, there is nothing stopping them from abusing their power. This is something that he particularly believes will be an issue with society and lawmakers because they prefer someone who will always assume responsibility for potential fallouts. He questions how that will play out if it becomes a reality. He then begins to discuss blockchains and how you can build one, even if the authorities don't like it, because they don't have much power over it as a self-sustaining system.

"Even if you prohibited Bitcoin all over the world, it wouldn't go away. But what would happen is that most people wouldn't be able to use it if it was illegal." After he discusses the blockchain, Lars references the way this similar issue occurred with gold during times of war. People in possession of gold were coerced into giving their gold to whoever asked as long as they said it would go to funding the war. However, there were no checks and balances to ensure that the gold actually did go to funding the war, and so some people would actually just pocket the collected gold. Christensen thinks this will be the issue for DAOs.

"If they get very unpopular with regulators, maybe people won't use them. I mean, big corporates certainly won't if it's not allowed, but maybe they're maybe not designed for that. If it's not, a lot of people do not interfere in your local organisation because you [have votes] about things and you [make] decisions. But of course, most of these things are not great big businesses either. I think it's an interesting way of running things. I do think you'll still see power concentrations, so some people have more to say than others. If something goes terribly wrong, who's going to fix it? That is a problem. If a regulator says, 'we don't want that', law-abiding people won't be able to use them. I don't see it as something huge, to be honest. It's just another spin-off of the technology, right?

My comments - DAOs will be a thing of tomorrow, but till now we have not seen the scenarios that it will bring. It is too complicated to understand when we do not even have blockchain rolled out in the public and private sector. The role of cognitive dissonance is clear here. But if you can imagine a scenario where we have blockchain incorporated into society, you can also see how DAOs will be minted into small and large contracts. Even the regulation from government has the same legal set-up as many private companies, including the rules on how a car works, or how a flight might take place with self-flying cars. This even applies to A.I. systems whereby you ask for contracts to be built for specific tasks and afterwards get sent with money in it. As I mentioned, if you have tried www.midjourney.com, where you can write a sentence like – 'Hobbits with swords, in a huge forest with a river and green leaves', you will get this. And it only takes 1 minute to generate.

Think about how fast it will be for an A.I. to build a contract that you can sign just like the ones lawyers have to use these days. I know the picture is not perfect, but it is A.I. at its best today. It is close to a real image, and it was generated in a few minutes. Think about what it will be able to do for contracts and even complicated rules and regulations?

How can we build autonomy in the organizations?

Because I work with a lot of freelancers who are trying to occur crypto up front, and because we're currently talking about autonomy, my next question is: How would autonomy in an organization that is fully autonomous by blockchain work? Furthermore, can it be done?

Christensen speculates that if autonomy is based on decisions distributed through tokens, it could be possible. But then, the question becomes whether or not it will still pay. He says that the person that has the most tokens, or the sub-segment of people who do, can still be potentially abused by something that a regulator, like a lawmaker, won't be so keen on. If this were to happen, Christensen questions what the outcome would be. In a normal corporate setting, a company will be comprised of the board, a CEO and a management team. If the company does something we as employees don't like, we go to the board and the CEO and file a complaint, which will then lead to an investigation. Depending on what the complaint is, it could lead to the shutdown of the company. Christensen explains that in dealing with a DAO this process becomes much more complicated. So once again, the question becomes whether or not anybody will use this platform if a real problem were to arise. Even if someone were to use it without any pre-existing problems, they still risk having extreme difficulty resolving a problem that may arise. Because Christensen doesn't see this as any different from the way that we do many other things, he likes to reference the real difference here and that goes back to the security of data. The security of data, whether with the

DAO or in a normal company, is imperative. Christensen would prefer to do this in a public sector; however, it is not for him to decide. It is simply for him to build something that works and that is both stable and credible, with an ID layer so that people can, under certain adverse conditions, be held accountable if they do something wrong. "I actually would like to make it clearly distinguishable between this and KYC... What we deliver at Concordium is a guarantee that there is a real person behind the account. That is a person who can identify himself to you. That's his choice. But if he does identify himself to you, you [still] know that what he tells you is true. So, that's the key thing here." Lars then discusses the building of a gaming company and how Concordium would make that process easier. For instance, he says that if this game were to include four people 18 years or older, it would be a KYC an inherent part of your business. Concordium makes this easier for you to do because they are completely confident in who they do business with. Therefore, The KYC is an overbuild. Because there will be millions of different types of KYCs, you will need proper assistance to ensure that you are dealing with reliable and trustworthy people. This is essential because if you use a sophisticated KYC on someone who turns out to not be who they claim they are, the KYC has limited value. Saxo Bank is one type of KYC, and it is therefore common for them to request certain information about you, such as the area you're from or where you live, whether or not you know how to play the game and if you know what to do. Regardless of your business dealings and what sector they are in, this is the cornerstone of all KYC and AML (anti-money laundering policy).

Concordium is designed to help you eliminate risk and make the process easier by assisting in creating categories for KYC that will enable you to ask specific questions pertaining to anything you want to know. This will be seamlessly combined with the identity of who you're working with at Concordium and who you wish to do business with, so you know exactly who the people you are dealing with actually are. This can result in a digital certificate that proves that the particular ID has gone through that particular KYC process. From there, you can use the data to show certification–based access control. This would allow you to monitor who has access to your game, for example, or who has access to a smart contract. "And that's the way I see our role. But we [still] can't predict what KYC you need for your specific game. For us, it's more about creating the building blocks that you can use to make that process as easy and as credible and safe as possible."

My comments - sophisticated autonomy comes down to the proof of who or what is sending the money. Identification has to be done to know your customers. And KYCs have to be made to make an Anti-Money Laundering policy. There are certainly different levels for this depending on whether it is a company, a paddle club or a government in a specific task that has to be done. Where is the money coming from, who is sending, and to whom and for what. When it comes to crypto as it is today, it is premature, and it would not be possible to do a solemn, firm KYC and AML on these transactions. But we now know that Concordium is working on this, and it will be doable in the near future.

What is your best advice to others when it comes to innovation and blockchains?

Finally arriving at my next question, after profusely thanking Christensen for answering these technical questions: What is some advice for people who are working with innovation and blockchain? And what would be your best advice for people looking to enter this field right now?

"First of all, you should decide whether you really need it. You know, I think in the industry, we tend to jump on every new flavour of the month and say, 'Oh, that's a blockchain thing, right?'" Lars says it is not essential for some companies to have a blockchain, simply because it is slow and has some other costs compared to an SQL database. Therefore, Christensen encourages people to use an SQL database when what they are seeking can be appropriately addressed with one. Nevertheless, he does encourage the use of a blockchain if the data has sensitive information, where the ownership and registration of that data is very important and therefore needs better protection.

"For example, right now one of the big buzzwords is 'Metaverse' when it comes to gaming. We're trying to make our own Metaverse that has something to do with a blockchain. Metaverse has nothing to do with a blockchain." However, he says you can easily build a Metaverse without a blockchain and there are many examples of this. One example of such a Metaverse is Second Life. In fact, you could say that most games are Metaverse. While they don't necessarily use blockchain, if someone was considering using a blockchain inside the metaverse in order to provide a degree of security for assets within the gaming economy, you would have to know who the users are or at least have the potential to know who the users are. If this were the case, then the blockchain becomes irrelevant as a piece of infrastructure.

"So, the first advice is, do you really need it? And what do you need it for? The second advice is that, if you feel you do need it, well then choose your technology very wisely. Because a blockchain is not just a blockchain; most of what's built out there is not very good. It's low [and] sharp with regular intervals." Christensen uses Terra as a good example of how using blockchain unnecessarily can go wrong. After billions of dollars were invested into the project, the information and developments pertaining to Tara went bankrupt and disappeared simply because the blockchain was deleted. Though the project remained intact, the information still disappeared. Christensen used

this example specifically because he believed it was a good one to highlight the necessity of sharing technology wisely. He further elaborates that because most people run full speed into making their idea a reality, they focus on how and where they can receive the biggest grants. Once they receive their necessary grants, they simply begin to build, receive a bigger grant, build some more and then seek to find a bigger grant once again, and the process continues. However, Christensen highlights an important detail; just because those sending the biggest grants have the financial capabilities, it doesn't necessarily equate to them having the best technology at their disposal for the project. "So, if you're building a serious project, I think you want to check very carefully what technology you use. And it's not necessarily the one that gives you the biggest grant; that's just the best solutions."
Christensen then confidently guarantees that big corporations wanting to enter the space will, of course do their due diligence regarding compliance, regulations, etc. Furthermore, they will also do their due diligence on the technology and cryptography required. He also points out that we should not forget the origins of crypto in cryptography, which is a very complicated, and to a certain extent, unprovable mathematics. Christensen explains, "because you can prove that a piece of cryptography doesn't work, you can break it. You can have something that worked for a long time, but you could break it tomorrow, potentially. So, you can never be 100% sure that any cryptographic thing will necessarily work, which is why people work with what we call cryptographic primitives (simple functions that have worked for maybe 10, 20, 30 years)." By using cryptographic primitives, Christensen says that they provide an increased probability of the cryptographic equation continuing to work tomorrow, but it still is not a guarantee. Further analysing blockchains, he says that they aren't really based on technology that exponentially precedes Bitcoin and its attempts at being used in the early 90s. Whenever a

Bitcoin was initially set to launch, it never succeeded until about 2008 or 2009. It only succeeded this time around because somebody configured it and marketed it in a way that appealed to enough people that it gained traction. This is why Christensen stresses that you must "choose your technology very carefully." Though he admits this is very difficult to do because you can't analyse every piece of code, his best advice is to pay close attention to the scientists involved in the technology. When doing so, he then says it's important to ask yourself questions such as: Are there serious cryptographic scientists involved? Are there serious people in general involved in the project? If there are, it increases the probability that the scientists and people associated with the technology will want to protect their reputations and build something solid that doesn't break the first time it is put under pressure. Once again, Christensen provides a few questions you should ask yourself once you have reached this stage. Do you need a blockchain? Does it actually suit your technology? Do the benefits justify the costs of using that blockchain? This final question is important because if the blockchain has a completely unpredictable cost structure, it might work for you for a while but then suddenly increase to such an extent that they are no longer feasible or justifiable. Christensen provide an example of this with Ethereum. "What do you then do [after] you build a lot of layer-two fixes that make it possible to still do most of your transactions and occasionally put them on the blockchain." Christensen argues that there is no sense in this approach because it just adds to your complexity and your risk. This is due to the fact that you now have to trust the theorem and the two-layer protection system as well as whatever else you're putting in the system. To Christensen, this begins to resemble the old world too closely because it creates a potential dependency on people that may not know what they're doing, and this may not be as secure as a real blockchain.

"And that is the real ambition of Concordium: to build a blockchain that is so scalable, and so solid, and so low in fee structure that you can actually put every transaction directly on the blockchain without relying on CK roll ups, [which] are extremely complicated. The technology is relying on two layers with very few notes and hence less security." The ultimate goal of Concordium is to allow corporations to be able to post everything they have onto a blockchain each day, regardless of the number of registrations and without compromising security. Currently, industrial sites need to upload thousands of registrations per second, which cannot be done without a serious compromise in security. To eradicate this issue, the blockchain Nirvana has been created. It is completely secure and completely immutable through real finality layers that we haven't talked about as of yet but are nevertheless just as important. Very few blockchains have this effect because, as yet, you have to wait for six blocks and Bitcoins to be reasonably sure that your transaction will work. For Lars, this is impractical. For him, that is akin to standing in a kiosk to buy a newspaper, having to wait for 60 minutes and still not being 100% sure of the protection against secure rollbacks. This is why he stresses the importance of finality. Through this you are able to know that, if someone gains control of the system, they will still have no possible way of changing the history before the point at which they took control. He stresses the importance of building secure things on blockchains and the reasons for doing so. He cautions you away from doing this if your motivations are because you think it will be a little bit easier to raise money or because it simply sounds nice. Once more, Lars leaves you with a few questions he encourages you to ask yourself before creating something on a blockchain. Do you need it? Will it sustain your business for the long term? Will it scale in a positive way? Will it ultimately allow you to post everything to the blockchain and not rely on various less secure two-layer solutions?

My comments - look into what blockchain works for you. But also, do not look into blockchain if you really don't need it yet. There are a lot of different blockchains out there already and you can go for one that fits your needs.

Gas fees - how do you control them?

Regarding this, my next question was how do you secure Concordium now that the gas fees are blowing up?

He explains that they are able to avoid increased costs because they don't have any costs associated with proof of work. Furthermore, they will develop sharding solutions (see explanation below) that will allow for infinite scalability, or nearly infinite scalability, so he can continue to avoid such a problem arising. However, Lars admits that this is a complicated thing to understand because nobody has truly solved the issues surrounding sharding. Nonetheless, there is no current alternative to sharding that provides a similar outcome. Lars wants to supplement sharding with the blockchain. By using the same approach as you would with sharding, he will continue until he has a blockchain that is full. Once it becomes full, he will move on and continue this process until he gets the same results with another blockchain, and so on and so on. Although it may sound tedious, Lars admits that it is relatively simple because it is simply a repetitive copy of the code. Nonetheless, a complexity arises due to the ability of the people associated with this blockchain to communicate directly with one another, while those not associated with the blockchain do not have the same capability.
In order to combat this problem, Christensen comments: "We have a lot of scientists working on this problem, and we believe that, theoretically, we [have] solved it." All that remains is proving this is possible in real life. Currently, Christensen's team is bringing out the blueprint for their

solution and will most likely begin early attempts at practical implementation at the beginning of 2023.
"But until that's properly solved, you will [continue to] have a problem of having to rely on some layer-two solution if you [go] above [a certain] number of transactions per second that the blockchain sustains." So, while Christensen has a well-developed plan to combat this issue, he confesses that they are not entirely rid of this problem. They still have a couple of big use cases that produce hundreds of transactions per second in which they will be required to perform a miracle of sorts with a three-site change. "But the ultimate nirvana is that you can post it all the blockchain way."

My comments - blockchain networks, like Ethereum, require several nodes to validate transactions, limiting their ability to scale. Ethereum, for instance, can process around 10-13 transactions per second (TPS). This pales in comparison to centralized systems like VISA, capable of handling up to 24,000 TPS.

To explain, a "shard" means a "small part of the whole." In database management, a shard is a subset of a large database hosted on a separate server. While each shard contains chunks of data, they all form one logical dataset. For example, if you group all city residents with surnames starting with specific letters on a unique server, finding information requires less computational resources, tasks require less time to complete, and the database becomes easier to manage.

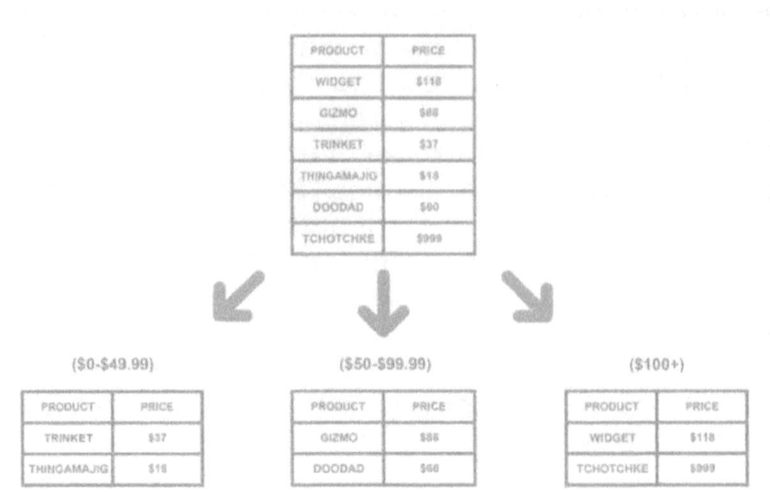

And if Concordium can do this for their blockchain, I believe it will be even stronger. Go deeper into this see LINK.

Nirvana in crypto.

Nirvana is a good way to end this interview. Once again, many thanks to Lars for bringing some hope into blockchain, which has been an up and down situation. Though it was temporarily down, it's coming up again because of the technology. Once more, I really appreciate your time here, Lars, so thank you.

Chapter 13: Evolution

Anthropology through times and the plastic frontal loops.

Doubt is the reason we explore and do science

Two scientists I admire are Darwin and Newton. Before their work was accepted, they pushed the limit on things that people in the churches and in the general population wanted to reject. All the scientists were against the missing link. Neanderthals were accepted as real, but Lucy was not; she would not have been accepted as an intermediate in the evolution process. Most scientists at that time did not want humanity to have evolved from apes. The admiration I have for Darwin is to due him refusing to compromise. He did not try to make a version that aligned with what the churches believed in, like Tycho Brahe. As described before, Tycho, The Danish astronomer, wanted society to adopt the geocentric model. His model had many intentionally skewed equations to adhere to the teachings of the church.
A few decades ago, we only knew about black holes in theory. Einstein had a belief that they could exist, but theories can be doubted until they are proven. Theories come to life through the philosophy in a scientist's brain and are often discussed with others, so they can form a theory together. This is even true of the standard model that is the name for the theory of everything LINK.

$$W = \int_{k<\Lambda} [Dg][DA][D\psi][D\Phi] \exp\left\{ i \int d^4x \sqrt{-g} \left[\frac{m_p^2}{2} R \right.\right.$$

$$\left.\left. -\frac{1}{4} F_{\mu\nu}^a F^{a\mu\nu} + i\bar{\psi}^i \gamma^\mu D_\mu \psi^i + \left(\bar{\psi}_L^i V_{ij} \Phi \psi_R^j + \text{h.c.}\right) - |D_\mu \Phi|^2 - V(\Phi) \right]\right\}$$

It is incomplete and does not explain everything, but it is a fine start. We might get more answers with A.I. and the James Webb Telescope soon regarding many questions that scientists are asking themselves.
We are still learning to understand the universe, and we still do not fully understand the human brain. Furthermore, we are only at the beginning of artificial intelligence. A.I. has been able to beat the best human chess player after only 4 hours of training, and that was with zero knowledge of the game. These building blocks led to the creation of Alpha Go, which beat the best human Go player, Lee Sedol, in 2016. Now Alpha Fold LINK A.I. has mapped 200 million proteins and may be about to solve one of the mysteries of how life first appeared utilizing proteins. Half a century ago, the number of calculations required to unveil the configurations of a single protein from its amino acids sequence, the basic building blocks of life, was inconceivable.

"If we do it right, we might be able to evolve a form of work that taps into our uniquely human capabilities and restores our humanity. The ultimate paradox is that this technology may become a powerful catalyst that we need to reclaim our humanity." John Hagel

It seems like we are about to reveal the building blocks of life. From amino acids, to proteins, and onto life. We are so close, but still in doubt.

The plastic brains

In order to understand human evolution, we must understand how the brain works. How do we obtain knowledge, and why do we get stuck on some ideas that are not backed up by any logic or factual proof?
The brain can create new neurons and create new pathways through your life. Functional plasticity is the brain's ability to relocate functions from a damaged area into undamaged areas. As I described earlier with the dogs that had their brains lobotomized, the center that lit up when they ran for a stick was removed, and later they did it again because the brain is also comparable to a hologram. All the parts contain a picture of the whole. Structural plasticity is the brain's ability to change its physical structure as it learns. We can learn through our life, but many people get stuck in one belief system. We also see that the entire society stops at a certain level. Some societies stop at level four and are strong believers in religion, others stop at level five and are strong believers in the individual and economic system; level six is when society believes in collectivism and a strong state.
But the conclusion must be that we can move on to level seven and eight soon.
During the war in Afghanistan, 320 marines were divided into two groups. One group trained in mindfulness for eight weeks at home and on the daily routine. They were trained to understand the signals from their body, like stomach behavior, increased heart rate or tingling skin. Part of the training was simulating real war scenarios that would be replicated in Afghan towns and soldiers. They were monitored by scientists during and after the drill for heart rhythm, blood pressure, breathing rate, and even

their neurochemical reactions to stress. The Marines that had been training mindfulness were calmer under pressure. Even when the Marines' brains were scanned with an MR scanner it proved that they had less of the stress-related activity patterns of the brain that integrate feelings, reactions, realizations and enteroception. We know that we can learn, and we know that young minds are a bit more sensitive and responsive to new learnings. And if you routinely keep your brain occupied with, for example, Sudoku or math problems, your brain maintains plasticity better than people who do not train the brain. We know now that you do not have to stay in the same mindset all your life.

Jumping levels

The reason I have comments on the different levels in is that there is a lot of information in it about why we react the way that we do. We react to the same sentence in different ways, and there is a larger explanation for this than your own personal reasoning. You also react to specific things because you are born in a certain area and in a specific culture. We know that environment plays a role in how we react to specific situations. But your own personality plays a role too will you fight or flee? Will you try to interpret or demonize what has been said? Are you living for your own wins, or are you living for the wins for others: society or mankind?
Power structures, as I mentioned earlier, are often set up by people who want the power. A structure has no innate power, but the people who keep it going and want you to be in it will benefit. The structure itself is just a structure; if you do not see any potential benefits to yourself, you might not subscribe to it. Now here is the thing with religion: some people try to keep you in their religion. They can be fathers who try to keep the women in a straitjacket and make them marry a man from a family they prefer. This gives the father power over their daughters and over their

sons. But why would someone do this to their own children? Do they believe this is good for them and that God will give them benefits? Or is it a structure that establishes them in the tribe? The power structure of level six is a bit different from religion because they are bound to group thinking and a consensus belief system. The strongest example here is what we see right now on so-called climate change. Someone called John Cook created a paper saying that 97% of all scientists state that global warming is man-made. We see people who will defend this belief/power structure in a way that reminds us of religious people, or as described here, as a tribal shaman. It belongs in the category of fraud. But President Barack Obama used the 2013 statement from John Cook in a speech, and then it became the solemn truth. Barack Obama knew it could provide his boat with some wind in its sails. His campaign would soar and appeal to the portion of faint-hearted people within the group of voters. Politicians use the voters' feelings to get them to vote for them. Populists have always been a part of political power structures. When climate change came along, they saw an option to use it to their benefit. In Denmark, it is used to increase taxation on the private sector so the public sector can grow instead. Is this a healthy economic structure? No, and the reason is that the public sector does not produce a larger enough profit but still consumes the money on welfare. If it had a surplus on the government's budgets, it would be beneficial. But in a consensus collectivistic mindset, the tribe is the public sector. They will protect it most of the time because they work in it. Denmark has one of the largest public sectors in the world, and we are also taxed the most in the world, competing with Sweden or Finland. However, in Norway they have the oil fields to pay for their public sector, and they pay well, so they drain the brains from other Scandinavian countries to their public sector and pay them well. There is a saying that a social democrat gave the oil in the North Sea to the Norwegians over a bottle of Whiskey. Norwegians also have the highest number of electrical vehicles per person in the world, but they do not rank on top of the least polluting countries. But again, a socialist did this, and again a socialist wanted to keep the taxation on the private sector with the narrative that electrical vehicles were the solution. Look at the new law in the EU where we must be carbon-neutral by 2030 and fossil-fuel-burning cars must be a thing of the past. This is a political decision; a power structure that will force a whole continent to go in a specific direction. However, no one can explain this with the laws of physics. Explain to me the thermodynamic second law and tell me that CO_2 can heat the globe. I have even talked to a professor at the Copenhagen University who is aiding the IPCC, the UN climate panel, who could not explain this to me. Nevertheless, I know that it is hard to jump levels, and this belief system is one of the hardest to overturn. Climate change is accepted in all the media. However, if we analyze 2018, with the coldest summer in a long time, no one with this belief would discuss it. Now we have a warm summer, and they paint all the weather forecasts red. When it comes to doubt there is none; they are true believers. When it comes to innovation, there is none; they are true believers. They don't even open their eyes to thorium fusion windmills and solar power is seen as the only solution. It has been proven that there is not enough copper in the world's mines to produce enough panels and mills for the whole world to go "green". The wind does not blow all the time, ensuring we have a reliable and effective power supply. But the power structure is strong, and we all know that it is going to push the production of electrical vehicles. So, is it the right decision from the "green" politicians, or are they running with faint-hearted voters?

1. Survival. It is easy to understand that the first primitive layer is a tough place to be. Your goal is to get some food, water, warmth, and to reproduce. Here, looking at the base level, it is again and again

showing up at the higher levels, until we change to tier two.

2. Tribal thinking is one thing that runs through all the levels in tier one. People tend to think they are a part of something. This started early in anthropological human development people try to be a part of some group. This is a force that turns inward; if you leave the tribe, they do not turn and ask where you have gone. They even had rituals to forget people who did something wrong and turned on them. In Scandinavia, there is a feeling that, if you are self-employed, you will feel this tribal sense right away. They will not turn around if you go your own way. Over 95% of the population swears to being hired. The tribal sense is a feeling of belonging you can find in the strongest hardcore religious environments, as I discussed with respect to level four. But it is all about a power structure. Someone will feel they are not in power when you leave and, therefore, they turn their back on you. They will feel that you did that to them.

3. Level three is a selfish level, as you see the levels go from 'we-thinking' to 'me-thinking'. So, this level is where we get our individualism; people started to work for themselves. Humanity was not on this level for a long time, but it taught us to stand on our own two feet.

4. This level is strictly religious. The people live with a mind of their own, but it is a religious mindset. So, the belief system is set in place. Nonetheless, it also means that you believe in something, in a specific place in the world, while you would believe in another religion if you were born somewhere else. Most people tend to stick to their religion because

the penalty for not doing so is too high. You stay with your belief system, even when you live on level five or six. Most of these people will pray, even if they are studying quantum physics or biology. Religion tries to find a reason for all aspects in life, and if you just believe hard enough, you're a good religious person. This level is hard to get out of, and if you do, you are a very rare person. Religion is stronger in places with higher poverty and hard times. People tend to pray for better times and believe that if they find money on the ground, it is God's will. If things go wrong, God is giving you a lesson. No matter what science says, God is behind it. For people who are not religious, it is a bit strange to watch these people stay with this belief system, as the barriers between them are high. We also know the numbers from the Middle East and north African region; religion stopped innovation in a region that was ahead for many hundreds of years.

5. Personal freedom means the world is a playground. Achievements, abundance, and enjoyment of material things are personal rewards. 'Me' is one of the strongest groups for innovation. 'Me' is also decentralized, meaning that is a drive for innovation because you want to do something in this world. For investors, the motivation is the same: invest and get more for me. But this also takes an entrepreneurial spirit, and the ecosystem must be in place. The strongest community around this is in Silicon Valley. Furthermore, the immigration to this place has been driven by some of the strongest people, from the settlers to the people who had leave everything behind and survived the harsh land of desert, snowy mountains, and all kinds of weather. Strong men

and women accomplished this, and I believe that their DNA is that of explorers. They wanted to explore, and they wanted to go further. Plenty of new inventions have come from the United States, and they have built an ecosystem around this. They know that innovation contributes to the whole of society. It creates new job opportunities, it brings wealth to the country, and it makes life easier and better. Innovation brings us prosperity, and countries around the entire world are now in a better state than just a few years ago.

6. People on this level have met their goals in life: a car, a family, a house, a TV, and computers, and all the phones they could dream of. But they find it very challenging to accomplish their own mission because they are busy listening to the opinions and perspectives of others. Consensus societies have adopted socialistic collectivism and the drive for prosperity is lost. Therefore, they think that the world is at the highest level it can be. Even though they see some people suffering, they really can't think how they themselves provide aid. In a country like Denmark, where you pay half of your income in taxes, you believe that it is something that the municipality or the government must deal with, not you personally. This way of thinking also ruins the individual who has a great idea that will help people thrive. Socialists don't like it when individuals get more than them; they have a large amount of envy. They try to think how they can tax people, so they don't get more than average. The focus is on a strong state and community. The focus is still the same as on level five when it comes to money, but now the money must be centralized. Centralization

is the worst thing that can happen for innovation. The money that flows into the space industry in the USA is a good thing for the individual; SpaceX, and Blue Origin have thrived on subsidies from the government. But we now know that NASA did not invent a way for landing modules for the rockets to be recycled that was Elon Musk and SpaceX who did this. It was an innovation that gave the industry a way to reduce costs exponentially. This can be one of the key changes in the space industry, like assembly line production was in manufacturing. Remember, this level is still tribal. People in this level think that consensus works and is the best thing that has happened for mankind. Jumping levels is thus even harder than before. Comfortable people can find it hard to move forward. People who live in consensus confirm each other in their beliefs. They even think this is the best thing that has happened to mankind and there is nothing beyond. If you ask them if things always work, they will probably say yes. When you try to talk to them about what could be changed, they often tend to think you are arrogant. There is a true cognitive dissonance when socialists think things can be done even better without tribal thinking. This applies to groups in a specific business category that they belong to. This category is presented as a specific party segment in the left or the right wing.

7. On level seven, people can first understand, use, and combine the benefits of the levels that have come before. They often seem arrogant to others because they do not need to win debates. They sometimes discuss things, just to understand the other

perspectives. Rank and status are unimportant. These people have a systemic way of thinking; they may set and work towards goals that are unlikely to bear fruit in their lifetime. This is an egocentric focus, but the concept of ego is expansive as it includes all of humanity. The innovation that spurs this level on has a higher goal. This could be the Mars mission for SpaceX, even though it will only be able to do this with the help of the US government. Otherwise, it would not be an option. However, the dream comes from an individual, and a lot of the innovation comes from a team and like-minded people who have the same goal. The tribal way of thinking is lost in these people; they don't feel the need to belong to a specific group. As mentioned, they can communicate with all the levels and accept them for what they are, but they do not feel the need to belong to a power structure. They create new systems, though not all will produce systems on this level. But they will understand that they do not belong to certain power structures that do not benefit their personal freedom, just as level five has a need for level seven to understand the freedom to express themselves and hate censorship and dogmatism. All other levels have dogmas even level five works under the dogma that having more is good; the buy and throwaway society was created by level five thinkers. We have a system in Denmark where we get money back from bottles. Denmark is known for its recycling of bottles. This started in 1922 because of World War I, to save money on the production of bottles. It seemed smart to use them repeatedly, until they broke. It was systemic thinking, but it was a level five version, as it was a result of scarcity. Today, recycling is part of production, but it is a mix between level five and six. That was a system similar to the corporations that sprung out of the farming industry, now called co-ops. They saw the benefit in owning the distribution channel themselves. Attempts to think in level seven are too often made on level five and level six mindsets. When we see these innovations built from scratch with only systemic thinking, we are at level seven. However, when you look at these innovative systems, you see that they make the pie larger; this is not what we see in the public sector unfortunately. Nevertheless, we would be able to get a larger pie if it was built by level seven thinkers, but that calls for a re-making of the public sector. Some of the greatest minds in Denmark are involved in infrastructure in shipping. I believe their thoughts on this matter could be beneficial to the new structure that we need in this country and in many countries around the world. Maersk, the second-largest shipping company in the world, is already going in on crypto because they know that, if all the goods that they transport have a unique number from the field to the table, then the distribution can be even more efficient. Efficient distribution will save billions of dollars each year. I mention recycling and corporations because efficiency and reuse of resources is effective and is one of the mindsets that will take us to Mars and other places in the universe. And the discoveries we make will help life on earth. Effective decentralized systems with longevity will improve this world, as seen in scientific research regarding the emergence of behavioral economics and the original development of NLP.

8. Holism is key to this way of thinking. Some see a world in danger of geopolitical collapse, others see a world that will prosper. As seen in the 'Gaia' philosophy, risks of alienation are the drivers for most of the population at levels 4/Blue/Justice and 5/Orange/Achievement. People have taken sustainability and a holistic approach as a guiding principle for their actions. Altruism is one of the drivers; you do not run a business only for economic gain but also to serve others in the best manner possible. Business has a bottom line that also gives a plus for wellbeing a plus for the good things the business does with others in the global order. Geopolitical movements are also seen in the conflict in Ukraine where companies move out of the country and stop doing business in Russia. Geopolitical good can be a part of level 8 now that there is more of a movement governed by countries. However, it shows signs of what to come. The geopolitical structures are still centralized economies battling for power. They get access to minerals and metals, so they can hold power over others. We know that China has bought a lot of mining access around the world to hold most of the minerals and metals, even rarely used metals. There is a reason for this, because we often do not know what metal or mineral, we will need to use in the production of the next energy source. The world is governed by powers that can withhold their own energy production. It is also governed by the countries with access to production on silicon chips. We know that TSMC in Taiwan is the largest producer and the most advanced in the world when it comes to chip production. Their revenue was

US$57.22 billion 2021 LINK. That is why there is so much tension in the Taiwan Strait. The US does not want China to get hold of this production. It will move the power away from them, so they can produce the chips in the same quality and amount as is done there today. Automation with robots is one of the key elements to bringing production into the United States and Europe. The world is still governed by centralized powers and will be until this is equalized. I believe we need thinkers like Bohr again. He revealed how to produce A-bombs for the different powers after WW2 because he saw that this was necessary to stop anybody from using it. Now the same solution of equalizing must come into the power structures of centralized countries. This must be equal in the right meaning of the word. They must not exist in a situation where someone feels that they owe another the other part anything. Holism cannot be whole if there is a bad basis for it. The perfect holistic power structure can be seen in the family where you love your children, but you still get to decide for them; if you do it with love, it is the right situation. I'm not saying we need to love each other in the same way, but at least we should not hate each other. This is the key to neutrality and a prosperous future. The geopolitical situation will change dramatically when fusion power plants are a part of our energy production and vertical farming is implemented around the globe. We also see options in hydrogen and the electrolytic process being improved so it is compatible with oil and coal. This is about to happen; the electrolytic process can now produce hydrogen at a cost that is comparable to, but will soon be less than conventional fossil fuel. In a globalized world, we will probably see decentralized autonomous organizations making a difference. At this point, we have not seen any successfully executed DAOs. It seems like the world is not ready yet.

9. Crossing borders with charisma will be used to solve problems for the whole globe. Even though such people are egocentric, with a 'me' approach to things, they see all the other levels before them and can make them work together to create a better world.

Different belief systems

You have probably been in a discussion with somebody who did not understand what was said. We all try this occasionally when a problem has more than one outcome. I have now tried to explain some reasons why people think as they do by extrapolating from Clare Graves and his 9 levels. We also know other systems that explain humankind like the Myers-Briggs type indicator (MBTI). However, this system is horizontal, where Clare Graves is vertical. The reason for the vertical approach in this book is because innovation is not a personal skill, it is a social skill. One example of a simple innovation is the leather bag. The bag is sold at a market, and each year you go to market and try to sell your bags. One day, someone comes along and really likes the quality of your bags because they hold a lot and last for a long time. Then comes the *BUT* – but why can't I carry more things in the bag; can it have a shoulder strap? The person who sells the bags and produces them at home goes back to the production table and creates a bag with a shoulder strap. Next year he sells even more to the people on the market. Supply and demand are a driver for innovation. The first smartphone was created in 1992, called the Simon Personal Communicator, invented by

IBM, and produced by Mitsubishi Electric. Most people think the smartphone is an iPhone. If you look at the hype cycle, it is after the chasm had been crossed that the iPhone was sold. The smartphone had to go through numerous phases before it became successful. Some people still don't even want it. Laggards are hard to discuss innovation with. However, all other levels can be hard to discuss levels with; they find it provocative to be told that they are not on the highest level in society, especially if they have money and success in the society that they are living in at the present time. Successful people are often hard to persuade, and a whole society that believes they are superior to other societies will argue against most other belief systems. Between the levels there can even be hate. The feelings are usually reciprocated, but it does not benefit anyone to be in conflict. When the different levels meet, a discussion can frequently end in harassment, or with someone trying to employ humor. This comes with an understanding of the belief system you're up against, if it is higher or lower than yours, it will not be understood. If their level is above your level, you regularly try to ignore what the person says to you, and often you think they are arrogant, mostly because you can't grasp what they are telling you. This means your belief system is simply not on this level, so instead of attempting to understand it, you have cognitive dissonance. I hope by writing this book you will be encouraged to go along the path with me. It is my hope you will set out to understand innovation and attempt to understand other levels. It is my hope you will change levels and level up with others so the whole society, and after a while the whole planet, will be at a higher level.

Cognitive dissonance

Values are often learned. It is something your parents should have taught you. Watching your parents gives you an idea of what values you must live with. In the book *Tipping Point* by Malcom Gladwell, he talks about the criminal mind that flourished in New York in the 80s, how graffiti spread, and how broken glass became a common part of the street life. This also involves the way families live in certain neighborhoods and how they raise their kids: the value systems you bring to your kids and what they think of this world shapes them. It is not up to everybody to think they can leave this world as a better place than when they entered it. Would you say you did something good for the world when you're on your deathbed? Will you try to change anything in this world? Are you a better person than your parents? Are you trying to do good? Well, if you are and you are trying, then there is hope. Hope for humanity. Because it all comes down to you, and me. We are the world. What we do to each other is also what becomes the next big thing. If you have any doubt about this, I have been in this place with you before: if you do not believe things can change, then your brain is not plastic anymore and your belief system is carved in concrete. This is often seen in level four, where religion is a part of the values that you are striving for. For others on other levels, it is also easy to see because they use a lot of symbols. Religions are full of stories, they are full of dogmas, and these fill them and us with thoughts. People often think we do not belong with other people. In any situation where one does not act as one's values prescribes, and this will give you cognitive dissonance.
When it comes to business, it can be hard to do business when you do not believe in the person, you're in front of. If that person has another belief system, you will probably feel discomfort, but you might do business with them anyway. There is a lot of doubt in other people, and especially in other people's attentions. When we look at the

interview with Lars Tvede, we know that people try to cheat in most cases. This can be lessened if you are at a higher level, but at lower levels it tends to be a problem. The lowest level is, after all, survival. The more you need to survive, the more you think about the short term and how you can get something to eat next time you are hungry. The spiral for the levels when we are going up in society from 1 to 2 or from 4 to 5 gets harder and harder because it is a belief system that has to change for more people at the time. The further we go down, the more we see people thinking of themselves, even in a belief system as religious level four. There is a higher 'we', but level four has strong convictions that the truth is in the sky with God. However, at the end of the day, it is me who must get something to eat. Religion is something outside of our selves. It can be God's will that I can't make things work. Up until tier two, survival is the main reason for you to do things like get up in the morning, go to the office, do the job, and go home. Then you have traded your time for a salary. But if you're on a higher tier, from level seven to level nine, your purpose for doing things is different. This will also require a new system when it comes to payments. Will it be centralized as it is today, or will it be decentralized? Most people do not understand the decentralized economy that crypto brings to us. Most people have cognitive dissonance in this respect. This is because most people are in tier one with systems that cater to central banks and central governments like today. Trying to explain decentralization to people who love the centralized world can be an uphill conversation at best, just as talking about innovation can be up-hill. I believe this is because most people love to use these innovations, but how they came about does not matter to them. When we look at the model on crossing the chasm, most people are in the majority. This means that they think smartphones occurred when the iPhone was launched and not when the first one came out in 1992. Discussing innovation with a person that thinks the iPhone was the first smartphone is a bit tough. One of the reasons is that they can be evangelists. These are the people who, in social media terms, push the messages to others: "Go buy the iPhone", "Apple products are the best", and so on and so forth. They also view these objects as a trophy. Well, I had one of the first iPhones, the number one, but I found it poor. The software was not stable and there were a lot of things you could not do on it. I had to hack it to get access to the root software so I could use other software options than they allowed. Even Google Maps was not in the software until later. Their own map system only worked in the US, so for all other nations you had no option. Even then, the map system was bad and still is, compared to Google Maps. Nevertheless, if you discuss this with an evangelist who has a belief system that the iPhone is built by the gods, then you can't talk about things that do not really work on it, can you? The picture I'm trying to paint here is that if you are an innovator or an early adopter, it can be hard to talk to people who are laggards. It can even be hard to talk to people who are in the majority about new innovations. When we add the Graves model on top of this, we know that people in level six often think of themselves very highly. This is because, most of the time, they think this is the highest level that exists in human history; they even agree on this with people at work and in their family. We see the same power belief system in religious people; they can also be hard to talk with about other religions, for example. We know for a fact that some people get hanged for their behavior in some religions. If we go one level down, we know that people can be burned alive in rituals. This was years ago, but back then it was a fact that you had to deal with. Now you must deal with iPhones being the better choice, or socialism being the best thing in the history of politics. That is often not the case. From where I see it, it is way too centralized. It often ends up with one ruler, and one ruler often ends up with bad ideas, mostly because they can't hold onto reality when they get the power, and therefore power corrupts them. It is seldom we have seen a country or a region where the one-ruler system has survived. In my opinion, it is often because the system gets rigid and overly complicated. It corrupts in more than one way. When the population starts to have troubles and can't withdraw money in a bank, for example, the population often loses faith in the system. We know that this has happened recently in China, and we know it is now happening in Russia, too. This is due to the pandemic, which resulted in global inflation. Some people lost their money because the banking system is corrupt. This led to people protecting on the streets. When the whole system is corrupt, the people start to riot and cease peaceful protests. This can, and will, happen.

Objects and objectivity

Anthropology can be hard for most people to understand. They are not wandering around each day thinking they belong to a specific belief system. We do not discuss with others out of the perspective that we are on level six and think that centralization is the best thing in the world. People on level six believe they are best suited to rule over the planet as they have wealth and a successful system. "Look at our GDP," they say. "Look how well we are doing in the Scandinavian countries." The people who are within the system, particularly, believe this. If you are outside this, you see something else. Often, you can see that they are overwhelmingly happy. It is as though they need to protect themselves when questioned about their belief system. Anthropology is used to help large corporations teach their employees how to understand their differences and to work together. Some thinkers have built systems on the horizontal level, so we understand how we are as a person. Most companies do this with the Enneagram, DISC Assessment, Goleman's EQ Test, and many others. They help us develop an understanding of each other so we can understand why people act as they do. Most of the time it is about YOU knowing why you act as you do, but it is easier to sell to you if you get to know others because you can understand their belief system and react accordingly. When you have worked with these models and personality tests, you know a lot about yourself. The more we know about our reasoning and why we act as we do, the more we reach a higher level in humanity. You are the object. You react to others. Others react to you is objectivity. When I went to film school, I learned about something called metacommunication. It is when communication either decodes itself or deconstructs itself. It is an analytic process for communication about communication. It sounds complicated, but when you start to work with it, you will lose some of the excitement for it. For example, when watching a good movie, you instinctively know what is coming next or even how it ends from watching five minutes of it. You know the plot, so to speak. When it comes to these test systems, they help organizations and the people within them to decode the signals that are exchanged between the lines when you work with people on a daily basis. It helps to better understand the power structure in the company, and the leaders can use it to communicate on another level than the one they could use before. Teambuilding courses have the same outcome. The employees have a great time solving puzzles in the woods with each other, while the leader watches how you work together and what communication level are you on. Do you communicate intelligently, or are you an aggressive hard knocker? The people on the team often also get to know each other in a new way. Objects are running around as planets in a solar system. Astronomers watch the constellations and find out how the universe works. On our planet, even the ants have a system for how to work together. Bees, as described earlier, know how to decode a dance so they can find the pollen to give back to the hive. You can be a worker who has fun with what you do. You know that you are a part of something bigger and you contribute a small portion every day. That does not mean you are able to be objective and see all the communication strings. It does not even mean you have an interest in seeing it. Depending on where you are in the Graves value model, you may not know where you are, and you may not even know about a value model. In Scandinavian countries, most people are highly educated. But, if you look it up, people in general are more highly educated in the United States LINK. People in, for example, Denmark do not know this; they think we are the most educated people on the planet. Although this is far from the truth, it shows us that belief systems for each level constrain themselves. A level protects itself as though it is the solemn truth. There are a lot of things you can't discuss with people who act as if they are at the highest-level humankind can manage. Those objects who do not understand objectivity will never have an interest in accepting this. I believe it is because they feel as if you are sabotaging their world view; you are also in a sense catching them with their hand in the cookie jar. In essence, they live by this system, and if you tell them that there is something rotten in the state of Denmark and they can't fee they fare. Again, even a friendly dog will bite if it is backed into a corner. When it comes to dogs, Pavlov knew even pigeons would learn the trick of pushing their beak on the button to get food. The hammer philosophy is also part of the picture. If you only have a hammer, every problem seems like a nail. If they do not understand your hard work as an entrepreneur and innovator, they will say you should get a job. In a consensus society, you will like the Scandinavian countries, where only around 4% of the population are self-employed; 96% think a job is the best solution for you. The object is a job; the objectivity is getting home from it. Well, jokes aside, 60% of people do not like to go to work. However, we see a mismatch in what they are offering others if it is hard to understand them. A lot of my former friends fell out with me when I became self-employed. This happened because they feel differently towards someone who does not have a job. The controversy seems to be the goal in life. If someone, even a good friend, does not match their belief system, then they would rather leave that person instead of watching them become successful. The negative result of this is envy.

-220-

A society at a standstill is doomed to die.

"You may say I'm a dreamer, but I'm not the only one. I hope someday you'll join us. And the world will live as one."
John Lennon.

Why innovation?

With most of the collective and consensus countries, we see that they do not succeed, become prosperous, or set an example to look up to. Typically, this leads to hunger and poverty. The results are lack of money, poor medicine and hospitals, poor education, and no innovation. These societies are not even at a standstill as the title of this chapter suggests, they are moving backwards. Standstill societies will see all nations around them get wealthier and move up to a higher level. Money is only a means of utility or security. When you trade with others you need to have something to trade with. Bartering was one of the ways we traded goods with each other in the past. It got better when currencies came along and helped us out, so we did not have to carry around a chicken under our arm to trade for a beer. But in some societies, this is the standard today. Innovation in the monetary system has helped us on many levels. It is the reason wealth was created in the first place. In order to achieve a society in which everybody receives the same standard of treatment, where no one feels less and all are "equal", all must agree. Once, I spoke with Lars

Tvede about this on a phone call we had about society. He provided a concrete example on how it works. Will you take the apple in the basket down at the supermarket with the brown spot? Most people would not take that apple with the brown spot. You will sort them out and take the apples without a spot or wormholes in it. You leave the bad ones to the next buyer. What is this? If you are a consensus-driven collectivist, you should not do so. But I tell you they do; you do find the bad apple, pears, bananas, and all other goods in the supermarket left for you if you're late. It is not like they take them; they do not go for these. There is not a one-size model that fits all. They won't take the apples and divide them in their basket so everyone will get a bad apple. No, they leave them to you, even the consensus-driven collectivists. They do not take the bad jobs either; they go for the best paid jobs. If you ask them about the economy, they want the low-hanging fruits to stay' in this analogy, they want the easy money. And they will push the bad jobs your way. It does not work. Innovations will be a product of this kind of pushing the bad stuff around society, where everybody is going for the best apples themselves. There is simply not that kind of surplus in the population. When the population agrees on a tax cut close to 50%, or higher in some cases, of their salary, what kind of money is left when you also pay VAT on 25% on all groceries and any other product? You even pay 15% when you want to give your inheritance to your spouses. You're taxed when you die too.

Controversies

I often meet people who argue that innovation is something that must be shared. They are of the mindset that all fruit in the basket must be shared. They are the same people who stand in line in the supermarket and do not ask for a new line to open at the next cash register. Then, when you ask the personnel politely in the supermarket about this, one will try to take your place in line and say you are cheating. I have tried this more than once, here in our civilized country, where consensus-driven collectivists have their own way of understanding equality. It seems kind of silly to me that I must share the apples that I found on the ground when they themselves can go and pick some up. When they see someone who gets something, they believe it belongs to everyone. They want you to understand this. In some countries under dictatorship, like in North Korea, we know that they are living in camps, they do not have electricity and they definitely do not have innovation. So, why are the apples not for everyone when I picked them up? They do not pick up their own trash when they come back from the yearly Roskilde Festival where 110,000 people go and listen to music each year.

LINK it is in Danish so I hope you can translate trough Google.

These are the same people who often vote for the so called "equality" where they take what you brought to life. This standstill gives us nothing, not morally, and no enlightenment or enrichment, and it is certainly not a great way to give back to nature. Yet they still vote green. These are often people with strong ties to collectivistic parties. People who think 'WE' first before 'ME', as they put it. This is not the only situation where this happens, but here it is easy to tell if they plan to do what they say they do. I don't think they really care that much. There is not an address on these tents, and they leave all of their trash behind them. There will be no address or phone number when they steal your idea or your innovation either. They will then think they are suddenly better than you, justifying their exploitation while knowing the laws will protect them. This is a standstill. It does not move forwards, though it is certainly moving backwards. When it comes to helping entrepreneurs, the same kind of thinking is overwhelming they have the so-called business houses. The amount of money they spend on this is, funnily enough, more, or less the same amount they get from taxes on 42% from share capital taxation. You may think, "What 42%, and how is it possible?" It is because they think it can be categorized as income, and income will be taxed based on this. Other people, who think by themselves, know that investments are not the same as a daily job where you trade hours of work for a salary. Nevertheless, consensus-driven collectivists do not see the difference. The apples are not yours; they are everybody's. But what does this have to do with innovation? Though they are innovators, they do not like crypto and avoid investing in it. They will have written a list of things to consider before investing in crypto. Funnily enough, the director of our centralized banks does not like crypto either. If you're looking for a system that is rigged to go in one direction for a socialistic society where everybody is "happy", this is the system. The highest you can become in life is an employee. If you try to become an employer, they will try to stop you. I have been in contact with the director of the business house in Copenhagen to ask her why they do this "early warning", where they try to stop companies from evolving. When you have a good idea, you need soft funding and funding overall. What farmer can harvest their crops without sowing? What person can build a house without a loan from the bank or inheritance to build it from? However, they do understand this option because they themselves just want a house. But if you talk about funding innovation, they have cognitive dissonance. It is like they simply can't see why they cannot exploit this from the beginning. If you take 42% of the money from people who invest in startups or other businesses, how many people will invest? When you sell a house, it yields 0%, so where do you put your money? It is a scandal for a country that is crying for more innovation. When I started 25 years ago, it was the same. I started with a good heart. I still have one, but people who only think of money themselves have the hammer problem; they think everybody else is also just looking for money. Why would you build a business if it wasn't to become rich and famous? Level five thinking. Level six thinkers will take your money, your apples, and everything else if they can; they also think of money. They legalize it by saying we are more than that. They make the laws, so it is OK that they take your money and ruin your startup. They will also stand in front of you in the supermarket at the cash register you asked to be opened and say this is queuing culture. They simply do not like people who can think on their own. They would rather stand in a 40-meter-long queue than ask the personnel to open a new cash register. When you finally open one, they steal it with a strange kind of logic. If you do not like the smell in the bakery, you can leave. This is what people do when they leave the country. Those who immigrate to the country are people who like the welfare system, and for some reason these are not the most innovative people. But this book is not about the downward spiral in this country, though it is a problem. It does not make the country better to live in.

We know that 11 out of 12 startups fail. So why do they make it even harder to start a business? It is like they are saying that the level of understanding and the level of living must be the same; if we can't understand, no one should try to understand it. Attempting to have a dialogue or discussion with these kinds of people in level six will often result in them using the phrase "we are better", or "we make the laws". We do not need this. The herd mentality was easy to see through the pandemic. 99% of the population removed the facemask as soon as they could at the end of the day. A newspaper conducted a survey on how many would continue to use a facemask to avoid Covid19; 30% said they would keep it on. That was far from the truth, though. However, the funny thing is that they are so used to mind-control that they all took it off once told to, as though a microbial virus would care about political directives. It reminds me of some historically scary things we have seen due to no one asking critical questions. If they are asked to march, they march. If you do something they don't understand, they turn their backs on you. If it is not understandable for them, you must be a crazy person or someone they must keep an eye on. This is happening with a point system in China now. I believe one reason prohibiting innovative people is that the power structure is structured to help a specific industry and demographic. We know that the Inno-Booster Link program will help you more if you have a green project. However, it is not only about this program; it is just the most discussed one. This is stated on their website – and remember this is the government's money. They are earmarked for specific sectors by people in the government. They say this is good for the country, but who knows what is good and what is bad? Centralized governments think they know, but do they? This means that they can use their power over others, and they therefore feel strong and good about themselves.

Innovation and strategy

Innovation is, without a doubt, challenging.

According to HBS professor Clayton Christensen, 95% of all product innovations fail, and according to the Startup Genome report, 92% of startups fail. LINK

In 2017 PWC found that 54% of innovation organizations had trouble bridging the gap from innovation to a larger business strategy. Another finding is that the best innovations are not always the ones with the largest R&D budgets. When you ask about Y Combinator, they often look for a company that is not a copycat of others with a red ocean strategy.
There are, however, a few success factors that have quantitative evidence.

1. You must measure it holistically and have a bias for action. The best performing innovators calculate the whole innovation process, as opposed to just the end results. They use metrics for assessing and improving the way they innovate.
2. 60% of global innovators are "need seekers". They focus on external trends in the market, like wearables and emerging technologies, and trends such as blockchain.
3. A pro-innovative culture is built into an organization in which innovation is part of the weekly routine. Using Google as an example, we know one day there is set aside for all employees to go and figure out something new. That counts for 20% of their time, and it leads to a lot of new innovations.

4. Alexander Osterwalder, the creator of the Business Model Canvas (LINK), says that it is more or less impossible to pick the big winners from the losers early on. Therefore, organizations or investors need to drive long-term growth and invest in a large number of innovation initiatives even though they will fail most of the time. One investor rule of thumb is that you invest in 20 startups, and one is a hit that produces profit 100 times over and also offsets the cost for the ones in your portfolio that failed.

5. Ambidextrous organizational structure is used in organizations that have structurally different teams for existing and emerging businesses. According to Michael L. Tushman (LINK), ambidextrous organizations have a 90% higher success rate on innovation. This means you have a structure where the emerging business is at the same level as the existing business.

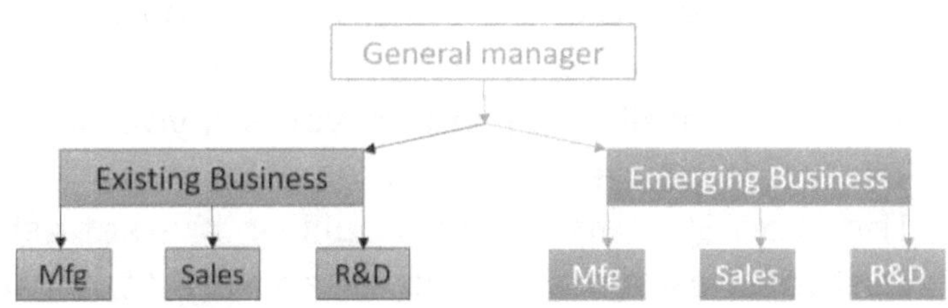

6. Open collaboration is a significant factor that separates the best from the rest 77% of the time.

7. The best innovators rarely base projects on approval based on future revenues. McKinsey's 2008 Quarterly article speaks the same language: The best performers were less likely (29% vs 37%) to base

innovation spending on the relative attractiveness of an innovation, or business case estimates.
The best innovators make sure that it works.

There are a lot of processes for innovators and innovation today. For example, the Phase-Gate process, or the waterfall model, as I have mentioned before, is one of the less well-known processes for product innovation. There are always more ideas than there are resources, but we still see this being used in organizations where there is "enough" money, or there is no focus on how it is spent. "It is the taxpayer's money, and we are doing this for the taxpayers," they say in the public sector, where the consensus-driven Marxists think that everyone must have the same options. They also think that everybody is better off with the same system. The waterfall model is probably the worst model for innovation you can think of. After all, the public will, and always has, picked the apple without the brown spot. They will pick the bag with the handles that fits their need, and you will leave a shirt in the boutique if it is too small. The market works: if you do not know this, you are not awake.
The Lean Startup Model is built on market risk and customer demand. You build an MVP (minimal viable product) that shows that the mouse trap works. Some investors are in on this phase, and often soft money from governments will also help the process – we saw this with the Tesla loan I mentioned earlier. Lean systems can also be used within the company, not only to make the organization more structured but also to make it a faster and better place to work without all the

clumsy case files and red tape we often see in the public sector but that can be removed in private companies. The Lean Startup model can be used for intrepreneurship within the company. Bots can be used to innovate new products, and also to innovate better tools within the organization.

84% of CEOs believe innovation is critical to growth.
McKinsey & Company

The statistics from early stage venture capital show us that we know we can't pick the winners without investing in the losers. Alexander Osterwalder (*LINK)*

We can try to find the winners, but the problem is the many unknowns. If you want to make a lightbulb, you will first try to make it work. Edison became known for being the one who made it work. In fact, he bought a patent from two other scientists who had a product that already worked. But did it work well? Edison made it possible to scale it up. Elon Musk was not the first person who tried to build an electrical car. The first electric car was built around 1900, when all other vehicles were born. The combustion engine won the race, as we know today, and it did this because of distribution. It would only have been people living in the city who could have electrical vehicles. The range of distributed electricity was one problem; the range of the car was short because of the batteries. We continued going into this instead of going with the business model. Yes, I know it works this way, but had we gone the other way, we would have had electric cars a lot earlier than now.

Pick the winners?

Politicians often want to have a goal to inspire people to vote for them. A politician's goal is usually designed to win an election. An election is won by gaining the most voters. The voters want a politician who gives them more benefits than the opposition. You might argue against me and say that they do not vote for this purpose. I believe you should scroll back a bit and read how and why the levels fight each other.

Winston Churchill once said that: "democracy is the worst form of government except for all the others that have been tried."
The Greeks said thousands of years ago that power corrupts. We know now that this is true. We have now seen so many countries where it applied. I think over 40 countries have tried socialism, and all of them have been deeply centralized. For some reason, it always ends up with the leader believing in his ideas most strongly. However, the opposite of innovation is when an idea is popularized

by combining all the best ideas, thereby ending up with the best combination of all of the ideas. Socialism will also neglect market forces; it will say that all people must have the same options. Therefore, you can't let them choose what they want on their own. This is what happens every single time. Here we are again stuck in the never-ending discussion between level four, five, and six. It is true that, if we work together, we will gain more than the consensus-driven collectivists who think they invented the best system in human history. They do not see the next level, level seven. They do not know about the tribal tire they belong to, nor that they try to help their own group over others. Furthermore, a politician would take in a company and give them a loan or subsidiaries to push a certain technology, like electric cars. Are electric cars better for the environment? No, not if you do not change the source of energy, often coal, to something else. This was the case in Denmark, where the lowered taxes were taken away from electrical vehicles because it was illogical to do so until we had clean energy resources. In this moment in time, we could have been the greenest country on earth if we had pushed on with fusion energy. However, Denmark is currently Green, and because Bohr was told by the Americans that he should stop telling others how to make the atomic bomb, politicians on the leftwing grew frightful. Therefore, they are willing to build an energy island that will be finished in 2070, costing the Danes around $34 billion to build. Remember, the Danish population is the same size as Barcelona, Spain. Oh, by the way, did I mention they think that the Earth will be one to two degrees warmer in 2100? By then, they will have had 30 years to stop this "global warming" from happening, with windmills and other copper-consuming technologies like solar panels. I mentioned thorium and fusion, which will be in a production line from a Danish company in the year 2024. They did not get subsidiaries or loans from the Danish government, but from the EU and private investors. You can read more about Seaborg Technologies here:

LINK. There are two companies with promising molten salt technologies working on this in Denmark; the list goes on: LINK. In 1969, the Oak Ridge National Laboratory shut down their molten salt reactor that was fueled by thorium. Just as the electric car was invented around the start of the century in 1900, thorium's benefits had been demonstrated. Materials, manufacturing, and instrumentations are now far better. This makes both thorium generation and electric engines feasible. However, will politicians understand this, or is it better to trust a student who can Google the consensus on climate change? Who are the winners when politicians find a promising way to get elected? If you think you will gain anything from it, you could be in one of the levels I have described. You see, even 2070 is many years from now, and there is ample time for them to wash their hands of this. They can greenwash and get elected for being the politicians who have a plan. You must remember that there is no solid proof to this, there is only consensus. This means that their so-called climate scientists say that the climate is changing dramatically; yes, we know that the climate is changing. It has been a long time since the earth had an atmosphere. Nothing new here. Then they tell us that the climate will get warmer, but what is the proof? Manipulated climate models made by Michael Mann who was the former author for IPCC who coined the phrase "Climate Change Deniers". No one denies climate changes. It is just another way to construct a straw man argument. We know that this guy worked for the International Panel on Climate Change for the United Nations, and we know that he created the hockey stick model that was used by politicians to scare the public off. This hockey stick is even used in primary schools in Denmark, being used to scare the kids from when they are 6 years old onwards. This happens as they are building their knowledge of the world, how it works, what is right and what is wrong. Indoctrination has been used for many years, but now it has moved into the classrooms. The children do not get to hear about the thermodynamics second law. They do not

know if infrared radiation can heat anything. They are told how the so-called greenhouse effect is working, but they are not told how small an amount there is in the atmosphere of Co2. You will not find many scientists who will tell you the truth about this because they are silenced. I talked to one and he currently has a hard time acquiring funding for his projects. Why is this? Because it is politically decided who will get the money. At the moment, scientists who will tell you that we are all going to burn up if we do not stop the industry polluting with CO_2 will get the money for their research. They will get money for their so-called science. Science is made with mathematical models that can be manipulated to do what Michael Mann's hockey stick told us. The Hockey Stick had to ignore a warm period in the forties around the Second World War, and a cold period in the eighties that was also minimised to make it look like the Earth will be overheated by the end of this century. The problem is that it is manipulation. For some people, this does not matter; fearmongers and politicians who see how they can use this to their advantage are on the bandwagon. Some countries do not go to the same extreme extent for this matter. However, if we build it with old technology, we might not reach the goal. The story goes like this: some people would like to build a rocket so they can travel to another planet, in another solar system, in a distant galaxy far away. The rocket sets off, and the astronauts' long journey begins. They travel for 20 years when, one day, they look out the window and see another rocket passing them at a higher speed. This rocket left the planet a decade after them.
This is what can happen if we start with old technology. We will spend too much energy and too much time to reach a goal that will be reached much faster just a few years later. I remember I once read an article in a car magazine back in the 90s; it said that the last supercar had been built. Lamborghini and Ferrari had around 450 HP, and for some strange reason, the journalist could not imagine a future with more horsepower than this. I was thinking that they

did not get it. And I was right. The super cars of today have between 1,000 and 2,000 HP, and this race will never stop until we do not drive anymore; horsepower will not always be the way particularly wealthy men show off their fortune. In the near future, flying cars are what will move us around. If you can't afford one yourself, you will be able to hire one on an hourly basis and get from A to B in a matter of minutes. Joby Aviation is working on solutions that fully achieve this (LINK). They are already building it with huge funds and backers. There are a lot of projects with flying cars (eVTOL) already; they have vertical takeoff and landing and can do this in around half a minute. Some of the larger airplane producers and aviation companies, like Airbus with CityAirbus and American Airlines, are investigating this space, too. Mercedes, Tesla, Toyota, Hyundai, and Audi are also building, as are Google and Uber, who are developing other technologies to use in this space. Even Slovakia, China, Germany, and Japan are in the race. There are several other startups, big and small, like Kitty Hawk, Terrafugia, Moller International, and PAL-V International, to name a few. These startups all want to conquer the cityscape. This is a booming industry without much focus, like it was in the days on Kitty Hawk when aviation started. The cityscape projects will give a lot of people around the globe new ways of transportation in just a few years.

Combined knowledge?

"You know it is hard to think. Most people can't even think at all. If you can think at all, you're not even good at it. I mean, think about what you have to do, technically, to think. First of all, you have to formulate the [scenario]. That is hard enough, and you have to formulate it precisely.

Then you have to generate a general potential solution to the problem, and then you have to let those solutions argue themselves into a hierarchy internally. In order to do this, you have to be able to tolerate that stress, right? You can't just be one thing if you're going to think, because thinking isn't just saying that what you think is right. That is not thinking at all. Thinking is questioning why you think something is right, and that's really hard. It's very demanding."

Jordan Peterson knows a bit or two on thinking because he is a clinical psychiatrist. He has written several books and is known for his sharp words on thinking and mental health. We need to think as a philosopher and an artist to create new innovations. The way we think has to be free; you cannot innovate if you are conditioned to think in a specific frame. Limitation on free speech is a huge problem for innovation. We observed this in the Islamic regions earlier on in this book, where we know that they limited people when it came to thinking differently. Think within the religious straitjacket and you will get a population who does not innovate or make new things; even the ability to help people in hospitals will be limited because of the way it is governed. I dare not think of what it gives a population in terms of degeneration. When it comes to people who are driven by wealth and greed (which, as we know is good, from the film *Wall Street*), we know that this kind of willingness to be persistent and take from others, or get rich by creating something, is the American way. Another film that shows this extreme is set ten years following real life events; this was about *The Wolf of Wall Street*, who got rich by selling penny stocks. People who thought they were getting rich buying these were cheated in many cases. We know that freedom of speech and access to learning resources has given the world better educational systems, better tools, better hospitals, better cars, better engines, and better everything. We live on this combined knowledge, but when it reaches a level where people start to become centralized and consensus-driven, we actually find that it takes more than it gives. Even though these people try to live for others, they can't and therefore must fail. Both level four and level six are 'we'-driven; we will thrive together. However, both levels are tribal, centralized systems that operate under a strong leader. Think about this: the wish or the greed for a better personal situation in level five gives the whole world better planes, trains and automobiles, and entertainment. It does this because someone tried to get more for themselves. They wanted something and they went for it, especially because a society like the American one does not stop you from the pursuit for happiness LINK. Actually, this movie is a classic example of what it takes to go in as the antihero with no chances in life and make it big. Happiness sometimes smiles at you; it sometimes come to you when you work or if you train to become good at something. Talent and training have made a lot of people happy and wealthy. If you have to look for happiness in an old written text that can't be changed, it is hard to find it. It is a 'We'-based centralized society that reads old texts that become the only way for you. It is a one-size-fits-all society. This is true when it comes to a society that tells you what you can do, who you are and what your limits are – and even more so when workerism and cancel culture become prevalent. A society that wants you to be in a specific class will also determine your future. This is what happens in strong consensus-driven collectivistic societies. They also have a one-size-fits-all model. For example, I got a parking ticket. I went online to deliver a complaint to the municipality. Well, after all, online is the fast way; it took me four minutes to fill this in with a photo I had taken five minutes before to prove where my car had been. They sent me a receipt for this, which stated it could take up to ten weeks to handle the complaint. For your information, the municipality of Copenhagen is the largest workplace in Denmark with over 25,000 people hired to serve the citizens of the city. This is not the teachers or the hospital workers, this is only the municipality, and they can't deliver an answer earlier than ten weeks. Service is not a word they use; speed is only mentioned if you drive too fast in the city, not when they work. So, what is this an example of? Combined knowledge does work in the private sector, but it does not in the public sector. LEAN is a concept that we use to innovate differently, to make an organisation produce faster and more effectively. LEAN is not used in the public sector. Maybe it is, but it certainly did not get implemented in this office and many others. If you want something to work for your customers, you ask them. You make surveys and you will find out what worked and what did not. For startups, it is crucial to find out about what the customers think about your product early on. For the public sector that doesn't care about the customer, the taxpayers are forced to compensate. They know that it is not OK to take longer than ten weeks to act, but they don't really care. If a politician would come into this system and promised to reconstruct the system, both the public sector and the press would jump on this person like wild animals. For some reason, a lot of workerism is implemented among journalists around the globe. We know for a fact that 80% of the journalists in Denmark are left wing, even communist.

People have to work together to find better solutions. This is what drives innovation. You have a problem and think something can be done better. You know you can invent an app for a mobile phone there are a lot of examples of these small ventures that exploded into social networks. It was not a problem, but when it came about, everybody was on social media. I mentioned the example to talk about the inefficiency in systems that have been built for a public who do not try to change anything. There is no combined knowledge when it comes to the public sector; it closes around itself. This is also how consensus keeps people rooted in the same beliefs. If you continue repeating the same lie, you will start to believe it yourself. This is the opposite of what combined knowledge is because it is indoctrinating and something that you have to learn within. Therefore, you can't discuss the fundamentals; there is no free speech. You may not ask specific questions. New discussions about the number of genders shows us what is hiding behind these organisations. They even defy science when it comes to gender and climate. They find a consensus and, if a large proportion of the journalists are left wing, they let it slip. The end justifies the means, and it will sneak up on you. This is knowledge being used in a downward combination. If you use knowledge in this way, you are a crook; you are hiding the truth. This is the opposite of innovation; with an innovative approach, you would work together to bring about the best of two worlds. But instead, you stay silent about your knowledge so others don't get their part of the pie. Then you can have more of it later. For a lot of people, the truth is something you create. If you can cancel some culture and some events to fit things into your narrative, you will do so, in order that you can have a larger piece of the pie. The mindset is not about building a better world; it is about getting what is rightfully yours, even if it means taxing those who make their money in a lawful way. We have to look at the example that Lars Tvede used earlier in the interview: people lie. And they can't stop it. This is one reason why people try to take other people's things. If they are not clever enough to practice combined knowledge and build a better world, it is simply easier to take from others, even if it means you have to go against science. Who is right when it comes to the climate "consensus" new order?

If you can dream it, can you build it?

Although there is some truth to this idea, not everybody needs to dream about building something. A lot of people are happy with being a chauffeur driving others around. A lot of people have one dream in life: to build a family and to live happily ever after. Some people just want their dream car. Others dream of cruises on the sea in their own boat.

Lots of dreams are about the easy life, the life without stress. A lot of people think that, if you want to build something and make it big, you only need to think about how to get more money in your pocket. Here is one of the biggest differences between people who are innovative and people who dream of things they can have. Innovators do not always dream of making things for others; often it is about solving problems. Like Jordan Peterson said, "It is not thinking at all to say I am right. Thinking is questioning whether or not what you think is right, is right, and that's really hard. It's very demanding."
People who are innovative think differently, mostly because they do not stop with pragmatism, they do not stop with dogmatism, and certainly not with consensus. Why is it so hard for a lot of people? It seems like it is easier not to come up with hard questions to crack or try to figure out how to build stuff. For most people, a dream is not a realistic thing to follow. There is a whole society, a family, an education, and other structures that hold you back from achieving it. A lot of people will tell you that you need something to fall back on it will be too complicated otherwise; it is not worth it. If you keep that belief, you will never be innovative and you will probably not think, "How can we do this better?"

Society plagues and wars

I have written about plagues, Covid, wars, scientists, the public vs private sector, and how all these give us innovation. When the horrible scenario of a war is over, the affected area is left in ruins. Everything that was is no more. Houses are bombed to the ground; people have died. A lot of factories, supermarkets and merchants must start all over again. It is a horrible situation for all of them. As we now know, some countries will use the situation to acquire the smartest people, and the brain drain will flow out of the place with the common people. There were two reasons for the US and USSR to take all the scientists who had war knowledge after the Second World War. One was to stop them from inventing weapons that could be used against them in future. The other reason was to get the best brains to help them build their war arsenal. For a society to be at a standstill after a war is not a good situation. After war, sometimes a lot of new options spring up, but mostly not in the country of the oppressor; they will still suffer for years to come. When we had Covid, a lot of science came to life: for instance, BioNTech, and Pfizer with a new mRNA system where you program the DNA by injecting the mRNA into your body. The company BioNTech became known because they had a vaccine that could work on the Covid 19 cases. The smart thing was that when the variations were caused by mutations, the mRNA could be reprogrammed to the new mutation. Innovation even cures viruses today, but most of the globe had to start over. A large number of countries were shut down in full. No stores were open, no one went to work and educational institutions were closed. A fun fact is that Denmark and Sweden followed the same pattern. LINK

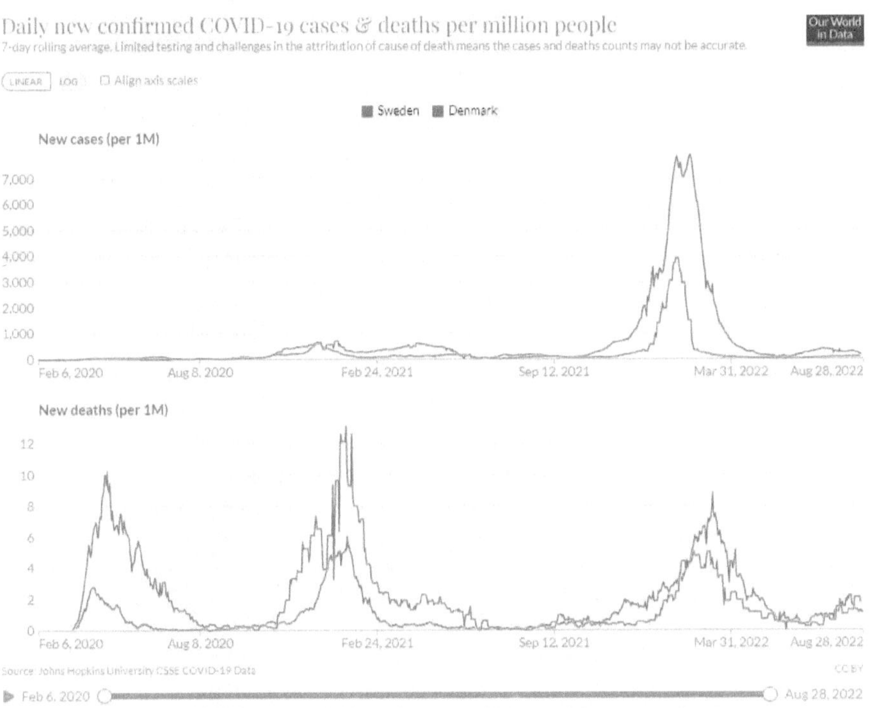

Sweden did not close supermarkets, factories or had a policy around facemasks. On this graph, you can see that Sweden had even fewer cases of Covid19 than we had in Denmark, but the test centres were also overpopulated, meaning more cases were found. So, that is also a part of the reason for numbers. Nevertheless, the death rate was nearly the same even for Sweden, although it was higher in the beginning. It actually looks like they had a smaller number of cases in the last phase. In 2018, there was a flu outbreak that caused more deaths on itch consciousness than Covid did. Most countries had more or less the same number of deaths over time. In the middle of this, people froze with fear; they got even more scared by what the press told them. On top of that, the politicians used it to boost their campaigns and received popularity for closing down businesses, resulting in billions in lost revenue. The lesson from this: people who found out that the graph is nearly the same concluded this was not a catastrophe. Many people still try to justify the use of facemasks and the lockdowns, even though the evidence and the numbers speak against them. It leads me back to Matthias Desmet, who wrote the book about mass psychosis and totalitarianism. When it comes to wars that start with mass psychosis and end up in a centralized totalitarianism, there is a reason why people do not innovate. They would rather go into a mousetrap and sit there afraid and shaking. But the world goes on; as if there is nothing to see here. We know it is like that, yet there is not much we can do about it. The world is not heading towards bad times; it is heading towards better times. Innovations will revolutionize the energy sector, the food industry and everything else you know. Even the central banks will fall sooner rather than later. The global society is not at a standstill, but some societies are moving extremely slowly. This is partly due to some parts of the world existing in poverty. For others, it is because of a consensus-driven collectivistic socialistic mindset. For example, in Denmark, as I mentioned earlier, blockchain and crypto are not seen as positive things. However, what is the logic in this other than that they conflict with the power structure? Nothing! This is where the problem resides; they won't move on this one until it eventually moves them.

Unlike the Neanderthals, we have brains that can create new innovations, communicate clearly and stay connected. Let's not forget who we are; do not live in fear. The world is an open place to be, with many opportunities.

Innovation cannot be stopped

Over the years, a lot of people have been bringing attention to the overpopulation of the planet, saying we will have too many mouths to feed. Statistic after statistic has shown that in 2050 the population growth will stop.

How do we know this? As I mentioned, the statistics professor, Hans Rosling, produced a fine video on YouTube about this: *The Magic Washing Machine*. The number will stop growing when we have sufficient wealth; there will no longer be the huge number of children needed to keep you alive when you get old. This demographic move is already seen in China, where the birth rate is below 2.2 children per family. The same is happening in India, too. Only Africa will see growth, but not enough to increase the amount of people on the globe. In about the year 2050, the population will start to decline. Doomsayers will also argue that the Earth will be one or two degrees warmer by the year 2100. They will tell you that there will not be enough food for everyone; there will be hunger, and we will have to share our resources and use consensus to become a better place for humankind. Socialism will try to make you believe in this consensus-driven collectivist (Link).

"Does population growth lead to greater resource scarcity, as argued by the English scholar Thomas Malthus and, more recently, by the Stanford University biologist Paul Ehrlich? Or does population growth coincide with, and perhaps even contribute to, resource abundance, as the University of Maryland economist Julian Simon has argued? The Simon Abundance Index (SAI) measures the relationship between population growth and the abundance of 50 basic commodities, including food, energy, materials, minerals, and metals.

The base year for the abundance index is 1980, and it is set to 100. In the last 41 years, this has risen to 448.5 percent. This is 4.24 percent per year, with a doubling of the global resource abundance every 16.7 years. In 2100, it can be expected that we will be around five times wealthier than today. In addition, most of the population on Earth will have a washing machine. They will have food to eat and electricity. When you look at the numbers, you cannot argue that we are in a worse state than years ago. You cannot deny that over two billion people are out of poverty. You cannot deny that people strive to have a smartphone.

Even in poor countries, they have smartphones today. One reason that the smartphone is so important for the whole world is information about better options elsewhere. It can lead to migration, but it can also lead to innovation in a region where there are none. For example, Kenya invented the m-pesa so you could send money through a text message before the smartphone was invented, and before crypto was an option with Bitcoin (Link). Smartphones give you the option to send and receive money or crypto easily like the m-pesa. They give you the option to be in contact with people on the other side of the globe. If you are familiar with services like Fiverr, where a huge amount of people works as freelancers every day, you know they find small jobs they can do for others around the globe. Web3 is already here, and it will grow faster every day. This is proof of globalisation in a decentralized manner; people find each other without interference from others. I predict that the abundance index will change, so the number of years it takes to double the abundance (currently every 16.7) years will halve towards the end of this century with a world economy GDP of $95 trillion compared to a predicted global GDP by 2030 of $1.7 trillion. These numbers are backed by PwC Link

Africa has waited for growth for many years, and now it is their time. This will happen in a new world, where the global economy is real. Trade will be conducted globally from Africa. Africa has a large number of resources, and they will prosper from these, but they will do it with Web3 technology. They have smartphones; there will be satellites like Elon Musk's Star Link and Mark Zuckerberg will invest billions (Link), changing the continent at a higher speed than the rate we saw in China. This will stop people from migrating; they will stay and prosper with their spouses. This is also one of the reasons why innovation will become even rapid when so many people start to innovate in Africa; like the rest of the world, it is becoming smarter and more educated. Education will become an online school where you can take small courses that fit the needs in your city, or in the company you are in or want to start. Everything will be like going on Amazon; an algorithm will recommend you products based on your past searches and those of others. Education will become monetized, so you get money to take the courses from those who need your skillset and brain. To all the doomsayers, I'd say just stop yourself. To all the exploiting socialists who will distribute the pie, instead of innovating and building a better future for all, just stop yourself. Your way of thinking is already outdated. It should have stopped with the fall of the communism in USSR, but you live on with fear and scaremongering towards a population that will wear a mask if a new pandemic comes about. Unfortunately, it is easier to scare than it is to understand prosperity and innovation.

Interview with Farzam Kamalabadi. "The Most Influential Foreign Figure in Modern Chinese History"

You will find the link to the interview in the notes.

What did you help China with?

Firstly, would you mind providing a brief introduction as to who you are, your vision and what you are currently working on? Also, having worked closely with both Dubai and China, what are the differences that separate them and how did you have to alter your approach when advising Chinese managers? Furthermore, how did you get into this type of work?

Farzam explains that after his arrival in the United States in 1978, he immediately became involved with helping Chinese refugees and people from Cambodia, Laos, and Vietnam. As he helped settle 5,000 families, he also learned English. He says that, during this process, he "wanted to influence the world, not case by case, but in a total arrangement." Because this was his goal, he sought out what he calls the Meridian points, or easy access points. Due to China being the most significant Meridian point, this is the path he decided to go down as he believed it was the most significant. Farzam admits that, though he could have chosen to learn Russian, he looked too similar to Russians and therefore believed that if he learned Chinese it would be more impactful. Therefore, he learned three Chinese dialects in Boston by reading, writing and studying the classics. He began with the classic *First the Hidden World*, and then *The Book of Tao*. From there, he began to work backwards in order to create his plan. When he first began in 1980, there were no overseas Chinese mainlanders in Boston, only Chinatown. However, he wasn't allowed to go to China because he was from Iran and during this time there was a revolution in Iran. Thus, Farzam was not financially independent. However, he made a promise to himself that if he could not go to China, he would continue to pray that China would come to him. Around 1979, the first group of visiting Chinese scholars, not yet students, came to Boston, more specifically Harvard and MIT. Immediately, Farzam became friends with as many of the visitors as he could. Because they didn't know English, it forced Farzam to learn Chinese faster. At this time, he wasn't aware of the new emerging demographic of Chinese immigrants.

"They were from the top intellectuals; children of the national leaders." Farzam wasn't aware of the visitor's status and therefore maintained an objective perspective. He befriended them and attended classes with them, and through this transferred their personal experiences and memories during the Cultural Revolution into his own. Farzam says that he felt as though he had already experienced living and growing up in China, even though he had not yet been there. This ultimately influenced his concepts and methodology. He quickly amassed a student base of 2,000 to 3,000 Chinese students and scholars because he went around different universities and gave lectures on the future destiny of China. Farzam recounts that during this time the events at Tiananmen Square we're taking place, and pessimism surrounding China grew. It was also during this time that a book was published called *The Ugly Chinese* and they later produced a television series called *River Elegy* about the death of the Chinese civilisation and decimation of the Yellow River. This affected all Chinese students throughout the US, Europe, and Australia as well as the entire leadership of China. Farzam took it upon himself to single-handedly change that. "I wrote many open letters [and] manifestos that showed that the society's rise and fall of the empires and of their civilizations is natural, and that the current, what we call superiority of the West and downfall of China is not at all permanent. I gave a lot of reasoning, and I wrote a lot of things about the future destiny of China." This was at the time when China was seen in the wider world as a second world citizen or third world citizen.

During his discussions, Farzam likes to use many analogies. For example, "the arrow kept in captivity longest, when it's released, will go the fastest and farthest" and "the entire oil well is dormant, and I need to be the match to cast in until it catches fire."

He idealizes the peaceful rise of China; it is becoming a new world with what Farzam likes to call imitators or receivers of beneficiaries and will be contributed. He references a 1990 article written in the *China Daily* that claimed China would have a leadership role in the new world civilization and new world order. However, at the time, nobody discussed China reclaiming a seat as a world leader because it was thought China was similar to modern-day Africa or India in the 1990s. And so, his single voice opposing this view reverberated in the entire US Chinese community and in mainland China. Nevertheless, after the Tiananmen Square incident Farzam visited the most conservative media outlet in Houston and became the single voice that proclaimed the glory and rise of China, and the pendulum change that would soon follow. However, Farzam stresses that there must be a balance; there can never be extremes of self-negation or self-glory.

 It was during this time that Farzam created the concept called 'harmonious society', 20 years before it was adopted as the national policy. "The harmony between individual and collective, between idealism and pragmatism, these are the things I wrote [about] in 1988, before Tiananmen Square. Also, what I call the unities between goals and processes, you cannot, through revolution and political downfall of nations or governments, raise the glory. It must be internal, from what I call the realm of possibility, which needs to shift."

Farzam single-handedly traversed China, visiting 1,000 counties and 500 cities over a 10-year period. During this time, he popularized a word never used before, Shi Ming 使命, which means the self-given mission and destiny. Because of Farzam, everyone had a word that they could use to describe their purpose in life, whether they were a cook or a village magistrate. Farzam further describes the way he altered some of the Chinese language. "Even the vocabularies, the dictionaries, and a lot of the Chinese phrases in my later calligraphies, I have changed. For example, the calligraphy of Chinese says that the people take the food as their heaven. I reverse only one word. I said the people take the heaven as their food." This references a subliminal change to the foundation of progress. There are other Chinese clichés that Farzam reversed in a similar way. "One of them was that China will serve the world of humanity. China for the service of the world of humanity. That means China will move from introvert to extrovert; from receiver to giver; from follower to leader. In this process, it must learn that it will hold ideals that will lead the world of humanity and contribute." China operated under Farzam's methods for about 30 years. However, China's current method has reversed some of this. However, Farzam says that it is still operating within the realm of ideal practice in China and that it will come back to how he advised.

Nevertheless, aside from the mental subliminal collective consciousness of the nation that he uplifted and changed single-handed; he became involved with policymaking alongside key figures in the modern Chinese leadership. Through his meetings with them, he was able to change their mindsets. "For example, with Mr. Dido, I asked him, 'Does China now need more friends or more enemies?' He said, 'Of course now we need more friends." When Mr. Dido proclaimed such a need, Farzam questioned him on why they utilized their communist motto when they have a class struggle. Once he was able to change their mindsets, the society became a harmonious one. It became an entire movement that Farzam had been preparing for 20 years in advance. He had foretold the quiet building of a consensus, and once it became dominant, some people could propose policy change to national leaders. Once the leaders discovered it and came to agree, they adopted it and began implementing Farzam's suggestions. There is a Chinese proverb that Farzam mentions that says once your contribution has received, and is now being implemented, you observe from behind the scenes; that we don't do it for glory or gratification.

Farzam didn't mention anything about the way he contributed to bettering the Chinese society until state figures themselves wrote about it in the media. With the blessing of the central government of China they mentioned him and his influence in the rise of China and proclaimed him to be the most influential foreign figure in modern Chinese history. The United Nations Pictorial Magazine also published their own blurb, It is also their statement.

Farzam recounts that "for decades, [he] was in the forefront, but again, also behind the scenes." However, he needs to mention once again that it was not for glory or glorification. He has only announced it himself to the world because they first published it. He notes that the simple fact is that his next mission is Africa. This is why he finds it pertinent to call upon his history, his resume, and the fact that he contributed to the rise of an entire Asian nation that affected the whole of Asia. China's purposeful, conscious, directed and collective rise affected and helped Indonesia, Malaysia and even Pakistan and India, and reached Dubai and the Gulf Cooperation Council (GCC). "One cannot deny that the rise of China has reordered and affected the whole of the world." Even though China has temporarily regressed, it is a phenomenon Farzam understands, and he recognizes it to be temporary.

Though poor, China was still a recipient of outbound investments in 1993. Around this time, Farzam began promoting China's outbound investments and had to prove himself to the entire leadership, one by one, until 1999. Then China reversed its policies and allowed investments in any city or province under $100 million to be accepted directly with no need for permission from the central government. Previously, the limit had been $10 million. This has been a decision that the central government has renegotiated multiple times, but it is still pertinent that the central government originally accepted this notion. As a result, many cities began focusing on outbound investment. Farzam notes that he contributed to the writing of a full-page article in which the chief editor of Shanghai Business Daily wrote about a joint venture between China and the US. When Farzam originally pitched this idea to the editor in chief, he asked Farzam how he had learned Chinese. Farzam told him and this gave great insight into his mind. "I want to do [the] most difficult things, so that easy becomes easy."

Because of this conversation, Farzam was able to influence him and to becoming one of the lead backers of electric and home appliances. For his lucrative aid, Farzam was rewarded by being invited to Shanghai along with all of the government and provincial leaders of the US. Though this is just one of many cases of Farzam creating economic opportunity, it also highlights the profound work he has managed to accomplish. The companies that profited from this were able to influence national policies regarding outbound investments in a way that was later recognized in Forbes.

However, before China's emergence and bringing end of the Chinese banks abroad, Farzam brought sovereign wealth funds of the Arab states to invest in China, the first time this had happened in history. The Kuwait Investment Authority in Qatar were responsible for one such financial investment. At the time the bank was unknown and its upskill was hidden. It had taken the bank leaders 10 years of persuasion before finally agreeing. Farzam made the investment proposal to the bank and supplied them with "thick, detailed feasibility studies." Farzam also mentions a multitude of projects outside of China from 100 countries. In addition, he accumulated between 400-500 mayoral and governmental delegations from all over the world, including Australia, US, and China and brought it to the Arabs and Africa. From there, Farzam systematically introduced China's outbound investments all over the world, including Oman and Vernon, California. In the case of Vernon, Farzam essentially adopted it and, within a 7-year initiative, brought 275 Chinese companies to invest and settle in the exclusively industrial city. Farzam implemented similar tactics in Oman. Over a five-year period, Farzam multiplied the trade volume between Oman and China 18 times, from $600 million to $11 billion. That resulted in the first ever China Television going to Barwani. Farzam and his team were involved in the entire process, from the first cement factory onward. Continuing with this success, Farzam brought Mr. Mohammed al Baluchi, who was Undersecretary to Shou Shi Bay, Prime Minister of Tourism of China, and was able to secure the most favourable nation destination for Oman. This led to the creation of an entirely new ministry, headed by First Ministry Madam Raj Shah. Farzam accompanied her to China on three occasions while she was still Director General of the Minister of National Economics, and later as the Minister of Tournament.

"After Oman, it was Kuwait, Qatar, and many other countries." During that period, there was no Consulate in any of the six GCC countries. As Honorary Consul, and on behalf of the Consul General of China, Farzam became African Colleagues Honour. He was on the receiving end. Farzam is responsible for the commencement of all the motorcades, and basically police motorcades, and received recognition for it at least 20 times. Now, with all of his knowledge and experience, he is taking it to assist in the collective rise of Africa.

My comments:
It is not often I bump into people like Farzam Kamalabadi, who I meet in Dubai. He is an open-minded person who understands all the levels in the Graves value system. It was a pleasure to learn from him. His history tells us that one person can move a whole country with wisdom and make them eager to change. The long road to change now seems shorter. But we still have some way to go before all humanity can prosper and all hunger is eradicated. One of the goals for Farzam is also to make all countries become one. We must thrive together to lift all out of poverty and into the new world of decentralized economy.

Question 2
Even though this is an amazing story with so much in it that we could discuss, it is a bit of a long explanation for one question. However, I did write that you knew the son and the daughter of Deng Xiaoping. So, these are some of the people that you have met, and they were actually in the family of the current ruler?

Farzam's answer
"Yes, Deng Xiaoping, son Deng Pufang, daughter Deng Nan, [who is also the] first general." This was one reason why the personal bodyguard, General Zhang Bao Zhong, helped Farzam to organize the bridge competition in the Diaoyutai State guesthouse something which had never happened before. "180 state leaders, ministers and higher-ranking officials were in the same room for an event organized by a foreigner. The reason why they were amenable to this, and to uphold the competitive tradition of Deng Xiaoping, was because I bestowed upon them many awards and wrote numerous proposals for China's peaceful rise and harmonious society, which were later adopted and endorsed by all of the ministers, the Prime Minister and the President of China. One condition of this signing was that after I received it, I was required to keep it private for at least 10 years. After that time, I could then

present it to the public." This became one of Farzam's many initiatives. So, yes, it is accurate that Farzam has met many royal family members. In fact, he is the only foreigner to have met them, which has been confirmed to Farzam by members of the royal family.

"I'm the only foreigner that has [direct] connectivity to the actual royal family of China [a dynasty that was continuous for 2,500 years]." Farzam was fortunate enough to meet both the last emperor and his youngest brother, Aisin Gioro Puyi and Aisin Gioro Puren (the younger brother who had actually lived in the Forbidden City).

My comments
It was a clever move that Farzam talked to so many people in China to get to know people high and low, and to understand the whole country and its habitants. It led him from Boston to Beijing to the central power and helped not only China but the whole region. It is a huge leap for mankind, and a fine step for Farzam. But it takes a leader to make other leaders follow him. This one accomplishment he has done several of times so far. I'm here to learn, Farzam.

It takes a lot of courage

In order to succeed in the way that you have, it takes a lot of courage, and most people do not possess this amount. This book is predominantly about overcoming doubt, particularly doubt within yourself. However, throughout this discussion I have noticed that you do not seem to possess much doubt in yourself. Furthermore, this book touches upon sincere truth, which is something you have garnered in order to make people believe in you. How do you go about this the right way? In addition, what are some of the eternal principles of humanity that intersect when it comes to the market?

For Farzam, it boils down to a thought process called non-ownership. In his mind, he owns nothing, neither the glories nor he has mentioned because he needs to use his abilities for the greater good. Furthermore, in his mind he is nobody and it is not all about him. It is about the destinies of the 8 billion people currently inhabiting the world. This is how he views his universe. When he is asked how many children he has, Farzam responds that he has 8 billion alive and one trillion in total to account for all of those who have lived throughout the 10,000 years of the Homo sapiens lifetime as well those lives yet to come. Although Farzam is unsure whether or not he can actually influence or affect those lives in the future, he believes that the destiny of our entire planet has to be in our own hands. If not collectively, then at least a few must rise to the occasion. We must acknowledge that we do not own this planet, and we are simply passing the energy through. "So, my number one job, and my only job, is not any of these events, activities, programs, businesses, and influencing donations." While these things demand much of his attention, his main focus is on the purity of his motivations. Currently, those with the least pure motives have the most potential to have the highest influence and more power than any atomic bomb. They have the ability to affect the greatest number of people automatically. Because of this, Farzam says we must pray and study, so a greater proportion of people strive to have pure motives. There is only one thing to focus on one thing, the smallest thing, the inner thing, the purity of motive. We must show these pure motives within our daily actions and become a source that has zero need and many solutions to any problem. "The more you manifest it in your mind and heart, [the more it] automatically spills over to your attitude and to your actions." Eventually people will recognize this and understand that this is as real as we can be. While Farzam candidly admits that he has raised about $30 billion, he has done so through direct investments via other institutions and hasn't spent any of the income he has received from it. He estimates the income received to be between $50 million and $100 million, perhaps more, but he didn't calculate any of it because didn't keep any of it. He calls this creation of wealth an immediate seamless distribution to create a circular economy with the rotation of wealth. He is of the opinion that you don't lose anything from this approach; instead, you continue to gain because you have the capacity for earning more money. Therefore, from the goodwill you have invested into society and into the business world, a lot of new income naturally occurs. This is why Farzam was never afraid of lacking money. "In fact, one of the spiritual powers is to overcome fear in any form that you will have. I call fear the number one plague of humanity. The plague of humanity is any fear of money, a fear of like, fear of death, fear of pain, fear of loneliness, fear of loss. All of those fears have to subside for [the] serenity it leads to.

My comments.
If you want to change the world within tiers and all wars have been tried. the knowledge must be, that war is over. Now we must go without taking but giving as Farzam is; he is a fine example for this.

"To win one hundred victories in one hundred battles is not the acme of skill. To subdue the enemy without fighting is the acme of skill."
— *Sun Tzu, The Art of War*

Victory is not war; victory is when we all prosper. Let´s not take from each other but instead make a greater pie for everyone. It is not only backers who know how to make a pie.

Politicians try to steer their populations

My next question pertains to the lockdowns under the Covid-19 crisis. The world witnessed politicians attempting to control the public through fear. From your point of view, what is the current situation of the world today and what is the global consciousness? Why will the Congo and Nigeria rise? Furthermore, why will the whole world rise when Africa rises? Compared to China, Africa has 50 times more minerals, how does this affect the rise of Africa?

Farzam originates from a culture that says, "One soul alone can be the cause of the spiritual and life attainment of an entire continent." He also admits that he never views China as a singular country, but as a continent. Subsequently, he was aware that by affecting the policies, current systems and mindsets, he was actually affecting the entire continent as well as the world. Two years prior to this, his younger best friend passed away. Farzam also hoped to be released from life after the conclusion on this project. As fate would have it, Farzam had several near-death experiences. After surviving reactive arthritis, heart illnesses, high blood sugar, a pinched nerve and many other ailments, he began to believe that he a specific purpose.

Farzam had been writing about China since 1981. He had also written in his diary solutions to help Africa. 41 years have since passed and now Farzam believes it is time for Africa. He wants to fight against all of the odds and setbacks caused by 500 years of colonialism, prevalent feelings of impotence and the lack of self-acceptance. Things are changing quickly in Africa. As he did with China, Farzam has selected two countries to begin his mission with: Nigeria and the Congo. Although his sphere of activities includes 30 other African countries, he wants to focus on these specific two. He has already met with leaders in Nigeria, West Africa, the Congo and several other countries. Farzam authored the manifesto for the future trends of Africa only a few months ago. Nevertheless, teachings from it have already spread among the leaders and community. It is gaining momentum, just like the vortex creation behind his common vision. While Farzam tells us we may be surprised, he is assuredly not, as he has done this and knows to track each individual or community, he presents it to. He notes that they have been receptive to it and have already begun to modify it in ways that best suit them. His teachings are trickling through the communities like watercolour dropped in a pool. Farzam states that he breathes "with the entire concept of the collective consciousness and the movements of nations, our societies, and for that matter, the entire world." Farzam is strategically embedding messages and methodologies throughout his target locations. Several generations of this creates the movement. Farzam has done this several times before and confidently observes the effects in each location.

My comments
Passion for change has driven Farzam to the point where he is today. He might be the businessman in the world who has spoken to the most state leaders in Asia, Africa, and the Middle East; he also had a meeting with Joe Biden years back when Biden was foreign minister. It shows me that his work is important. This mission will be one of the gamechangers for the way that we see the world and how we live. Speaking to a true level nine gives me food for thought: on how we will try to live together without fighting, but with the options for all to prosper.

Question 4.
Having met in Dubai, I am aware of your influence there. As I read Clare Graves, the convergence and merging of the levels integrate, aggregate, digitalise, multiply and distribute, I wonder how we can bring nations into the next state of mind.

Farzam's motto is integrated, aggregate, and "convert, integrate, aggregate, digitise, multiply wealth and distribute across seven or eight stages at the same time." He explains that means we convert and merge all of the classic assets obtained from agriculture, ground minerals, oil and gas, energy and then environment and forest. In addition to this, services and health education will be included along with processing. This is how to get industry to converse, merge and supply finance to then become digitalised. By layering the economy through Farzam's method, one that only he knows, one curates a stable wallet comprising of two coins, a hybrid, and sandwiching and investment coin. The securities lie in tokenisation. Furthermore, Farzam explains that fiat currency is like a stable power grid. The underground digital data coin will be discovered by the artisans on the blockchain's daily logging. The daily logging, which becomes economically accountable for, has five houses that you can endorse to become a financial producer to then be rotated and floated, becoming liquid in the financial markets.

"This is what I call the analogy of an iceberg, where not only the top 2 - 3% [is kept], but the body of the iceberg can become monetized." This is one of Farzam's methodologies for accumulating wealth in Africa. He mentions that there are many methodologies included in the manifesto to tackle future trends. Another among them is the concept of collecting assets, including domestic ones which can be triggered to become monetised locally and globally. The trigger would be just a few foreign investments; the rest will be done by Africa itself. With Farzam's approach, a nation reliant on aid can become self-supporting and an exporter of aid within 10 years. "You help its own domestic dormant economy to become alive, including oil and gas, mining, minerals, agriculture, water resources, forestry, and all the other assets in a new ecosystem, of what I call excitement; this arises through the enterprise community in a peaceful manner, always with humility and dignity."

It is important to Farzam to remember where we come from. Poverty in rural areas of Africa can be as high as 90%. Nevertheless, he is confident that this will change soon.

Liabilities will become assets able to produce a multitude of beneficial forces. From this point on, the national economy, magnified by the digital economy, will be open for contributions. This will create the first ever sovereign wealth fund for future generations within the digital economy and produce more wealth through the exporting of wealth to other nations. This, Farzam says, is how you make a third world country prosper. Within a decade, this could revolutionise Africa's fate, and show its people glory with humility and peace, and without hatred. By doing this, it invites beneficiaries to the banquet table, so to speak. As there will be no animosity between France, the US, Canada, China or even Russia, it is Farzam's hope that a neutral zone may be created. "This is how the whole world has to be anyway. Let's do it correctly, from the place [that] is least expected to create a miracle [so] that humanity will look upon itself [and say], 'wow'."

Farzam believes that the entire fate of humanity, "which is in disastrous order," can easily be altered. Although humanity is crippled by a few blind spots, Farzam believes we can counteract them once our discovered self is understood and popularised, so we can reverse the damage inflicted. Only then can humanity rise. Farzam insists we must think of ourselves as contributors to everything, even to the farthest villages lacking any means. Touching upon how history is written, Farzam notes that our view of the victors and the vanquished of the 10,000 Years War (the period for which civilization has existed), with all their glory, is wrong. Humans must realize that every war is wrong, that those who created the wars are in fact the weak ones. For Farzam, the logic is simple: they lacked the necessary skills to effectively negotiate, communicate or create mutual benefits. In essence, they did not know how to raise others up, even if they are the enemies. They were poor, weak and so incapable that they resorted to violence. "When knowledge becomes simple, and basic, no leader in the world [would] dare to go to war, because that means [they're] the weakest [with] no community of that nation." Farzam emphasises that we

don't need to be militant against our own leaders. We must be supportive and encouraging while also exemplifying a new paradigm with other, better, tools than war and the slaughter of the masses. Even the victors of war do not truly win. If this mindset becomes predominant, the blind spot disappears, allowing humanity to forever change.
"There is no just war. Every war is unfair. In war there [are] no winners, both sides always lose." There are only relative victors and losers but both sides have lost in the middle. And if that becomes a very simple predominant mode of mind, the blind spot goes away and fate of humanity will change.

My comments
Napoleon Bonaparte warned the world about China when he said, "China is a sleeping giant, let her sleep, for when she wakes, she will shake the world." And so she did. Over the last 30 years we have seen more people come out of poverty and into to a middle class. China has surely changed how we live and given everybody in the western world more goods than before. Both sides have been prosperous in this process. It is a good thing if it stays this way.

How does decentralization help people?

As a globetrotter who has travelled throughout the African continent as well as China and also Dubai, how can a decentralized economy actually work within all of these different hubs around the world? Also, how could the potential fear surrounding a third world country like the Congo seizing power affect future wars that should not happen?

Farzam says that there is no fear of the rise of other nations. For instance, if Africa became richer than Saudi

Arabia, Kuwait or Qatar it would be seen as a contribution to all of these societies. He believes the transition will be peaceful, orderly and result in more wealth being redistributed. "So, there is no competition in wealth except [in] what we call a rotational rising [of] wealth." His focus is never solely on the cities and developed nations; it is always on the rural areas and villages, as in Iran.

"When I left the country, I went to at least 500 villages, travelled on foot over the summer as a child of 13 years old, 300 kilometres away from my family." He undertook this journey sometimes alone and sometimes with a group. It led him to villages where they still believed the moon came from nowhere. Farzam recounts that even when he went to Boston, US, he wanted to go to the ruler of the area. So, he visited all of the Native American tribes, and even went to the outback where there were no real villages or tribes. This is why he left and went to help the Vietnamese and Cambodian fishermen and farmers. This is also why he left for China and went to 1,000 counties. This again means that he visited villages where they had never seen a foreigner in their entire lives. These villages lived without technology, meaning no electricity, no light, no power nothing. His friends became the brothers of the emperors or national leaders as well as beggars and village children who had never seen someone from the city. He repeated the same process when he went to Africa, becoming close friends with the Minister of Rural Development in the Congo. During his next visit, Farzam plans to consult with the minister about bringing state-of-the-art technologies and the blockchain to all of the realms under his supervision. He hopes to use the blockchain for water, forestry and even microeconomy. He says that this is one of the areas people visit and believe it is a lost cause. But in reality, this is the exact type of place in which you should encourage development and bring the tools for it. He did the exact same thing when he went to China and visited the 1,000 counties, giving them their first donations for the use of electricity. His donations allowed for the villages to have their first ever fax machines and telephony. His reach extended into the mountain Xinjiang, beyond the Kaçkar into what we call Tashkorgan county, near the border of Pakistan and Afghanistan, where there was no electricity at the time. Along with the help of others, Farzam was able to donate an entire library and audio-visual library.

When you go to these places, Farzam says you not only affect them physically but also in their hearts, their minds, their spirit and their psyche. It becomes symbolic for them. Once business deals begin to take place, the people learn the methodology so they can create their own wealth to sustain themselves.

Farzam says that he is now in fact creating his own automatic modelling concept called embedded benevolence. By integrating embedded benevolence into the underlying software protocol of the blockchain in order to create wealth, the distribution of KYC will be applicable and compliant with regenerative models so that it can be adopted by the mass population. It will also support better programs, creating a complete circle of benevolence. "I call it humanitarian and hyper [and] distributed ledger, or philanthropic and smart contracts." These are some methodologies that will automatically affect what Farzam has done as a person, creating his own wealth and redistributing it at the same time. Farzam encourages people to give their wealth to the world, in the same way it happens when they pass. But he does not want people to wait until they die to financially help others. This once again touches upon certain fallacies that perpetuate the idea that we must change blind spots, create wealth or become wealthy, when we should in fact learn how to distribute it at the same time. So, to again, fallacies that we have to change blind spots, create wealth, become wealthy, but learn to distribute it all the same time. "No need to keep even a penny if you have confidence and reliance on the power to be that you can refurbish and furnish yourself." Farzam states that it is this fear that inhibits people from distributing wealth, and therefore creates selfishness. This fear also creates its own blind spot.

He says it stems from an environment accustomed to loss or the fear of losing, fear of scarcity. However, it is only through the rejection of the fear of death, the fear of illness, the fear of poverty, the fear of loneliness and the fear of being misunderstood you can become the real source.

My comments
The blind spot is also based in cognitive dissonance. It can also be a lack of knowledge. But it takes some courage to walk the many miles Farzam did when he was a young man. The knowledge he gained from all the people he met, gave him an insight that few people have. A lot of people think others are only there to take their money. Farzam has seen that there is more to it than this. Only poverty and famine take people to the edge of life where a lot of people only see one way out, and that is to steal from others. The opposite would be to build and find out how we could build together. This is where innovation comes in. We will become a far better world if we all accept that innovation and teamwork are the way to become a better place for all.

How does the digital economy help the world?

The real source of technicalities in the digital economy stems from unstable tokens. So, what is blockchain to you? What is the zero-knowledge proof and how will this help the world to prosper?

Farzam begins by stating that the world imperative is only traveling in one direction, and that is upwards. He says you cannot deter this upwards trajectory even in areas of science that could be seen as harmful or detrimental. Therefore, Farzam is not against any form of science, he is simply in favour of doing it correctly and learning the maturity to do so. He says that any form of science is good if you do it correctly. This leads him on to his next point, which is blockchain, the digital economy, the spatial web and the quantum. He says that these things are only going farther faster; the world is bound to continue on this trajectory just like it did when adopting the Internet. He says that when internet technology was first created nobody believed in it. Everybody was ignorant of it and fearful of it, so they rejected it. Farzam believes we will see the same thing with blockchain and the digital economy. Although it is inevitable, in Farzam's opinion, the first generation of blockchains was faulty. He explains that the set-up of a blockchain should be horizontal and then vertical, not vertical first and then horizontal. This is why the first generation was faulty. He blames this on crowd financing, the benchmarking of value creating coins and then promoting it without any substance. When the blockchain was announced, the financial gain was simply promised, and for Farzam this is a form of cheating. Naturally, this approach must cease and be replaced by backed assets, or operations-backed orbiter combination ecosystems. He then says that the development of horizontal and operations of industrial integration through the assimilation process must occur. This will create efficiencies within an inefficient market. Next, benchmarks comprised of tokens with values that increase need to be created. Because this process was not adhered to during the first generation, 99% of all past blockchains, whether with benign or malignant intentions, were faulty. However, this doesn't mean that the entire ecosystem will collapse. Instead, a new generation with the correct process will emerge. This next generation will include real operations and processes, whether it's from mining, agriculture, health or service industries; everything will be on the blockchain and will subsequently integrate and aggregate many global resources. Regarding the information age and economy age, Farzam foresees these tools being possessed by the wealth generation. This would allow for the creation of unity and dichotomies.

Pertaining to decentralization, Farzam does not think we should be anti-government or against centralization. He believes that we can always create a hybrid, centralized and decentralized, government with blockchains and private institutions that utilize both blockchains and cryptocurrencies. However, these private institutions who don't have mass adoption should learn five forms of adoption: government adoption, institutional adoption, public adoption, corporate adoption and mass adoption. Farzam states that if you are not able to roll out your blockchain to be accessible and adopted in many countries, then it simply will not work. This is where the real work begins. Therefore, an in-depth plan worked out on paper that focuses on real delivery should be produced before any coin is. Farzam predicts, "This will be prevalent, permanent [and] popular. Many governments [and] many institutions will jump into the digital economy. They will start with a layer of what I call stable coins and data coins. [Then] there will be investment coins and utility coins in between, so that the full package will rise. One key message: stable coin does not mean stagnant coin. Stable coin means it is stable; it is not fluctuating." Because the coin will not fluctuate, Farzam says there will be no volatility as the entire grid capacity rises like water. This approach also happens to be his solution to the unstable African and Latin American economies:

"By the way, Latin American countries have come to me [asking] 'why don't you write a future trends manifesto for Latin America?' So, they are doing it for me actually and in several of the countries we are in communication [with] that will be the next chapter." Even high-level leaders from Japan are requesting Farzam's expertise. He of course agreed, because it is not only positive for the developing or underprivileged, but also the entire global system. However, he must enact this piece by piece until he has more successful cases to provide credibility. For him "the whole plan is the major fundamental change of the fate and the [destiny] of the entire human race." When discussing the blockchain business economy, in terms of practical tools, Farzam relates it back to the realm of ideology and thoughts. He then reverses it because he is a believer in a dichotomy between idealists and pragmatists. The more idealists want higher and better ideas, the more they become introverted and less involved with business and finance. They look at money makers as money mongers and subject themselves to the feeling of being marginalized. However, they created this reality for themselves whereas money makers view these types of people as inferior. Therefore, these two worlds are becoming more divided. Farzam initially originated from the idealist camp but moved to the practical camp and was able to curate his own wealth. He is now a chairman in over 50 companies and has completed over 100 successful transactions within projects. He has also affected the destiny of the economic planning of many nations. While he shows the world that he is a practitioner, his heart is still in the idealism. These two ideologies interplay with one another. 40 years ago, he had a certain image of himself and therefore invested all of his energy into it. Whenever he accumulated more wealth, he always referred back to his idealism to dictate how he would spend it. He calls this the eternal law. No dissipation: just energy turning into movement and movement turning back into energy. This is the perpetual law of the preservation of energy.

"So, on a tactical level, yes, I myself have my future trends, an umbrella organization, [and] my business is to create growth for other companies, entities, even countries. My business model is [based on] all the vectors of growth. So, global sales and distribution systems, global partnerships, global government support branding, centres of attraction where we do conglomerate creation and accession of shares, and then capital raising and mergers and acquisitions." He repeats this process with every company he assists. As the companies grow and become successful, he kicks them back to the country in order to help the country's economic growth. It is a very hands-on economic approach in which the money generates itself beyond a certain level of success. Regarding centralization, Farzam says it needs to be like the heart: to pump out and receive. "That's true protection of wealth."

My comments
There are not a lot of people I have met who have built so many successful companies through their network and thoughts. But there is a true businessman behind Farzam Kamalabadi. He sees the world as his playground. And bringing all the state leaders together in Africa will also bring him some options and he will also prosper. But his main goal can't be only based on me-thinking, it must We-based. Otherwise, he would have stopped earlier as his oil and raw material business could have given him all the wealth in the world. I believe more people would prosper if more people started to think like Farzam.

The whole world in a grain of sand?

As you are a true level nine in the Graves Values, you understand the holistic viewpoint, seeing geopolitics and the world as one. As this is something unattainable for most people, I would like to take a moment to thank you.

 "Thank you. I call it a system-oriented mind, plus a process-oriented mind. Yes, [a] system-oriented mind is everything interconnected, and [in a] process-oriented model, each state [is] interconnected and the dynamic changes. On top of that, you [can] guide and direct [it] to the right direction."

That's perfect, because tier one is all tribal, concentrating on the self and, and smaller things; it's so hard to go to from level six to level seven. But the systems are all in level seven.

"It is called wider and wider loyalties. Yeah, [I] don't think of humanity as evil, even though we'll go fight and kill in the name of justice. It's only because their loyalty is limited." As Farzam continues to explain why it is so difficult for people to move through the levels, he says that fighting amongst or for your tribe is due to suspicion and love for one's tribe. So, he says, because he may love his family, he will fight other families to protect his own. Likewise, because he loves his clan, he will also fight for them should the need arise. If the innate loyalty to one's clan leads someone to fight and kill others, Farzam says they are acting out of fear. When one loves all of humanity and its interconnectivity, Farzam says you begin to only wish others well, even above yourself. From this perspective, he says that wellness you wish unto others will come back to you without you even wanting it. This blind spot, Farzam says, needs to be changed. He says it doesn't need to be the entirety of the population, only a mass of a few critical individuals; a few million in key positions can affect the entire world enough to change the systems.

"That's why I'm a believer that in one generation, I will [create] a fundamental change [to] the entire system of the human race. That's the only goal; we should have nothing less... not [just] a little bit of change here, a little bit of change there. I say the enemies of peace are those who believe in peace, not their enemies."

My comments
We need to change the entire system of the human race. As stated, I accept, this book is one small step for a man. It can sound a bit hippie, but the hippies had only a few goals in life, initially just to get the damn war stopped in Vietnam. And then the movement seemed to fell apart. The greater goal is for everyone to prosper. Not only one specific group as it is in the many-faceted governments around the world. It must a higher goal than just taking money from one group to give to another. It must be more

than going to war for own winning; it must cross border benefits. just as it is when true innovation come to life.

How does web3 run the world from now on?

Now, after having amassed a community from such a young age which you both learn from and teach, how would you relate this to Web3? From my perspective, your approach is very holistic in nature, and I believe Web3 is similar.
Then, we have the blockchain and decentralised autonomous organisations where we can integrate electronics with humanity and create an organisation that is governed in a similar way. What is your take on all of this?

Farzam likens this development of Web3 to many natural progressions throughout history, such as the telegram evolving into the telephone; then radio, television, computers, internet, laptops and mobile phones, ultimately bringing us to being capable of creating blockchains and quantum computing in the spatial three-dimensional web. The fact we are adopting new technology such as this doesn't surprise Farzam as he points out that the EU has already adopted an IEEE. This will soon spread throughout the world, and Farzam plays a major part in this. He has introduced Dubai to the digital authority, which he expects will dominate the world through enablers. The result of this, Farzam explains, is that the world will be contracted into smaller sectors, which is precisely the objective. However, Farzam questions the tools necessary to unify politics, the economy and finances, and how the collective wealth will be distributed.
He emphasizes that technological advancements occur at a rapid pace; the transportation age of today will soon enable travellers to venture wherever they please across the planet in an hour's journey; through the Internet and quantum communications. the Air Force method, along

with infantry style, will be utilised as tools to create unity amongst humanity allowing for physical realities to be prioritised. Unfortunately, this means the mental reality will lag behind. Nevertheless, while we have made, and plan to make, such advancements, our way of governing has not changed. Farzam says that our blind spots remain the same, and this will only be changed either willingly or forcefully.

To accentuate how far humanity has progressed, Farzam briefly provides an overview of nomadic life until current ways of living. Less than 10,000 years ago, humans entered a migratory nomadic phase. Over time, we learned to settle near rivers, which led to the possibility of creating villages. Ever since the first nomads began to settle, it slowly altered our perspective of physical reality. Firstly, this was because of the development of agriculture, then it led to the eventual alterations of lifestyle this new way of life allowed for, and to clans forming and ultimately developing into cities and then national. Considering the timeline of humanity, Farzam states that the act of building nations is still relatively young, only about 3,000 years old. Though it took time for cities to merge and create nations, the follies of national building have come to an end. Farzam credits this to space exploration and the discovery of interplanetary unity. It is his belief that the physical tools of telecommunication, transportation, smart contracts and seamless transactions and auditing are all connected. For him, this is justification for why you don't need to resist central banks and commercial banks.

"If you can't beat them, join them." Farzam never vibes with this motto because he believes the only people focused on beating anyone are poor, weak or narrow minded. When people lead their lives in this nature, Farzam recognises it as a tell-tale sign that their mental reality is limited. This becomes an issue, he says, once the physical reality migrates into the mental reality, because the physical will preside over the mental. For Farzam, the mental reality must lead, and the mission of the mind, heart and soul must mature. However, when the physical reality leads, the components of the mental reality cannot improve. As a result, the suffering of humanity will increase, deepen and expand. In a healthy environment, the body grows beneficial physical tools, while the mind learns how to utilise those tools in a positive manner. When this fails to occur, Farzam likens it to an underdeveloped, almost child-like, adult, ill-equipped to deal with the challenges of the world.

My comments
Collective intelligence will become real in a few more years when more brains have built better A.I. Because where do the bots learn from. Diffusion, DALLE 2, Midjourny: all of these you can go and play with. But they will all learn from you. When you finetune your picture and what else you ask them for, they will remember what you as a human looked for. If you wrote clown in a room with funny hat, and it looked like a goat, you would eliminate the picture from the four it represents with. Collective intelligence is when we all participate in the training of an A.I. bot. The first trails are here. I find Midjourny the best so far but go and try it out yourself. When in a few years we have doctors, scientists, and many other jobs functions training A.I. it will become far more intelligent than we are. It will remember everything, and it will gain knowledge from a billion brains, and be trained 24/7. As you can imagine, exponential innovation is here to stay, and it will come faster than you might think.

Why is it hard to get funding?

As the mind of a child is naive is pure, we need to build a society where kids don't need to steal in order to survive. This mutual observation leads me to my next question: what is your best advice for innovators and, of course, startups to best succeed.

Lastly, due to the difficulties of acquiring VC capital and obstacles with crowdfunding, how would you advise start-ups to acquire these?

Farzam's best advice is to never chase after it. If you are, he interprets that to mean something is missing from your equation. In order to avoid begging for funding, he states that we "have to think, plan, reflect and find [an alternative]." Furthermore, he adds that "if you're creating a team on your own merit, with your own resources, or creating something that is working to solve solutions in a unique manner, sure, the money will come to you." Therefore, this has become his mantra. There are so many start-ups and projects nowadays that are bogus, he encourages you to maintain your authenticity and believe things will come to you. Once you do, Farzam reckons the money will come to you.

This approach is fundamental to his relaxed mindset. Even throughout, and despite, all of the hard times in which he was almost penniless or without a bank account for 10 years while doing humanitarian work, Farzam remained steadfast in his thinking. He recounts how sometimes companies would fall through due to lack of funding, and yet, miraculously, money would still arrive from unknown places. These experiences have led Farzam to become a firm believer in this approach. And so, he lives fearlessly when spending his acquire wealth on his orphaned (adopted) children, initiatives or anything else he chooses. Due to this being his motive, Farzam knows it will make him more money. Regardless of who receives money from him, Farzam does not invest financially but also mentally and spiritually so that he is also building their character. However, as he helps build them up both on outside and the inside, he makes a point of saying that he doesn't "want to make a whole group of people reliant." He says it is your job to "let them breathe and eat, drink and eat on pure thoughts." The world is comprised of both practical and spiritual ideology, both physically and mentally.

Farzam stresses that a little bit of money and little bit of the correct love inspire improvement and independence. So, Farzam concludes this section with his wisdom: "all must come together and not at the cost of others."

My comments
Belief has brought Farzam to the point where he is today. He speaks with world leaders as if it were a Sunday supper. He has influence on them by showing a possible route, without force; he channels them with him and many others. He has tried to lose it all, and he has found diamonds on the bottom of the sea and brought them to the surface. This is not for everybody to do. A lot of people seek freedom in the known and in what they were taught was security. Not for Farzam, he is a true explorer, and I will follow.

What do you want to add?

At the conclusion of our interview, I asked Farzam if there was anything else that he wanted to add as it is so rare that we are privileged enough to discuss these topics.

 "I have two messages. One is to the rich; have no fear of loss, and no fear that if [you] give money to people, they will become dependent." By continuing to keep the money and refusing to disturb it, Farzam says you are doing a disservice to all of the excuses in your mind. You must wash them away and start giving in a regenerative way by contributing to the lives of millions. This is his message to the rich, while also sympathising with the plight of someone redistributing one's fortune because he did the same thing. Now, he leads by example. He avoided accumulating his wealth, only to later give a minute portion of it to charity. He says that "you don't need to do it that way."

Farzam's message to the poor rings an entirely different way. He explains his message through the fable of an illiterate man. The story, told to Farzam by his father, is: An illiterate man lost his father at the age of five. Now forced to be the breadwinner of his family, he often ventured into the countryside with an old man on a mule to collect thorns. The thorns pricked their skin so often, it was not uncommon for them to return home with blood trickling down their hands. The man also battled against the pains of 100 killer diseases, while also being illiterate and unacceptable in every one of his low-level jobs, from masonry to quarterly to shoemaking until the age of 20. Suddenly, he became inspired and completed his schooling; he studied sixth grade in one year, ninth grade in one year and 12th grade during the following year as well as three years of Unified School. The man exhausted himself while attending two universities, but successfully became the doctor of 100 villages and saved a minimum of 300,000 lives. His triumph affected the whole history around him. He was a villager; he was poor; he had nothing. He had no inspiring employment, but he still succeeded. So, Farzam's message to the poor is "if he could do it, all of you in the villages can do it." You don't need to be reliant on anyone and you don't need to think that you are a little cat that needs milk. There is no need to complain about why the world is not giving you the milk you are crying for. Farzam says that you are responsible for unlocking your highest potential.
"All must be the believer and utilize the tools of modern economy and finance to create the greater good for all."

Thanks

Right, thanks, Farzam for participating and being a part of the book. I hope that you gave more hope than doubt to readers, and I know you did to me.

Farzam's answer
A new culture of humanity, new civilization of humanity, the divine civilization being deployed on Earth and being practiced by all believers and non-believers and by poor and rich and by rich who are non-believers and poor people that are believers: you all have spectrums. Don't think the poor are better than the rich or the rich are better than the poor; neither the rich person who is not pessimistic because of their wealth nor the poor person who is not proud of their situation should lose any direction and become suicidal. I know too many poor people who are suicidal because they have no direction in their lives. You're all wasting your life. There is so much good in everyone, so much contribution, so much creativity in the poor and wealth alike. Please route it correctly in the right direction and clear your blind spots; as simple as that.

Steffen answer
That's why I created this this book as well.

Farzam's answer
I know your book and congratulations for being a leader in the mind world but connected to the practical. We are of the same breed. That's why I'm serving you and am at the service of all your readers. Best wishes to you!

Doubt

Innovation is built on doubt

First, you think this can be done better. Why has no one thought about this before? It might be a bad idea since no one else has done this. It might be the greatest idea ever. Why did I not think about this before Can I do it? Should someone else not build it? Will I be able to make a life out of this? Can I make money from this? Is it feasible? Will I need funding? When will it be finished? Should I set a deadline if it does not work?
Well, the Wright brothers did not have a deadline; they tried for 12 years before they flew just 4 miles / 6 kilometers Link. How many wing shapes had they tried before they identified the specific shape that gave optimal lift? The reason I keep on using this example is because they must have faced a lot of cognitive dissonance from people around them, and at this time there were not a lot of investors who thought this was a great idea. Commercial flights might have been a thought and balloons at this time could fly people around. The larger balloons became the Zeppelin nearly thirty years after the Wright brothers' first flight. We know that some of them exploded because of the use of hydrogen, so they were not a good innovation. We live in a world where bureaucracy is killing ideas. There are public sector players who take over startups and insert their own people or who won't support a specific sector like crypto, as they think it is bad. The public sector is full of people who try to preserve the system; they try to hold on to the status quo so they can get others money for this project. Most of the time they do not even like their job and they try to get the most out of it; they have more days of being sick than in other businesses. Some of them even think you can stay at home if you have an off day, even if

you are not sick. They also argue for a Global Basic Income. Well, there is nothing wrong with these thoughts in a society where we have enough energy. We are on our way with the new energy power plants based on thorium. There are many other options in the pipeline for fusion energy consumption. When that happens, we will see a large number of people who do routine work today without work; but will we need to work in the same way as today? No, even gaming will be a job and that is one of the reasons I'm building Gamer´s Gold. Having fun will be a job, not like today when most people do not like their job. We will also see many new ways of making a life function when we have only spare time to spend. A lot of people are afraid because they believe in the great reset and the climate crisis. This is not how it will be, because we have innovation. The innovation is exponential, one leads to two, two leads to four and so forth. And, as Søren Kierkegaard told us.

The paradox is really the pathos of intellectual life and just as only great souls are exposed to passions it is only the great thinker who is exposed to what I call paradoxes, which are nothing else than grandiose thoughts in embryo. – Søren Kierkegaard

To sum it up for me, we are on the brink of a better and brighter world. Not the opposite. But the human mind is worried; people have doubts. Doubt is the source for something bigger. When 99% of the population in a country like Denmark takes off the mask at the exact moment when they are allowed to by the government, as if Covid 19 ended that day at 14.00 PM, you are not with a lot of people who understand this way of thinking. They follow order, not logic. Exponential thinking on innovation is a rarity, but it is not that I want to be different; it is not as if I try to differentiate myself from others. It is simply just that I can't help thinking like this. Maybe you think I am a mad man. Or maybe I'm a dreamer, but I'm not the only one. I hope I will find more likeminded people in the future. Thanks for reading this book. And let´s get in contact if you think alike.

Notes.

Chapter 1.
Psychology Matthias Desmet Mass Formation
https://www.youtube.com/watch?v=dPisp_VgEO8

Black Death - Wikipedia
https://en.wikipedia.org/wiki/Black_Death

Chapter 2.
www.midjourney.com Midjourney is an independent
research lab exploring new mediums of thought and
expanding the imaginative powers of the human species.

OVERVIEW OF GRAVES' VALUES LEVELS - Institute of
Applied Psychology (iap.edu.au)
https://iap.edu.au/overview-of-graves-values-levels/

8 Things You Need to Know about the Graves Model
https://www.artofwellbeing.com/2017/09/05/gravesmodel/

Chapter 4.
Bee Dance (Waggle Dance) - YouTube
https://www.youtube.com/watch?v=-7ijl-g4jHg

Asch conformity experiments -
https://en.wikipedia.org/wiki/Asch_conformity_experiments

Asch's Conformity
https://www.youtube.com/watch?v=sno1TpCLj6A

Wernher von Braun - Wikipedia
https://en.wikipedia.org/wiki/Wernher_von_Braun

Chapter 5.
Bohr model - Wikipedia
https://en.wikipedia.org/wiki/Bohr_model

2021 Corruption Perceptions Index - Explore the... -
Transparency.org
https://www.transparency.org/en/cpi/2021

EPR paradox - Wikipedia
https://en.wikipedia.org/wiki/EPR_paradox

Chapter 6. The full interview with Lars Tvede can be seen
here. https://youtu.be/irj55UAPflg

Chapter 8
List of firsts in aviation - Wikipedia
https://en.wikipedia.org/wiki/List_of_firsts_in_aviation

Timeline of online video - Wikipedia
https://en.wikipedia.org/wiki/Timeline_of_online_video

V236-15.0 MW™ (vestas.com)
https://www.vestas.com/en/products/offshore/V236-
15MW/V236-15MW

Seaborg Technologies
https://www.seaborg.com/

Chapter 9.

Crossing the Chasm, 3rd Edition: Marketing and selling.
https://www.amazon.com/Crossing-Chasm-3rd-Disruptive-
Mainstream-dp-
0062292986/dp/0062292986/ref=dp_ob_image_bk

The Man Who COULD Have Been Bill Gates: Gary Kildall
https://www.youtube.com/watch?v=sDIK-C6dGks

Just How Much Does Tesla Get In Subsidies Anyways? - CleanTechnica https://cleantechnica.com/2020/08/03/tesla-subsidies-how-much/

Tycho Brahe - Wikipedia https://en.wikipedia.org/wiki/Tycho_Brahe#Observational_astronomy

Action of 4 June 1565 – Wikipedia https://en.wikipedia.org/wiki/Action_of_4_June_1565on

Frederick II of Denmark - https://en.wikipedia.org/wiki/Frederick_II_of_Denmarkedia

Stephanie Kwolek - Wikipedia Known for the innovation on Kevlar and spandex. https://en.wikipedia.org/wiki/Stephanie_Kwolek

Nicolaus Copernicus – Wikipedia; https://en.wikipedia.org/wiki/Nicolaus_Copernicus

Chapter 12.
Managers Account for 70% of Variance in Employee Engagement (gallup.com) https://news.gallup.com/businessjournal/182792/managers-account-variance-employee-engagement.aspx

Chapter 13.
Interview with Lars Seier Christensen – Chairman of Concordium https://youtu.be/dcm3DBnbzAY

Web3 - Wikipedia https://en.wikipedia.org/wiki/Web3

Chapter 14
Denmark vs United States Education Stats Compared (nationmaster.com)
https://www.nationmaster.com/country-info/compare/Denmark/United-States/Education

Fact Checking The Claim Of 97% Consensus On Anthropogenic Climate Change (forbes.com)
https://www.forbes.com/sites/uhenergy/2016/12/14/fact-checking-the-97-consensus-on-anthropogenic-climate-change/?sh=48499c8a1157

The Plastic Brain.: Training Marines Johnson D.C. Thom, N.J. Stanley E.A., Haase, L. Simmons, A.N. Shih, P.A.B., Thomson, W.K., Potterat, E.G., Minor, T.R. and Paulus, M.P.: 2014 Modifying resilience mechanisms in at-risk individuals a controlled study of mindfulness training in Marines.

AlphaFold: How Google's AI Helps Science Answer a Biology Problem | by Rui Alves | Geek Culture | Medium https://medium.com/geekculture/alphafold-how-googles-ai-solved-one-of-life-s-greatest-problems-8a0d1f0ecca7

The theory of everything Can you explain this 'Theory of Everything' formula? | Physics Forums https://www.physicsforums.com/threads/can-you-explain-this-theory-of-everything-formula.817623/

John Cook Fact Checking The Claim Of 97% Consensus On Anthropogenic Climate Change (forbes.com)
https://www.forbes.com/sites/uhenergy/2016/12/14/fact-checking-the-97-consensus-on-anthropogenic-climate-change/?sh=48499c8a1157

Chapter 15
Press Release | Seaborg | Funding
https://www.seaborg.com/press-release-nov-2020

Top thorium companies | Venture Radar
https://www.ventureradar.com/keyword/thorium

Thinking is hard. Jordan B. Peterson
https://www.facebook.com/watch/?v=1689469234755331

The Pursuit Of Happiness: Job interview
https://www.youtube.com/watch?v=UUDKEbX5OQw

Why Do Startups Fail? An Analysis of 3,200 High-growth
Technology Startups
https://techli.com/startup-genome-project/32391/

Denmark to build 'first energy island' in North Sea
https://www.bbc.com/news/world-europe-55931873

The Simon Abundance Index 2022 - HumanProgress
https://www.humanprogress.org/the-simon-abundance-
index-2022/

Joby Aviation | Joby
https://www.jobyaviation.com/

Flying vehicles of the future: Companies racing to develop
eVTOL "air taxis" - YouTube
https://www.youtube.com/watch?v=1YUv0AMq0x8

Fonde – Innovayt
https://innovayt.eu/da/fonde/

The Ambidextrous Organization (hbr.org)
https://hbr.org/2004/04/the-ambidextrous-organization

COVID-19 Data Explorer - Our World in Data
bit.ly/3PZXWst

M-Pesa - Wikipedia
https://en.wikipedia.org/wiki/M-Pesa

PwC: Blockchain   Tech Could Add $1.76 Trillion to Global
GDP by 2030
https://beincrypto.com/pwc-blockchain-tech-could-add-1-
76-trillion-to-global-gdp-by-2030/

Facebook Will Bring Expanded Internet Access to Africa in
$1 Billion Project
https://www.nasdaq.com/articles/facebook-will-bring-
expanded-internet-access-to-africa-in-%241-billion-project-
2020-05-22

Chapter 16
Interview with Farzam Kamalabadi
https://youtu.be/_D7Wyfv_omM

Epilogue
The Brilliant Engineering of FIRST FLIGHT ! - YouTube
https://www.youtube.com/watch?v=LigpsX1KoQE